THE CONTEXT OF
ENGLISH LITERATURE

1900–1930

EDITED BY
MICHAEL BELL

HOLMES & MEIER
PUBLISHERS, INC
NEW YORK

First published in
the United States of America 1980 by
HOLMES & MEIER PUBLISHERS, INC.
30 Irving Place, New York, New York 10003

Library of Congress Catalog No. 80-7792

ISBN 0-8419-0423-5 cloth
     0-8419-0424-3 paper

Printed in the United States of America

Contents

Illustrations

1 Introduction: modern movements in literature

MICHAEL BELL

Literature undeniably reflects in some sense the life and thought of its time, but to determine how it does so is the delicate and continuing function of criticism. It may address itself to 'life' in a greater or lesser degree but its value as literature is not in any simple sense contingent on such a criterion. The vitality or meaningfulness of literature hinges on its internal intensity rather than the quantity of historical information in a factual sense that it may include. It is a delicate matter, therefore, to mediate pertinently between literary experience and its putative contexts; to discuss 'influences' and preoccupations without collapsing the tension of this vital heterogeneity. This general consideration has an especial importance in the modern context since it is precisely from the influential modern writers that we have inherited the insistence that literature be seen as literature and 'not another thing'; that it is not simply a vehicle for 'ideas' or 'content' which could be expressed in some other form. In fact, this discrimination is one of the defining strains of literary modernism.

The approach in this essay reflects that perception. Rather than attempt to sketch the manifold interrelations of modern literature with contemporary life and thought in a one-to-one, quantitative way, I have tried primarily to establish what kind of a literature it is. In so far as a distinct body of characteristics can be detected, this provides the perspective on its extra-literary relations. That amounts, in effect, to offering some definitions of the modern element in literature. I say definitions because I do not believe there is a single principle or

movement covering even the range of literature we feel to be pecu
liarly modern. 'Modern' may strictly refer to any work produced
within the given years though it naturally implies a special contem
porary pertinence. Lawrence and Galsworthy both write within these
decades, but of the two Lawrence is clearly the 'modern' writer. The
term 'modernist' generally refers to something more specialized
again. Though it is in no way an organized or unified movement, there
is a corporate effect produced by the highly self-conscious European
and American *avant-garde* of the time such that the understanding o
Proust, Joyce, Mann or Pound is helped more by awareness of one o
more of the others than by knowledge of their personal and nationa
contexts. As I have said, this does not imply a single movement so
much as a series of discrete centres whose effects widely overlap. The
modernisms of Pound, Eliot, Joyce and Proust turn out in fact to be
quite differently animated. Without wishing therefore to impose a
rigid scheme, I use these terms to distinguish constantly interweaving
yet crucially different, strands in the literature of the time.

Hence, although modernism in this sense of the international *avant
garde* seems to me to have the deepest and most problematic relation
with its time, a relation through its forms and techniques as well as
content, it does not cover the whole range of possibilities. I proceed
therefore, by concentrating on Joyce's *Ulysses* and then moving
through different, in some measure opposing, forms of modernism
such as Pound's, towards writers like Shaw and Wells whose concern
with their time does not manifest itself in *avant-garde* technique. To
some extent this shift in focus coincides with a turning from the inter
national context to a specifically English one, and the particular
quality of English literature over these years should appear by contrast
with the preceding consideration of modernism at large. In sum, the
essay moves from one pole to the other using the large overall discri
minations to clarify more elusive shadings and overlappings. I hope
too, that these different elements will provide a mutual critique. Since
among other things modern literature is a dispute over the nature o
literature itself and its relation to the world, a critical assessment of its
achievement is intrinsic to our topic. To ask how this literature relate
to its time is surely to ask how adequately it does so. I want to suggest
the achievement and limitations of both international modernism and
the native product.

Having indicated the general shape and purpose of this essay, I should account for the choice of specialist contributions. The purpose of the historical and philosophical essays is, I take it, clear enough but the desire to balance these general surveys with discussions of individual thinkers or specific art movements involves an inevitable arbitrariness. Film, music or sociology could just as reasonably be represented. I believe the topics chosen not only focus on new and philosophically far-reaching developments but they to some extent balance, or supplement, each other. Cubism is primarily a matter of form; Freud's new model of the psyche affects the traditional material of literature, the human personality; and the anthropological study of myth and archaic man opened new perspectives on the nature of literature generally as indeed on civilization itself. While limited in their individual focus, therefore, these three essays are intended to converge from different angles in keeping with general approach outlined above which is to provide close examination at some representative points rather than sacrifice detailed critical perception to historical generality.

Modernism and realism in Ulysses

'...something solid *and* artificial' (Cézanne)[1]

James Joyce's *Ulysses* (1922) seems to me the most substantial and comprehensive expression of literary modernism by a British writer and it conveniently exemplifies more general techniques and aspirations. There are four broad aspects on which I want to focus here: the transcendence of realism; the presentation of identity; the treatment of time; and aesthetic self-consciousness. In some form or other these would require commentary if the author were Proust, Mann or Woolf.

The first issue, realism, subsumes the other three and the problems of this term in fact provide a comprehensive perspective on our whole topic. Realism as a literary mode implies a body of assumptions about the human relation to reality. Philosophically, therefore, it is a nerve centre of the relation to other intellectual fields. However we seek to explain the fact, literature and the visual arts in the early twentieth century are strikingly characterized by a departure from the conventions and assumptions of realism in the sense of verisimilitude used as a means of understanding. Since the Renaissance the minute depiction of the world, whatever particular stylistic developments occurred, had remained the primary mode of the literary and visual arts. It is also striking that this continuing endeavour towards accurate depiction is contemporaneous with the apparent triumph of the kind of physical science associated with Bacon and Newton as well as with the success of an expanding bourgeois capitalism. The compelling verisimilitude of Defoe is not just a matter of accurate description in some neutral and quantitative sense, it expresses an active curiosity about what can be made of things. The solidity of his world is an aspect of its availability to use. Hence a shift in the artistic representation of reality has extensive implications; it offers a spiritual paradigm of shifts felt, if not so articulated, in scientific and social spheres; its manifestations will be likely to shade from physical and metaphysical principles to more nebulous changes in social confidence and purpose.

To get a focus on this, I am initially concentrating on the novel form since this has had historically the most intimate involvement in the assumptions and practice of realism. To approach the break up of fictional realism from a pertinent perspective it will help to see first what *Ulysses* positively does. If we begin by posing the crude question, 'is it a realist novel?', we immediately see its duality in this respect for clearly the answer must be both positive and negative. Consider this passage:

> Hot mockturtle vapour and steam of newbaked jampuffs rolypoly poured out from Harrison's. The heavy noonreek tickled the top of Mr Bloom's gullet. Want to make good pastry, butter, best flour, Demerara sugar, or they'd taste it with the hot tea. Or is it from her? A barefoot arab stood over the grating, breathing in the fumes. Deaden the gnaw of hunger that way. Pleasure or pain is it? Penny dinner. Knife and fork chained to the table.
>
> (Chapter VIII, 'Lestrygonians')[2]

Leopold Bloom has met Mrs Breen outside the baker's shop just as he himself is about to look for some lunch. In the series of impressions and thoughts comprising Bloom's consciousness there is a characteristic merging of inner and outer worlds. Hunger conditions his response to his environment; the clear-cut external perceptions are governed by a bodily need. And the sense of the world as mediated by a perceiving mind is reinforced by the stylistic pitch of the two opening sentences. It is clearly not language Bloom himself would use, yet it gives his sensuous experience with mimetic precision. The vivid, but initially undefined, sensation of warm, smelling vapour is followed by a further differentiation of taste, after which the long-delayed main verb is felt enacting rather than stating its meaning. The proper name, Harrison's, denotes a precise experience by the time we get to it. Note, too, how the vowel and consonant sounds flesh out this structure with the word 'roly-poly' again introducing, as well as delaying, the verb. Then the rest of the paragraph modulates into Bloom's own expression so that the authorial density of the opening sentences is assimilated to a general sense of Bloom's mind as the theatre of consciousness.

As an immediate dramatic effect, therefore, the passage renders its moment and place with sensuous specificity and in that respect it could be called realistic. But its realism as one-to-one local correspondence with possible actual experience does not tell us how the passage relates to the rest of the book, and the striking feature in this regard is the fortuitousness of Bloom's impressions. From this passage in isolation one might suppose the book to have no structure beyond that of a flow of impressions and associated ideas. In fact, of course, *Ulysses* is a highly structured work and even here the authorial self-consciousness of the language might alert us to that dimension of it. While faithfully reproducing the moment to moment feel of randomness, the novel carefully constructs a pattern as complete and precise as a vast jig-saw puzzle. In the present instance, apart from the preoccupation with food as an aspect of Bloom's somatic personality, the whole chapter is an elaborate play on the idea of eating with a metaphorical extension to mental forms of ingestion such as reading. Taking off from the cannibals episode in *Odyssey*, the chapter raises eating to a general metaphor of greed and egotism; attitudes that Bloom, despite his sensuality and curiosity, is seen to avoid. And the whole work is structured in this way. Using the story of Homer's *Odyssey* as the model for a comprehensive spiritual cartography, Joyce plays the random foreground of Bloom's day against a symbolic background of permanent human values. Bloom's story is contrasted, yet also suffused, with this larger vision and his own unwittingness of such a perspective on his life, even while he is intuitively in accord with it, reinforces the reader's sense of a dual perspective such as we have already noted in the prose. The sense of a perspective *on* Bloom as well as *through* him is conveyed by all those elements of organization which are so clearly the author's and not his.

It could, of course, be said of many literary works that the author's perspective is different from the characters' and that there is a corresponding duality in reading. But the special quality about Joyce is the way the two perspectives are kept on separate planes philosophically. We may understand this by contrast with the realism of Balzac or George Eliot based on an organicist conception of life in which the interconnections of the book's structure, for all that they are created by the author, are modelled on the supposed interrelations of life itself. The Victorian novelist inherited Wordsworth's understanding of the world in terms of 'what we half create, and what we perceive'; an understanding that has behind it historically the magisterial argument of Kant's *Critique of Pure Reason* (1781) which brought home philosophically the extent to which the human mind constructs the world in perceiving it.

Hence George Eliot could understand the world and the self as existing in a kind of symbiotic relation; a relation that creates values as well as being mutually sustaining. A right perception of the world recognizes the self as part of it, as a branch is of a tree, and the indissoluble nature of the relationship is constantly expressed in such organic metaphors. Consider a cardinal passage from *Middlemarch* in which Dorothea Brooke experiences precisely that recognition:

> It had taken her a long time to come to that question, and there was light piercing into the room. She opened the curtains, and looked out towards the bit of road that lay in view, with the fields beyond, outside the entrance gates. On the road there was a man with a bundle on his back and a woman carrying her baby; in the field she could see figures moving – perhaps the shepherd with his dog. Far off in the bending sky was the pearly light; and she felt the largeness of the world and the manifold wakings of men to labour and endurance. She was a part of that involuntary, palpitating life, and could neither look out on it from her luxurious shelter as a mere spectator, nor hide her head in selfish complaining.   (Chapter LXXX)

Like Bloom, Dorothea is invaded by the experience because of her receptive disposition towards it at the moment in question. But otherwise the passages are in sharp contrast. Here there is nothing random; or at least nothing that is allowed to feel so. The whole description is framed by the window and the 'bending' sky while the moral archetypes of road, burden, family and shepherd seem to arise from the emotions of the character which are supported by the felt interrelations of human and natural processes. Eliot's realism is based on this organicist assumption that the world is, as it were, the mind's home and that there is a proper relation between them which is not arbitrarily determined by one alone but by their interaction. The physical structure of the scene reflects inherent moral relations and the same elements of window, light and nature form a comparable structure in the book at large. Hence the vision at this moment is continuous with the whole and individual objects come to us imbued with an inherent moral meaningfulness. Eliot's world is value-laden whether or not the character at any given moment is capable of responding to it as such.

In the Joyce passage, on the other hand, the psychological subjectivity of the character's response, rather than being objectified by the external world grouping around it, is heightened in its pure subjectivity. The physical world is solidly there all right but the mind floats over it by its own volition. And, correspondingly, the larger patterns created by such passages throughout the book share this arbitrary, or volitional, basis. The overall structure is composed of the parts but is not in the same sense *derived* from them as Eliot's is. There is not only, therefore, a disjuncture in scale between the randomness of the detail and the order of the whole, there is a disjuncture in kind. The randomness of everyday life is seen in a perspective of serene order but the order is always a creation of the book, of the perceiving mind. For all the minute depiction of Dublin the structure is not strictly derived from external reality but from a consciously artistic creation. We end up with a teasing duality by which an extraordinarily solid and detailed world, a closely literal depiction, in fact, of an actual city, spins on an axis of arbitrary artistic volition. If we now look at the other features I have suggested, we can trace out further aspects of this dual vision. Firstly, there is the presentation of identity.

The general difference I have been outlining bears equally on the presentation of character. Dorothea seems to exist before, and independently of, her momentary consciousness. From the beginning of the book her physical person, her family history, her social context are all modes of definition that locate her solidly in time and place. In Bloom's case the personality is more nearly conterminous with his own play of consciousness. Even such external glimpses as we have of him are largely through the perception of other characters such as Molly, Stephen or Gertie McDowell. Bloom, of course, exists in a distinct time and place, but the outline of his personality is never given that objective edge. The technique is not original to Joyce nor exclusively modern but it has come to feel so because of the conception of personality it is made to embody. The unframed presentation goes with an open-ended sense of the individual psyche. Stephen speculates to what extent the self of seven years earlier is really identical with the present one when the body has completely changed its cells. And conversely a man may have many possible personalities latent within himself just as Shakespeare was able to create a stageful of possible selves from his own head. Stephen's speculations hint that the felt presence and individuality of the personages in *Ulysses* is achieved within a radically questioning and malleable conception of human identity. In evoking the figure of Odysseus, Joyce suggests the unwitting presence in Bloom of an heroic archetype.

Some such questioning or expansion of personal identity is evident in some way or other in most important modern writers. Freud's naming of the 'Unconscious' provided a focus for a variety of intuitions in the latter part of the nineteenth century to the effect that the psyche includes an unwitting domain by which the patterns of past experience, both personal and racial, affect involuntarily the conscious self. It is a convergence from several sides, scientific, philosophical and literary. Samuel Butler developed such perceptions out of Darwin; Schopenhauer's philosophy of the 'will' based its influential and tragic world view on a related idea; and various strains of romanticism had sought to penetrate, through nature or through mystic symbolism for example, areas of experience beyond the personal consciousness. Hence the contemporaneity of Freud with modern expansions and questionings of personality is neither fortuitous nor a matter of simple influence and this consideration underlies what are often effectively territorial arguments between Joyce and Jung or between Lawrence and the Freudian ideas he encountered after his marriage. For, apart from the personal values and purposes involved, writers of literature, as the traditional purveyors and interpreters of dreams, have frequently proved unwilling to yield this function to what Nabokov later called 'shams and shamans'. Such tensions indicate the felt overlap as well as the importance of the issues involved.

The important point here, though, is that Freudian theory is not a simple substitution of a new model of personality but rather, as in the matter of literary realism, already discussed, a duality. Just as the post-Freudian magistrate habitually weighs psychological factors against the moral responsibility of an alleged offender, so the novelist has to accommodate two levels of personality which may be not only discrete but at odds. Consider even these two often quoted statements of intent by modern novelists:

> You mustn't look in my novel for the old stable *ego* of the character. There is another *ego*, according to whose action the individual is unrecognisable, and passes through, as it were, allotropic states which it needs a deeper sense than any we have been used to exercise, to discover are states of the same pure single element of carbon.   (D.H. Lawrence)[3]

> Life is not a series of gig-lamps symmetrically arranged; life is a luminous halo, a semi-transparent envelope surrounding us from the beginning of consciousness to the end. Is it not the task of the novelist to convey this varying, this unknown and uncircumscribed spirit, whatever aberration or complexity it may display, with as little mixture of the alien and external as possible.   (Virginia Woolf)[4]

Both passages are iconoclastic, arguing for a radical departure from the conventionally 'realistic' presentation of character. Each appeals, however, to a sense of reality as the basis of its criticism. That these revolutionary and difficult conceptions of human identity should appeal to the standard of verisimilitude, or truth to life, suggests the phase in the evolution of realism that most characterizes the important new writing of the period. The attack on literary characterization as artificial or limited is not with a view to destroying it in principle so much as transcending its present limitations. There is no suggestion that fiction as such cannot engage pertinently with reality. Lawrence and Woolf are seeking precisely a more penetrating and comprehensive engagement. This is in marked contrast to such later inheritors of the modern tradition as Beckett or the French 'new novelists' whose anti-novels question the very possibility of such an engagement. The Beckettian enclosure within a mental world is latent in his predecessors, Joyce and Proust, but in them it co-exists with other elements. The characters of Joyce, Lawrence or Proust have a solidly detailed presence by ordinary standards yet exist within a context that enforces simultaneously a different, even opposed, perception of them. It is as if one were to meet someone socially and have simultaneously a moving x-ray vision of him. This is more than a colourful way of saying that their dramatic presence is accompanied by the author's analytic discussion for such a method, as practised by George Eliot for example, reinforces the common sense perception. Proust radically undermines the notion of a continuing personal identity; Joyce increasingly dissolves individual personality first into mythic archetypes and eventually, we might say into the 'mind' of language at large; Lawrence's symbolic scenes rehearse elemental motions of the psyche beneath the conscious self. Yet in all these cases the 'common sense' aspect is not belittled, or undermined. The meaning lies in the duality of perception.

In Bloom's case, apart from specific episodes such as 'Circe', the expansion of identity is not so much into the Freudian personal unconscious as into the Jungian domain of racial archetypes. *Ulysses* attempts an encyclopaedic summary of essential cultural history based on the figure of Odysseus/Bloom flanked by the somatic woman, Molly, and the cerebral artist, Stephen. That the whole world of the epic should be located within the mind is itself a measure of where human culture has come to by Joyce's time. Joyce's fictive world is not solipsistic, but the prism of individual consciousness is the formal and philosophical precondition. It is in other words as much an expansion as a limitation of experience in the world.

The three opening chapters concerned with Stephen exemplify this. These address themselves in turn to Stephen's immediate situation as an aspiring Irish writer; the historical dimension of that situation; and then the basic philosophical structure of experience in the world. The questions become more universal as the focus progressively closes into Stephen's own consciousness. For Bloom, who lacks Stephen's education and speculative intelligence, as well as pretension, the epic expansion properly occurs around rather than in the character. The cultural resumé is not comprehended by Bloom yet intuitively he acts from the centre of the book's perspective of values. The 'equanimity' with which he accepts Molly's infidelity towards the end is not indifference, but the absorption of his personal anguish into an impersonal perception of it that chimes with the creative impersonality typified by Shakespeare. It is an impersonality not of withdrawal but of all-pervading sympathy. An essential heritage is in him and perhaps the more effectively for being habitual and intuitive rather than conscious. Or we might say the heritage is in the reader, is a universal possession, and is hence independent of its individual forms. It rightly subsists, like the Cheshire cat, as a ghostly presence mysteriously in and around the central character. But however we define the relation precisely, Bloom and his archetype give us two ways of looking at the same reality; each modifying and expanding the other. The unbounded definition of Bloom's personality allows it to expand indefinitely as the book's allusiveness spirals outwards.

There is in fact a hint that the Bloom/Odysseus relation might be even closer. Molly's questioning of Bloom about the word 'metempsychosis' raises an idea used to comparable effect in Proust and in Mann's *Joseph and his Brothers*. Each opens up the mystery of personal identity to suggest that it may become the medium for reincarnation of the dead. In Proust's case a past self of the narrator is called into being by the incident with the madeleine; in Mann's case it is the racial ancestors; in Bloom's it is a general archetype of the questing voyager. This seems in Joyce, as in Proust, to be a suggestive metaphor rather than a literal belief in reincarnation but in each case the move into the unconscious, as for Freud and Jung, is a freeing from time. Hence the dual perspective with which we view the world and the characters of *Ulysses* applies also to the third large issue to be discussed: the treatment of time.

The conscious focus on the nature of time in so many of the generally accepted major works of modern literature implies a cultural and historical context that will be expanded later. At present, I want to concentrate on its actual manifestations in literary form. It is by now apparent that Joyce's decision to superimpose his modern character of Bloom on a figure from archaic legend, and on a Renaissance dramatist, has many implications and one of them is the conflation of an immense time span. The effect is to suggest that, if only it can be seen from the required angle, life in Bloom's time, or Odysseus', or Shakespeare's, has essentially the same structure. It is as if a tall tree were to be cut in cross-section at widely separated points to reveal the same pattern of rings. The book reveals a hidden structure to human lives which, though only manifest in time, is essentially timeless. We feel it standing above any of its particular historical embodiments and the whole structure and technique of the book reinforce this intuition of the timeless. Just as the apparent randomness reveals itself as a vast order, so the apparent passage of time secretly traces a timeless pattern. Once again the mind flickers constantly over two planes. The familiar foreground is made just sufficiently rebarbative and unfamiliar to make us constantly reconstruct it in terms of a teasingly elusive further perspective which could perhaps be grasped more directly only as an abstraction or a cliché. And such an abstract reduction is indeed the chasm that yawns beneath the works of Joyce's maturity, although in *Ulysses*, I believe, the liveliness of the foreground sets up a proper resistance to the abstract structure, imbuing it with a sense of mystery and surprise. Like some mystical or religious experience it is only glimpsed by a creative leap.

The desire to create an intuition of the timeless within, inescapably, the condition of time will often exploit musical form, as happens in T.S. Eliot's 'Four Quartets' and most explicitly in Thomas Mann's *The Magic Mountain*. Joyce takes the musicality of form to an even further and more literal degree. The techniques of individual chapters in *Ulysses* are generally microcosmic of techniques and qualities pervading the book at large, and indeed other areas of modern literature. The 'Sirens' episode is a case in point. Joyce opens it with a page and a half of words and phrases making no connected sense. Subsequently it becomes clear that these expressions are all leitmotifs of the episode. They represent an abstract of it not in terms of narrative, but musically. Music is a medium that involves the literal passage of time for its expression yet the fleeting moment of its presence in the ear is meaningless without the ideal totality, or spatial form, in the mind. Music, therefore, brings into focus the interrelation of the temporal and spatial modalities of form. To set out the key phrases of this chapter before the narrative begins is to enforce the spatial perception of it against the generally temporal bias of fiction. This quality pervades the book as a whole. In the third chapter, for example, Stephen thinks of an unnamed man: 'That man led me, spoke. I was not afraid. The melon he held against my face. . . . ' This turns out to be Bloom although there is no way in the first, or purely timebound, reading in which this could be known. In sum, the intuition of the timeless in *Ulysses* is a product of its moment by moment technique and its overall structure, so that the treatment of time is intimately bound up with the other feature to be discussed: its aesthetic self-consciousness.

Joseph Frank's essay 'Spatial Form in Modern Literature'[5] argues, rightly I believe, that the kind of spatialization I am indicating in *Ulysses* is a distinguishing feature of modern literature generally. We will want to say more about the implications of this but we should first take further stock of the literary texture it implies. It commonly requires a high, one might say creative, degree of self-consciousness in the reading, and another study helps explain why. Wylie Sypher's *Rococo to Cubism*[6] discusses a comparable spatialization in a more concrete medium and also attempts to relate it to a broader cultural context. Sypher argues, in fact, that cubism is the central style of the visual arts in the early twentieth century and distinguishes for this purpose 'style' from 'stylization'. 'Style' for him is a distinct formal mode embodying a distinct perceptual or philosophical framework; whereas 'stylization', under which he includes nineteenth-century painting at large, is a formal mode applied externally, as it were, to an essentially unrelated material or mode of seeing. I have already suggested that modernism has discrete if overlapping manifestations, but I think Sypher is right to see a cardinal importance in the formal mode that implies a new philosophical basis and hence to understand the cubist outlook in this culturally pervasive sense. Furthermore, he explains the conscious constructivism of the cubist mode partly in terms of its treatment of time.

What I am calling the cubist style developed rapidly through several phases and branched in different directions; hence the inclusion of Cyril Barrett's more detailed essay in this volume. However, we can say that running through, particularly its early development, there is a preoccupation with time. On the face of it painting might be thought a medium, as compared with music or literature, for which time is rather unimportant. And if the subject is a classical mythological scene or a social portrait, this may indeed be the case. The Impressionist painters of the late nineteenth century, however, as well as being in competition with the newly invented camera, a machine that could fix momentary appearances absolutely, were independently interested in catching the effect of momentariness as part of the reality of perception; as, for example, in Monet's series of paintings of Rouen Cathedral at different moments in the day. Such techniques, however, commit the artist, condemn him one might say, to catching only the fleetingness of an object. How can he convey permanence, the grandeur of the unchanging, without returning to older modes that will now seem rhetorical and subtly untrue? The development through post-impressionism, Cézanne and then Picasso can be followed in the light of that question. A kind of painting emerges that has structural solidity as painting, as an intrinsic logic of design, rather than as an imitation of solid forms in the world. Where the painter's genius is fully engaged the object painted, even a human sitter, may find expression in the structural design newly created by the artist. But this kind of painting does not seem to falsely impale the subject on canvas because the object is represented not through one of its fleeting aspects in time but rather through its mode of construction in the mind. When we look at a bird from the side we do not see its other eye, though we know this to be there so intuitively that this knowledge could reasonably be counted as part of the 'perception'. And it is largely the fact that our vision constantly moves around such objects in time that affords this intuition of the world's solidity. Hence a cubist painting in which the two eyes appear on the one side can exploit precisely the limitations of perception in time to construct a more radically fixed and spatialized, as well as more comprehensive, apprehension of the subject.

Hence, the structure of *Ulysses* by which the details of the temporal flux only become meaningful in relation to a supra-temporal perspective is cubist in principle. The smaller scale, stylistic correlative of this is an effect that was precisely defined by Eisenstein in the context of film technique, but which has since come to be applied to the arts generally.[7] Montage is the sharp juxtaposition of different images – the baby carriage that rolls down the Odessa steps amid shooting and carnage being the classic example from Eisenstein's own film *The Battleship Potemkin*. Eisenstein repeatedly pointed out that this was not new; it was only a filmic expression of poetic metaphor. But where poetic metaphor is likely to be mediated and qualified by the rational and grammatical orderings of language, the film deals more directly in images. In that respect it is a distinctive technique and provides a helpful model for what was happening contemporaneously in literature in a less immediately tangible way. Here, too, a constellation of images and impressions impinge on the mind, successively it is true, but without their meaningful interrelations being primarily defined by this succession. Instead the discrete elements relate in multi-directional ways that are constantly intuited with a cubist simultaneity. The pattern is suddenly seen as whole or not at all.

Joyce, in fact, sets one of the chapters of *Ulysses* in a newspaper office and imitates the prose and headlines of popular journalism in the technique of the episode. The newspaper is a kind of unwitting montage that sets out the most disparate events side by side on the grounds merely that they have all occurred on the same day. Joyce's novel also consists of a juxtaposition of events that happen in one day but constructing from its very randomness an intuition of wholeness and order. Apart, therefore, from the metaphorical tightness of Eisenstein's usage, or the simply decorative possibilities of this technique, montage can be a way of perceiving or maintaining order in the midst of chaos. So, too, in the poems of Eliot and Pound based on such technique the images do not so much group around a single point as maintain an equal distance from each other; the method seems appropriate for marshalling large groups of impressions where the controlling idea is exploratory or uncertain. However, poetry will be treated later and enough has been said to indicate the moment by moment technique of 'montage' simultaneity and the overall 'cubist' spatialization through which *Ulysses* constructs its timeless dimension on a highly self-conscious aesthetic plane.

All this should help to clarify the book's dual relation to the world. We have seen how some cubist pictures construct a synthetic account of an object by exploiting the multiplicity of its appearances. From the point of view of conventional verisimilitude, the 'solidity' it now acquires is in *contrast* to that of the object itself while from the point of view of the painting it is felt *directly* in the architecture of the design. This dissolution and synthetic reconstruction of the 'common sense' object parallels the ambivalent realism of Joyce. There is both a departure from realism and a more thoroughgoing fulfilment of it. *Mutatis mutandis, Ulysses* fulfils the aspiration of Cézanne, from which cubism largely developed, to create '...something solid *and* artificial'. The solidity of Joyce, though, comes out not so much in a geometrical design as in his respect for the existential integrity of the materials of his design: Dublin itself and its people. What is meant here can be explained by invoking a later development of the cubist idea: the collage. The emphasis on the artist's design, which can imply a godlike dominion over the material, is at the same time, because of its very purity as formalism, its overtly mental ordering, a mode that does not impose on the material world at all. In a collage, where actual fragments of everyday objects are arranged into a design, it is explicit that the original object was not existentially dependent on the artist. Similarly, in the use he makes of the randomly 'given', Joyce anticipates later 'found' poetry or, more pertinently, the literary constructions of Nabokov which do not interfere, as it were, with nature. In effect, the emphasis on the artist's purely invented construction relieves the material, the external world, of the realist burden of meaning. Hence when Joyce writes home to Dublin to ascertain the height of the railings at 7 Eccles Street for Bloom to climb over in the 'Ithaca' chapter, he is not being a realist but constructing a collage. The elements become part of a design but were not in themselves designed for this purpose. Their 'meaning' in the work is distinct from their 'being' in the world, however much the artistic design, as in a cubist painting, may lead us to see the original in a new way. The effect once again is to produce a teasing duality. The world is solidly and externally there but it is apprehended through an ordering construction which is essentially mental. Just as Bloom and Stephen within the book construct their own worlds out of Dublin, so the whole work is an elaborate rehearsal of essentially the same process. Joyce's triumph is to preserve the existential integrity of Dublin and the prism of consciousness while making them fit as hand to glove. The 'reality' of the book is constructed but not solipsistic.

*

Hence, to summarize the argument so far, the three elements just discussed, personal identity, time and overt aesthetic constructivism are aspects, progressively, of the book's departure from traditional realism to affirm an ordering of life that is frankly and essentially an act of arbitrary aesthetic volition. Yet the parallels I have drawn with cubism, montage, etc., do not imply that these were Joyce's sources. His aesthetic transcendence of realism is a development from within the literary tradition itself. The broader philosophical import of this shift may, therefore, be defined in relation to some of the dominant tensions and oppositions of late nineteenth-century literature: particularly the complexes of intellectual stance and literary mode suggested by the terms '*symbolisme*' and 'naturalism'.

Where the English term 'symbolism' can refer quite generally to a poetic device the French *symbolisme* commonly denotes a specific literary movement that deeply affected most modern writers; modernism is in many respects a second generation *symbolisme*. The movement is not easy to define and even the notion of 'symbol' is not so clearly central to it as the term would seem to imply. Broadly speaking, however, the *symboliste* writers in France, like the aestheticists in England, accepted art as an absolute and autonomous value rather than as an imitation or criticism of common experience. Philosophically, this reflected the status of art in Schopenhauer's philosophy of the will. Art, in that context, is the only mode of release from the blind, impersonal process of generation and destruction by which life realizes itself. Art is not a creative acting on life but a contemplative remove. This idea also took mystical, theosophical and other quasi-religious forms, and can be seen as a non-religious response to the implications of Marx, Lyell and Darwin who seemed to swamp the individual fate into vastly collective processes socially, historically, and even biologically. Naturalism on the other hand, is the literary correlative of this opposite world view. The naturalist, and Zola is the classic example in the context of European fiction, sought to express precisely the social and biological factors that determine individual lives. The minute substantiation of environment, education and heredity becomes a way of explaining human behaviour leaving little room for the free play of personality or the independence of moral will. With the waning authority of the Christian world view the theological paradox of foreknowledge and free will is not removed but shifts into the secular terms of social or biological determinism, with the difference that there is now less of an overall metaphysic by which the poles of the paradox can be held in simultaneous focus. Where the Christian tradition, for the most part at least, provided a basis for meaningful moral destiny within the submission to a larger entity, these currents of late nineteenth-century thought offered respectively an aimless spirituality and blind process. What needs noting here is that although these two poles may find expression in such apparently opposite forms as oriental mysticism and scientific enquiry each takes its meaning from its polarity, implicit or explicit, to the other. Determinism takes its importance from an implied ideal of moral freedom just as the desire for an aesthetic or contemplative remove implies remove *from* something. Zola's personal friendship and sympathy with artists on the other side of this notional divide, such as Cézanne, suggests the broader truth that these movements are to be understood as opposite sides of a coin. Hence it is not surprising that both *symbolisme* and naturalism are generally felt to be one-sided. For most readers, the theoretical integrity of each, its abstract coherence, still leaves a sense of experiential incompleteness. Part of the achievement of modern, and especially modernist, literature is to respond deeply to both these poles rather than to one at the expense of the other. Whether or not modern writers achieve an equivalent for the morally pregnant mystery, or paradox, in the major religious traditions, they have created syntheses within which these abstractly opposed philosophical outlooks find some kind of co-existence. This seems to me the angle from which to approach philosophically the duality of *Ulysses*; the book does not answer the major questions we may pose about our lives, it rather suggests in what frame of mind we may live with them. The ordering of art, without carrying the freight of a religious meta physic, takes over something of its function.

This brief historical excursus suggests how we may view the modernism represented by *Ulysses*. Realism, with all that may imply socially and philosophically, had reached by the end of the nineteenth century a point of crisis. There was an apparently unresolvable cultu ral bifurcation between *symbolisme* and naturalism. No alternative world view of comparable comprehensiveness seemed to present itself. Hence there is in modernism a radical criticism of the old mode without a complete rejection of it. In this respect, the notion of a modern renaissance, whether or not it is justified in the quality of the literature, does point to its nature. For apart from their personal genius, Cervantes and Shakespeare are authors whose range and pene tration is intimately bound up with an historical moment in which they could be inwardly responsive to modes of thought and sensibility both modern and medieval. Though all historical moments are 'transi tional', some seem to our retrospective understanding more cardinally so than others, and the early decades of this century have a comparable sense of conflicting commitments held simultaneously. By contrast mid-twentieth century attacks on realism seem to me to have produced a less substantial literature and partly because the attitude of say, Beckett or Nabokov has settled into a coherently different, and more exclusive, stance. Proust, Joyce and Mann transcend the veri similar mode while still retaining much of the relation to the world that sustained nineteenth-century realism. Proust's creation of the childhood world of Combray has strong affinities with *The Mill on the Floss* or *David Copperfield*. Mann produced his squarely realistic *Buddenbrooks* at the opening of the century before going on to the elevation (*Steigerung*) of realism in *The Magic Mountain*. And Joyce's *Dubliners* takes up where Flaubert left off, poised between realist notation and aesthetic autonomy, before their interactions are explored in *Ulysses*.

This should indicate in a general way why the duality of perception I have indicated in *Ulysses* is important. So far, however, I have concentrated on the technical means by which the synthesis is sustained. More is required to justify the final suggestion that art be raised to a quasi-religious status in a more philosophically substantial sense than the aesthetes and *symbolistes* had in mind. I believe that such a philosophical justification is implied in several modern writers and to define it we may relate all that has been said so far about the modernist features of *Ulysses* to another problematic area that had acquired a new importance by the period in question: the concept and use of myth.

Myth, art and belief

> ' . . . for in the life of humanity the mythic indeed presents
> itself as an early and primitive step, but in the life of the
> individual as a late and mature one.'
>
> (Thomas Mann)[8]

If the critique and transcendence of realism imply shifting and relativistic conceptions of reality then it is not surprising that many modern authors have shown a deep interest in myth precisely because of its ambivalent truth value. It is somehow more than a story yet less than a proposition. To follow this development aright it is necessary to see both what myth had come to mean by the early twentieth century and why so many writers were especially receptive to it in their different ways. The point of conjunction is all important here since anthropology is generally of use to the artist where it confirms and expands his own independent intuitions. Much of the anthropology of the time has since been superseded and was in any case seen through the prism of literary purpose. Considered in itself, the rise of the new science of anthropology in the late nineteenth century is clearly an important and complex matter; hence the inclusion in the present volume of a separate essay outlining this development. And apart from its general information, this essay may have the further usefulness, by looking at anthropology in its own terms, of promoting reflection on

how far the mythopoeic consciousness of archaic man is itself one c
our potent modern myths. For the present, however, I want to consi
der this subject as it is manifest in literature.

Myth in its original form as the mode of thought in archaic societ
was taken to express a pre-analytic mode of relation to the world, th
community and the self. As its underlying mental process wa
explored, myth ceased to be a collection of rituals and superstitions o
an allegorical device. Instead it began to reveal an extraordinar
psychological wholeness in primitive life. The radical conceptualiza
tions of time and space, which Kant saw as conditioning the whol
engagement of mind with the world, seemed not to pertain for archai
man; or at least not in the same way. The archaic self related to it
environment, and to its past or future, in terms of identification
which we may call mythic but which for it were literal and efficacious
Hence the ritual dance before a hunt would affect its outcome, or
dancer wearing an ancestral mask would be literally imbued with th
dead man's spirit. Similarly, sexual possession in the fields could affec
the fertility of the year's crops, for the world was alive with 'mana
and magically responsive to human influence. The Western mythi
inheritance, for which literature was the principal repository, came t
be seen in a new light from such anthropological findings. Vergil'
'golden bough' from the *Aeneid* could hardly now be encountere
without the resonances of archaic ritual and belief created by Sir Jame
Frazer's then prestigious study of the same name.

As myth was increasingly revealed as more than poetic metaphor o
mere error but rather as the underlying structure of a coherent worl
view, so the traditional literary notion of the golden age, or the primitiv
good life, acquired what appeared to be a scientific validation. Her
apparently was the mode in which archaic man enjoyed the sense of
unified world view so notably lacking in modern life. But, in fact, thi
contrast is fraught with further irony for the modern in that he is onl
able to encounter the archaic mode, it seems, by the exercise of precisel
that analytic, scientific intelligence that debars him from inward partici
pation in it. If he can experience it inwardly at all, it is only by a poetic o
imaginative projection. There is an inescapable dilemma here tha
modern writers have repeatedly and variously engaged but I see tw
principal strategies underlying these endeavours: either to seek a retur
to archaic modes of sensibility or to create an equivalent within th
terms of modern consciousness – either return or progress.

The attitudes to myth in this respect reflect a larger opposition etween trust in the sophisticated evolution of the mind and distrust of he possibly alienating effect of abstract thought and highly developed elf-consciousness. I have discussed elsewhere the primitivist impulse n D.H. Lawrence as the signal British example of such distrust.[9] Vithout advocating a literal return to the primitive, Lawrence saw omething vital as lost to modern man and for Lawrence the recovery f wholeness and spontaneity lay through contact with the primitive man within the self. Lawrence was not opposed to intelligence but his onception of it as the 'whole man wholly attending' was in explicit pposition to a scientific standard of precise thought which he saw as a rogressive commitment to abstraction, a continual mentalization of xperience, at the cost of the felt 'otherness' of people and things. For he present purpose of defining a modernist use of myth I want to onsider more closely the opposite strategy: a use of mythic models hat can accompany a positive and even celebratory attitude towards he power of mind: an acceptance of self-consciousness as an expansion ather than dilution of experience.

The most direct and comprehensive formulation of this I have found a remark by Thomas Mann in his memorial lecture on Freud quoted t the beginning of this section. In fact Thomas Mann's philosophical xplicitness and his way of building this into his works in discursive orm makes him an especially helpful focus through which to define he general issue even as it bears on the comparable British authors. Ve might even begin by considering the form of the remark just uoted. It expresses the basic venture very pithily: the highest achieve- nent of sophisticated individuality is to recover a form of the primitive elf the race has struggled to transcend. The sentence has an air of onfident solidity and precisely controlled opposition; each part upporting and defining the rest. Yet as soon as you try to make sense f it more closely its outline becomes hazy and the words begin to issolve. Cunningly, Mann uses the key term 'mythic' only once which suggests it has the same meaning in both applications. But if ither application is held fast, does it not produce a different *meaning* r the word? Is this elusively adjectival abstraction really the same ntity in each context? My reason for submitting to this apparently ostile analysis a remark that is in any case taken out of its context is ot to dismiss Mann's idea but rather to indicate the characteristic 1ode of thinking in which his ruminations on myth take place. The

language wishes to engage, or at least to suggest, philosophical issue
while evading conventional philosophical criteria. It is a kind c
juggling with ideas by which a pattern is sustained visibly in the ai
while depending on the rapid mutual substitution of its constituen
elements. The effect is to tease us with a superposition. The momen
tary merging of the two meanings leads us to intuit by a verba
trompe-l'oeil the possibility of a third meaning encompassing both th
primitive and the sophisticated applications of myth. Our languag
preserves in the word 'conjuror' an association between sleight c
hand and supernatural power and such verbal juggling can have
comparably serious purpose of transcending everyday terms. Thoma
Mann is one of the most adept jugglers with ideas; creating constantl
revolving paradoxes that finally seem, to use his own word, 'bottom
less' rather than merely hollow. The novels themselves are the onl
test of that, of course, but his family pet name of the 'Magician
reflects his awareness of this quality in his work and, significantly
places it in a context of pure entertainment. As opposed to the mor
earnestness of Lawrence, Mann approaches myth as a self-delightin
play of ideas.

The difference in spirit emerges more clearly in the comparison c
specific works. It is a significant reflection of their respective presup
positions that Lawrence's view of contemporary civilization darkene
progressively while Thomas Mann's humanistic optimism persiste
even despite the dark years of the Fascist dictatorships reflected i
Doktor Faustus and other works. Lawrence's affirmation in *The Rain
bow* (1915) is almost negated by the subsequent desperation c
Women in Love (1920). Mann's *The Magic Mountain* (1924) i
close to being his *Women in Love* for it also studies the psychologic
corruption, the secret orientation towards death, of contemporar
civilization through a small but representative group of personalitie
and it even makes symbolic use of the same snowy mountain regior
The two novels have also a parallel genesis in that both were conceive
before the Great War and by the time they were completed they ha
assimilated into themselves the consciousness of a historical catas
trophe which the original conception had already in some sense antic
pated. Yet Mann went on to write *Joseph and his Brothers* which w
might call his version of *The Rainbow*; it is his way of affirming th
value of life. The separate volumes of the work were actually publishe
over a span of years starting after 1930, but the initial concept and th

background reading, particularly in anthropology, date from the late 1920s so that for our purposes the work does belong to the period under discussion. To see myth used with a method and spirit in polar contrast to Lawrence's we may look more closely at *The Rainbow* and the Joseph sequence.

The two works are a curious mirror image of each other; at once parallel and opposite. Lawrence tells the story of an English yeoman family passing an emotional and moral heritage through several generations down to Lawrence's own day. As the title suggests, the story of the Brangwens is modelled on *Genesis*; the meaning of the heritage and the mystery of its transmission are embodied in a biblical structure, symbolism and language encompassing the whole work. Mann also effects a fusion of the *Genesis* tale and modernity but in an opposite sense. He retells part of the biblical narrative transposed into the language and assumptions of a modern psychological novelist. The abrupt, mysterious statements of the biblical style are given elaborate psychological and anthropological explanation so that the sheer disparity in volume between the few biblical pages and Mann's monumental tetralogy is itself part of the point. Mann is not seeking to 'modernize', still less to improve, the biblical version. The significance of his retelling may be understood rather in terms of a recurring issue in the German literary philosophical tradition that bears on the paradox of modern myth-making and the value of self-consciousness.

Schiller's essay 'Über Naive und Sentimentalische Dichtung' (1796) is the classic announcement of this central modern theme; a fact that is rather obscured by the common mistranslation 'On Naive and Sentimental Poetry'. We may call it 'On Spontaneous and Self-Conscious Poetry' for Schiller argues that ancient poetry, such as Homer's, implies a spontaneity, a oneness of thought and feeling, that has been superseded by an habitually self-reflecting consciousness embodied in a different kind of poetry. In principle, at least, Schiller sees these as equally valuable, but the crucial point is that they are polar; the sensibility that adopts the one foregoes the other. This is a classic theory of historical modification of sensibility based on poetic language. T.S. Eliot's 'dissociation of sensibility' took seventeenth-century poetry as its basis to argue something comparable but with a more negative slant. And Lawrence's *The Rainbow* and *Women in Love* also trace an historical shift from spontaneity to alienating self-consciousness. That such theories have been frequently accepted as

simply cultural facts reflects, I should think, a serious spiritual truth,
but historically speaking the issue is strictly speculative and can be
seen quite differently. Goethe, in his late conversations with
Eckermann, for example, remarks that Schiller's excitement about his
important idea led him to force it too far and thereby miss its main
point. For self-conscious poetry, Goethe remarks, in so far as it *is*
poetry, will necessarily include the spontaneous element. Thomas
Mann's vast reworking of the biblical narrative is, in effect, an exhaus-
tive vindication of this Goethean perception with application not just
to poetry but to self-consciousness at large. Mann recognizes the core
of myth within even the most scientific and rationalist modes of explanation. His modern style tugs the archaic tale into the light of a
psychologically and anthropologically sophisticated consciousness and
in so doing demonstrates that the tale does not thereby lose its
mystery. The elaborate structure of modern understanding grows out
of the same ground of the unknowable as does the ancient legend.
Hence Mann views the evolution of our civilization with less hostility
and suspicion than Lawrence does. The mythic mystery is expanded
rather than dissolved by the play of analytic consciousness.

This general difference is apparent in the more detailed features of
The Rainbow as compared to the Joseph sequence and these parallel
the features already considered in *Ulysses*. For Lawrence and Mann
also transcend or expand the conventions of realist fiction in ways that
involve more open conceptions of personal identity and time and they
reflect these attitudes in their different registers of authorial self-
consciousness.

In each work characters weather the crises and transitions of their
lives by intuitive recourse to the past manifest as an impersonal, or
supra-personal, mythic identity. Mann's Joseph, Jacob and Isaac
behave consciously as characters in a story the general form of which
they know by its repetitions since their ancestor Abraham's time.
Their conscious seeking of such mythic identification is directly opposite to the experience of the Brangwens. These latter pass into the
impersonal alignment with the family identity by a lapsing of
consciousness. The collective emotional pattern characteristically
asserts itself for them when the personal consciousness has failed to
cope.

So too, in each case, the constant transcendence of the personal self
implies a corresponding transcendence of linear time. The Brangwens

ive with the experience of the past in their blood, as it were. Apart from the occasional play of memory upon the past, Lawrence's narrative language handles time itself in a fluid way that frequently foreshortens it. The general effect is that time is never an abstract issue for characters or reader yet the experience of the book has an especial density arising from the constant cyclic superimpositions of past and present; there is a mythic livingness of the past in the present. Mann, too, shapes the structure and texture of the novels to modify the reader's sense of time in a comparably subliminal way, but he also brings time into it as a conscious philosophical issue. In fact, the opening chapter entitled 'Prelude' is an explicit rumination on the human sense of location in time. For example:

> Thus there may exist provisional origins, which practically and in fact form the first beginnings of the particular traditions held by a given community, folk or communion of faith; and memory, though sufficiently instructed that the depths have not actually been plumbed, yet nationally may find reassurance in some primitive point of time and, personally and historically speaking, come to rest there.[10]

It is notorious that the new vistas of evolutionary time opened up during the nineteenth century had threatened the *Genesis* account of the origins of man and reduced him from a divinely appointed moral essence to a randomly historical process of becoming. Both *The Rainbow* and the Joseph sequence effectively adopt an anthropological standpoint to reconcile an evolutionary with a religious view of human history. Yet as Mann introduces his theme, far from relying on a mythic blurring of the conceptual elements, he gives them explicit and abstract formulation. 'Historical' origins are as arbitrary as the opening of a folk-tale with its traditional formula of 'once upon a time'. Yet the moment is not entirely arbitrary if it affords a point of rest within the structure of the narrative itself. The starting point for legend is the moment *in illo tempore* that the spirit intuits as an intrinsic necessity rather than an historical fact. Typically, Mann treads an exact line here between a scientific and a mythic perspective and the effect of his language in a long-term way is to reinforce this dualism stylistically. It is both elaborately abstract and yet an informal personal voice. Its elaborate structures of quizzical philosophizing move around a centre of touchingly naive faith; the one register qualifying but also animating the other. Hence in this passage the finding of a haven in a mythical point of origin is seen in a conceptual way as arbitrary, yet in conjunction with the imagery and syntactic structures of the preceding paragraph it embodies the subjective movement of the mind searching and coming to rest. It is this open-eyed, yet inward, acceptance of the mythic mode in a context imposing such an explicit philosophical burden on it that characterizes the mythicizing of Thomas Mann as opposed to Lawrence.

The further implication of this is that whereas Lawrence keeps within the formal tradition of realism in accepting the complete actuality of his characters, Mann exploits their fictionality. The reader, in fact, stands in the same relation to Joseph's story as Joseph does to Jacob's within the book and to Abraham's yet earlier again. In composing the sequence Mann constantly reread that classic of self-conscious fiction, Laurence Sterne's *Tristram Shandy*, and it is vital that he places the whole story within, not so much a conscious fictional frame, as a conscious and continuing fictional creation. Just as the sentence quoted is poised between the 'objectivity' of science and the 'subjectivity' of myth so the whole story explores the ambivalence of man's 'creation'. Man is mysteriously created, he is not his own originator, and yet as part of the whole process he comes in some measure to define and create himself. When the work ends with

... and so endeth the beautiful story and God-invention of
JOSEPH AND HIS BROTHERS.

the typographical highlighting of the title completes and epitomizes the spiralling ambiguities. The book has both given and received the power of the pre-existing story. And just as we do not know where the original biblical figures and Mann's fictions shade into each other, so we do not know whether 'God-invention' refers to the characters' invention of God, which is a major element of the whole tale, or to God's invention of this tale and thus of the human story at large. Here, of course, the German word 'Geschichte', like the French 'histoire', preserves a suggestive ambiguity where English discriminates between 'history' and 'story'. Hence the two views, invention *by* God and *of* God, the religious and the rationalist, are woven into a seamless cloth of legend. And withal it *is* a beautiful story whether we are its readers or are included in its larger historical frame. Whatever misery and wickedness it includes, the human story, Mann suggests, s beautiful for the constant turning of men to the 'highest', and the retelling of the story in itself celebrates and promotes this aspiration. Hence the fictional self-consciousness is not merely showing off on Mann's part but a proper and lovely expansion of the book's meaning. Mann's story, in transcending the realist form, is our mode of access to myth.

I have allowed myself this digression from the purely British situation because the discursive explicitness of Mann illuminates much that is only implied in a work like *Ulysses*. Despite their differences, the family likeness is revealing: the features of modernist transcendence of realism can also be seen as modes of modernist mythopoeia. Yet the mythic or legendary dimension of *Ulysses* is far less prominent than in Mann and still further aspects of modern, self-conscious mythopoesis emerge from comparing the 'cubist' constructivism of Joyce with the commitment to traditional narrative structure in Mann.

The eighteen episodes of *Ulysses* invoke by their diverse techniques the highly specialized activities through which we collectively organize and comprehend our experience. The arts, science, economics, history, theology, etc., are all attempts to survey the whole of life but only from the fixed perspective of their own terms, and this clear demarcation into intellectual specialisms is a development particularly of the last few hundred years. While accepting their separateness, Joyce has grouped them around the single focus of a day in Bloom's life and given them a further interlocking unity of a cross-word-puzzle kind. This collage-like unity is at the opposite pole from the unity of archaic myth, yet Joyce, like Mann, evokes archaic legend as his analogy. For primitive man art, science, religion and history are not yet separated. A rain-making ritual might be said to involve poetry, music, dance and the plastic arts as well as implying a view of history, religion and science. And all these activities would partake of the sacredness of the whole. No such unity is possible once these elements have found separate definition, but Joyce, like an archeologist restoring a jar of unknown shape, places a sufficient number of the fragments in a mutual relation so that we can intuit the form of the whole. In this respect the invocation of Homer, unlike Mann's use of *Genesis*, suggests as much contrast as continuity with the archaic mode. Epic is a literary form containing the historical legend and world view of a people. For its original audience the response to it *qua* poem was presumably not distinguishable from the response to it as history; it is the point, looking backwards, where history and poetry meet and blend in myth. But Joyce's use of Homer implies not so much a return to myth as an equivalent for it in the modern mode. If literature is our form of myth, Joyce, as opposed to Mann, works through the discreteness of the two modes.

Hence the overt constructivism of *Ulysses* affirms its creation in the present rather than its survival from the past; it is a product of aesthetic will rather than legendary inheritance. And Stephen's aesthetic theorizing within the work, notably in the 'Scylla and Charybdis' episode, emphasizes the Joycean ideal of aesthetic impersonality in a way that implies a similarly distanced relation to the human material as in the archaic mode of the epic. Homer and Shakespeare, the authors on whom respectively Joyce bases his book and Stephen his theory are highly impersonal. Homer is so close to an oral formulaic tradition that his identity as a single poet has been a matter of scholarly debate Shakespeare, a Renaissance dramatist, does not inherit historically such an impersonal perspective. In fact, his character of Hamlet is the classic embodiment of the modern experience of alienated, self conscious personality. Yet, Stephen suggests, Shakespeare as a drama tist is able to see life steadily and as a whole in a way that neither his characters, nor he himself perhaps in his personal life, could do *Ulysses* embodies that wholeness of perspective and recognizes from within the work the enormous difficulty of this for the modern consciousness. Impersonality, for Joyce, is the high point of literary evolution. Hence Joyce's attempt to disappear as author behind the impersonal artefact has a common significance with Mann's overtness as a story-teller. Both are means of recapturing an archaic impersonality; the one directly and the other by an elaborate equivalence.

*

For Joyce, then, the mythic equivalence lies not so much in the simple continuity of legend as in the impersonal, even serene, perspective of aesthetic creation as he understood it. The emphasis, in other words shifts from the cyclic recurrence of content in Lawrence and Mann to a philosophical disposition manifest in the form itself. This is why for Joyce, as for Yeats, the significance of myth emerges more from the *symboliste* and aestheticist views of art than from anthropological sources. These movements had imbued in Joyce and Yeats the sense hat art stood in contradistinction to everyday experience and had ience for them pushed art closer to myth in having an ambivalent ruth, or meaning, value. We might go back to Coleridge's formulaion and say that poetry as a 'willing suspension of disbelief' is a model or how we respond to myth. But this would be a clumsy conflation in hat Coleridge's phrase sets out precisely to discriminate between ioetic belief and belief at large. It is the latter phase of romanticism, he broadly *symboliste* version, which prepares for the characteristic hift in modernist myth-making we should now consider more closely: hat 'poetic' truth becomes the model for truth generally.

To pick up this aspect it is helpful to move to Yeats[11] who not only ived his first thirty-five years in the nineteenth century and was leeply committed to aestheticist attitudes but who also, partly as a esult of his concern with Irish political events, fought hard afterwards o engage the life of his time in his poetry. I have suggested in connecion with fiction that if much modernist literature is to be seen as a econd phase of *symbolisme*, its distinguishing feature is to carry the iestheticist principle into a new relation with life. In Joyce, as in 'roust, the poles of aesthetic autonomy and referential verisimilitude neet. We can see a corresponding transformation of aestheticism, and it a more explicitly philosophical level, in Yeats' views on myth and ielief; particularly as these are embodied in his mature poetry.

The principal mentor of the aestheticist movement in England was Walter Pater and in his 'Conclusion' to *The Renaissance* he adopts a tance of wide, if problematic, import:

> What we have to do is be forever curiously testing new
> opinions and courting new impressions, never acquiescing in
> a facile orthodoxy of Comte, or Hegel, or of our own. Philo-
> sophical theories or ideas, as points of view, instruments of
> criticism, may help us to gather up what might otherwise
> pass unregarded by us. 'Philosophy is the instrument of
> thought.'[12]

iven this brief extract is a *pot-pourri* of modernist attitudes and hemes, to some of which I will return later. For the present we may iote its espousal of perpetual relativism not as a fallen condition but as i positive ideal. The phrase 'point of view', which becomes so crucial n the discussion of modern fiction, is here attached to an ideal of :onstantly shifting frames of reference. Truth is defined in relation to a

given frame, not by universal principle. The statement invokes a sense
of thought specialisms comparable to the chapters of *Ulysses*. Yet in
suggesting the pertinence of the aestheticist outlook to the modern
situation, this passage also exemplifies its limitations. The objection
one feels to Pater's relativism is not so much logical as empirical:
behind its active curiosity is a passiveness that seems ultimately naive
in its grasp of actual human motivations. This passivity is a point of
difference from Yeats and it relates to a further difference in the very
mode of discourse. Pater expresses his idea here in a language that,
however crucially interlarded with rhetorical imagery, is basically
conceptual. Poems, like myths, can evade such modes of formulation
and their ability to do so can be an important aspect of their significance. Yeats, like Lawrence, was a man capable of the highest quality
of intellection by conventional standards, yet deliberately eschewed
this in much of his most serious 'thought.' For him 'knowledge' and
'belief' were intuitional; allied, as he put it, to the 'wisdom or instinct'
of 'a migratory bird'.[13] To so conflate wisdom and instinct is verbal
juggling akin to Thomas Mann's remark on myth already discussed:
the most crucial questions and discriminations get conveniently
blurred. Yet in Yeats' poetry, as in Mann's novels, this blurring of
categories is a conscious creative element by which he can say things
he could not otherwise say. In Yeats, the aestheticist inheritance is
manifest not in a remove from life but in seeing life from a perspective
that cannot be formulated conceptually, or in any other terms but the
experience of the work itself.

We can see the force of this in Yeats by briefly following from its
earliest to its latest manifestations his treatment of the subjective
experience he called 'dream' or 'vision'. His early poem 'The Stolen
Child' in *Crossways* (1889) enacts the enticement of a child by the
'faery' to a dreamily painless other world. The incantatory rhythms,
particularly of the refrain, express the hypnotic attraction while each
of the four stanzas makes more plain the sinister implications. The
child will forfeit the solid and familiar world of reality. Using a conventional nineteenth-century dichotomy of 'dream world' and 'reality',
Yeats makes poetry out of his ambivalence. The whole assumption
here, though, is that the two worlds can be clearly distinguished. In
'Ego Dominus Tuus' from *The Wild Swans at Coole* (1919), these
categories have been elided:

The rhetorician would deceive his neighbours
The sentimentalist himself; while art
Is but a vision of reality.
What portion of the world can the artist have
Who has awakened from the common dream
But dissipation and despair?

However we take the word 'reality' here, which seems to have the sense of a platonic ideal, the human choice is now between 'vision' and 'dream'; two subjectivities. And note too that the distinction hinges not on fixed categories but on art conceived as quality of expression and on the artist's awareness of the potential deceptiveness of his medium. You cannot test it in terms outside the poetic act and that act includes a consciousness of its own truth status. The kind of thinking about subjectivity, truth and art expressed here found quasi-discursive form in *A Vision*;. a work that was already occupying him now although not published till 1925.

Shortly after his marriage in 1917, Yeats' wife began automatic writing in which mysterious supernatural 'instructors' dictated largely incomprehensible notes. Out of this material Yeats pieced together a systematic 'philosophy' of human history and individual temperament based on twenty-eight psychological types. While individuals might be of any kind, the collective psychological orientation of a civilization passes through the twenty-eight phases in recurrent cycles of about 2000 years. The question of Yeats' debt to his wife's 'instructors' would be immaterial if he had not built into *A Vision* a conscious ambivalence concerning its truth status. He leads into it by a long story of the discovery of its principal diagram in an old book and, apart from this stock device of fictional mystification, he concludes by saying that the whole system amounts to a 'stylistic arrangement of experience like the cubes in the paintings of Wyndham Lewis. Yeats develops for use in his poetry, and generally, a comprehensive classificatory system that enables him to characterize individuals and historical periods with considerable acuteness, yet which evades, ostentatiously evades, questions concerning its philosophical status. The rather awkward explicitness with which he confronts this issue in *A Vision* arises from its discursive mode, but in the poetry based on the visionary material he is able, at his best, to make this discursive limitation work as a positive dimension of the poem's meaning. Of the many poems using this material, the very late 'Lapis Lazuli' in *Last Poems* (1939) is, I think, the most paradigmatic in this respect.

In 'Lapis Lazuli' Yeats asserts the artist's, or we might say the myth-maker's, 'gaiety' in the face of the anarchy and violence of contemporary history. The poem consists of four movements. A brief but forceful recreation of the contemporary agony in the first section is followed by a study of tragic experience as recreated in art, specifically that of dramatic tragedy. In the third section the focus is once again on 'real' life in the generalized perspective of a historical summary and in the fourth, through a description of the lapis lazuli carving of the title, the argument is resolved in terms of art. The movement of the poem, then, in its overall progression from hysterical women to the poet's gaiety, is a continual transposition from life to art and back again. Considering this constant transposition more closely, we can see how it provides a context in which Yeats defines the delicate interrelations between the two apparently inimical orders of being.

The poem's strategy begins to emerge in the second section as the tragic experience is contained within an aesthetic frame affirming the power of the mind to make the suffering inherent in the human condition an object of ecstatic contemplation. The full force of this, though, derives from Yeats sustaining a suggestion that the ecstatic sense of tragedy realized in dramatic art is not just the creation of the artist, but is somehow identical to, or continuous with, that of the hysterical women of the opening section.

The second section opens with the general statement, 'All perform their tragic play'. As so often in Yeats' poetry the rhetorical shaping of the sentence seems clear and definite while actually leaving syntactical relations suggestively open. As I have said, this is revelatory of Yeats' cast of mind and can, as in the present instance, play a crucial poetic role: as indeed we might expect from his comment on similar technique in Blake: 'The form of sincere poetry, unlike the form of popular "poetry", may indeed be sometimes obscure, or ungrammatical, as in the best of the *Songs of Innocence and Experience*.'[14] In the present instance the syntax is formally clear enough but it only gradually asserts itself over the rhetorical movement. Only as the sentence continues does it become evident that the 'tragic play' of the opening line refers syntactically to the formal or literary tragedy while its early position, and apparent generality of reference at that point, imply at first that it efers back to, or at least includes, the contemporary tragedy of the first section. This initial ambiguity concerning the location of the tragic play', whether it refers to life or art, would be only a momentary distraction if it occurred in isolation but in fact while it is still in the course of resolution a further, and comparably suggestive, ambiguity reinforces it and is then developed through the whole section.

In the line 'Yet they, should the last scene be there', the subject 'they' clearly refers to the dramatic characters named in the preceding lines. Yet when ostensibly the same subject pronoun recurs four lines later, apparently as mere recapitulation, in 'They know that Hamlet and Lear are gay', its meaning has undergone a subtle but important change. Considered in isolation the line would be taken to mean that some other consciousness, such as the actor's, possesses this knowledge. Earlier suggestions in 'part' and 'lines' are thus picked up and the implication is that the dramatic character has such a reified sense of his own role that he transcends it to become his own actor or author. The statement that the tragic figures 'If worthy their prominent part in the play/Do not break up their lines to weep', reinforces this duality. Whether we choose to see 'worthy' as applying more to character or actor, breaking up the lines to weep would in either case remove the existential grounds of the weeping. If the character weeps he is no longer the character created by those lines: if the actor weeps he dissolves the whole illusion of character and suffering. With a deceptive simplicity of image Yeats catches the discursively inexpressible complexity of an art emotion created out of two worlds that can never directly meet. Yet while they cannot meet, neither can they, within this emotion, be taken apart. Harold Bloom's observation that 'the gaiety of Lear is, of course, non-existent'[15] is strictly accurate, but there is gaiety in the *enacting* of Lear; and this latter gaiety is necessarily predicated on the suffering of the character. Hence for the actor, or the sympathetic spectator, the mind suffering the agony is not separable from the mind that holds it in being and experiences it with exaltation. As I have suggested, this delicate superimposition of actor and character grows out of the initial superimposition of tragic experience as encountered both within and outside the dramatic frame. The final effect, therefore, is to suggest that the inextricability of the agony and the transcending exaltation as demonstrated within the dramatic context extends outwards to imply the same relation pertaining generally between tragic circumstances and the human mind. The poetic action expresses in a vividly concrete, if discursively elusive, image both the transforming power of the tragic vision and its larger relation to experience.

This definition of aesthetic emotion is picked up in the final section which enacts something very similar except that the direction is now reversed. Instead of life contemplated in an artistic frame, we now have art figures contemplating life outside the work that contains them; the movement inwards towards art becomes a movement out towards life The crucial figures in this section, the carved Chinamen, are intro duced with a momentary ambiguity parallelling that of the 'tragic play'. At first mention they seem real people until the second line makes clear that they are part of the carving. Once again this momen tary suggestion is only the first stage in the development, for with the line 'The third, doubtless a serving man', an intricate double action begins. The word 'doubtless' implies that the scene the poet is describing depends in part on his imaginative interpretation of the carving. This is the beginning of a shift from the carved scene to an independently existing realistic action; a shift from the stillness of art to the movement of life. Yet at the same time the word 'doubtless' by the very fact of implying interpretative activity, is a reminder that the scene is in fact a piece of carved stone. This double suggestion is deve loped in the next four lines as the arbitrary imperfections of the stone are transmuted into the details of a more and more vital natural setting; 'water-course' and 'avalanche' leading to actual movement in 'it still snows'. Following this, the word 'doubtless' again introduces the next phase as the Chinamen are seen to be in motion too. Only in the last six lines does Yeats allow his imagined scene effectively to take leave of the carving. The final scene is freely and explicitly created by the poet's imagination: the Chinamen are now seen as having arrived at their destination; they are moving, speaking and smiling. Consider ing this vantage point as a poetic as well as a literal one, they can be said to stare on the 'tragic scene' with an ontological as well as physical remove. What the Chinamen stare at is the tragic scene of life outside the boundaries of the work of art that contains them. Yeats has created for his tragic gaiety a standpoint that looks out on life yet which is made possible by a work of art.

If we now relate this final section to the second, we can see that the overall strategy is firstly to contain the tragic experience within an aesthetic frame while still keeping it continuous with life, and then to use the aesthetic vantage point, the capacity for transcendence, in order to look out on the tragedy of life. This systematic interweaving of art and life is a necessary condition of the poem's final affirmation and it gives that affirmation a characteristically elusive basis. Indeed, the elusiveness is so emphasized as to be an important element of the meaning. The gaiety is attributed directly to the Chinamen only; the Chinamen created by the interaction of the observer with the carving. It is as if Yeats' affirmation, the very nature of which necessitates a singleness of expression undisturbed by irony or qualification, could only accommodate itself 'unsentimentally' to reality by locating itself at this elusive ontological remove. Yeats provides a structural qualification for his rhetoric; within this he can express unreservedly what he could not otherwise say.

Yeats' poetic deployment of the historical system of *A Vision* enabled him to face and transcend the tragic aspect of history in a manner comparable to the Chinamen of 'Lapis Lazuli' who look out on life with an emotion defined in terms of art. When he suggested that his visionary system functions as a 'stylistic arrangement of experience' like the cubes of Wyndham Lewis, he might have adduced the cubist paintings analysed by E.H.J. Gombrich in *Art and Illusion*, which superimpose different planes in a contradictory manner so that the eye, seeking a realistic rationale for the pattern, finds no point of rest.[16] As Yeats puts it in 'The Tower':

> O may the moon and sunlight seem
> One inextricable beam
> For if I triumph I must make men mad.

He does not say that moon and sunlight, his terms for vision and reality, could *be* one beam, only that we might find a way of seeing them as such; of orienting ourselves morally and emotionally as if they were. Like Thomas Mann, Yeats came in his maturity to feel the need for a principled engagement in the political questions of his time after having been deeply imbued with a spirit of aesthetic isolationism; indeed, as Yeats 'gaiety' suggests, they have a common inspiration in Nietzsche. Without abandoning their earlier principles both developed a mythopoeic conception of life that enabled them to affirm what they felt to be its enduring values without mere dandyism in the face of contemporary anguish. Mann's achievement seems to me on the whole more convincing in this respect than Yeats', and this may be

connected not only with Mann's relation to more central currents of
European history in his day, but also with his German literary and
philosophical heritage which had so thoroughly digested the issues of
myth, art and belief as well as charting the involutions of romantic
irony. Yet Yeats, despite his weakness for emotional rhetoric, something of which can be felt, I think, in 'Lapis Lazuli', is manifestly a
major twentieth-century poet able to express important spiritual
perceptions within, and because of, his mythopoeic elusiveness.

I have dwelt at some length on the question of myth as this seems to
me a point where literature meets other intellectual fields in a recognition that all world views are human constructions. Any belief, so
perceived, becomes mythical and questions of its adequacy or truth
value must be dealt with from inside this assumption. The literary use
of myth focuses ways of making the necessarily subjective construction of the human world not an epistemological blind alley but a
positive and reality-engaging dimension of the mind. Tolstoy in *What
I Believe* expresses his realization of the moral precariousness of his
earlier world view in a striking, if unphilosophical, image of being
suspended on a bed-spring over an abyss. To use a comparably
picturesque analogy, we might imagine a child born in a wooden
building and never leaving it. He might suppose the building to be the
world. On more mature analysis he might deduce from the form of the
building that it is constructed. It exists independently of him yet is a
human construction and he might even intuit the possibility of a world
outside it. This stage we could equate with the Kantian recognition of
our mental creation of the phenomenal world. Supposing one day a
flood comes. The inhabitant expects the building to be destroyed but
in fact it floats and proves to be a boat. This is a further radical
retrenchment of the stability of the initial 'world'. But the home holds
together and, as a boat, has the advantage that it can be made to move
from place to place by the volition of its inhabitant. Compare this with
modern mythopoeia. Philosophical aspiration has settled for a new
subjectivity, but having lost its stability in the world the boat comes to
be judged by other standards of construction and purpose. Philosophical subjectivity can accompany an active engagement with the world.

*

The literary creation of mythic world views is a spiritual or humanistic correlative of other metaphysical retrenchments that also,

paradoxically perhaps, could accompany an enormous expansion in the human mastery of the world. For apart from the emotional subjectivity of poets, the apparently hard-headed world of science found itself in the early twentieth century expanding its empirical knowledge at the cost of a new metaphysical uncertainty. But this is a large topic which I think is best discussed in the context of general interrelations between science and literature in the modern period. Once again, as with anthropological material, we need to understand the other field in its own terms as well as seeing why certain literary contexts should have felt a real or apparent affinity with it.

The passage from Walter Pater's *The Renaissance* already quoted in relation to Yeats' mythopoeia is pertinent here. Pater's remarks are replete with the scientific language of 'testing', 'instruments' and 'microscope'. That the devotee of absolute art should model an essential philosophical position on science is a useful key to the relationship to science of the modern inheritors of aestheticism. For we most commonly, and I think rightly, see science as a quite different sort of thing from literature and it is only certain kinds of science and literature that coincide. There is also a further twist to the matter, I think. Over the course of the nineteenth and twentieth centuries there is a sense in which we can see science and literature defined as opposites and then curiously changing places, or at least stealing each other's clothes. Consider, for example, Wordsworth's remarks in the 'Preface' to the *Lyrical Ballads* (1798):

> Poetry is the first and last of all knowledge – it is as immortal as the heart of man. If the labours of the man of science should ever create any material revolution, direct or indirect, in our condition, and in the impressions which we habitually receive, the poet will sleep no more than at present; he will be ready to follow the steps of the man of science, not only in those general and indirect effects, but he will be at his side, carrying sensation into the midst of the objects of science itself.

In Wordsworth's time the word 'science' referred more generally to systematic understanding, but the polarity he assumes here already points to the later bifurcation. In the face of this split, such an arch organicist as Wordsworth, in contrast to Blake's bitter and radical rejection of the abstractive thinking and materialist assumptions of physical science, envisages for the sake of poetry itself the necessity of assimilating scientific to poetic understanding. Truth must ultimately be one and denial of the part weakens the whole. In the event science and literature have indeed interpenetrated but in a very different sense from that envisaged by Wordsworth, with his assumed polarity of scientific fact and poetic imagination or feeling. For literature has increasingly come not just to assimilate but to model itself on science while science over the same period has come to recognize its own status as a mental projection on to reality. Let us first follow up the scientific side of this.

The change in the view of science was a concomitant of apparently paradoxical revelations, particularly in the latter part of the nineteenth century, about the basic structure of the world. According to some experimental observations, for example, certain sub-atomic elements appeared to be discrete particles yet from other, equally valid, observations they were waves. In time physicists have come to accept that their interpretations of reality at these microscopic levels have to proceed through mathematical deduction without models, such as waves or particles, drawn from everyday macroscopic experience. Even before Einstein's relativity theory and Planck's quantum theory brought this home forcibly at the astronomical and sub-atomic levels respectively, it was already apparent that the notion of 'observation' was deeply problematic. Rather than the scientist observing nature and then explaining it, it becomes necessary to devise an interpretation in order to have significant observation. The basic structure of the world is not actually seen, but deduced. This raises a serious question concerning the cognitive status of scientific theory. Such theory is not purely subjective, it is after all held to the criterion of experimental verification, but there may be competing theories of equal utility and demonstrability with no otherwise available external reality by which they can be judged.

In view of this high level of hypothesis and indirection in scientific theory, some scientists and philosophers of science began to see science as an elaborate summary of what happens rather than an explanation in principle of why it happens. Karl Pearson's *The Grammar of Science* (1892), which went through several editions and was addressed to a lay as well as a purely scientific readership, argued that science in this sense *describes* rather than *explains*. This account of scientific theory as the instrument rather than the object of thought, as something that does a job more or less well but is not therefore to be described as true or false, is a form of creative scepticism analogous to Pater's view of philosophical theories as 'instruments of criticism' or Yeats' use of his visionary system as a 'stylistic arrangement of experience'. There are differences, too, of course. Pater and Yeats positively rejoice in this state while science suffers it, and their modes of testing truth value are quite different, but the conceptions reflect a similar mental stance: the mind makes active and genuine engagement with the world through its own essentially arbitrary frame of reference.

Furthermore, Sir Arthur Eddington in *The Nature of the Physical World* (1929) suggests a duality of perception for the modern physicist akin to that we have discussed in literature. Eddington speaks of the physicist sitting at his desk and knowing that the solid plane surface he is using is in fact, at a sub-atomic level, a conglomeration of particles in a continuous motion. For the orders of size and velocity at which relativity and quantum physics changed the Newtonian system did not invalidate it within the range of everyday perception. Paradoxically perhaps, the 'uncertainty' of quantum mechanics at the micro-level does not apply to macro-phenomena even though they have this micro-structure. Hence the new physics both denies and yet co-exists with the Newtonian and its stance towards reality has the duality of commitment we have seen in the literary transcendence of realism. The two levels sharpen each other and the engagement with reality is not necessarily the less for being recognized as invention as much as perception.

In pointing out this affinity between literary and scientific stances *vis-à-vis* reality, however, we need to make important qualifications. It should firstly be noted that this was a common but not universal interpretation of modern physics and proponents of this view, such as Karl Pearson, Henri Poincaré, Arthur Eddington and Werner Heisenberg have been refuted by Ernest Nagel's magisterial summary of these issues in *The Structure of Science* (1961). Nagel indicates that modern physics does not in fact enforce a more indeterminate metaphysic than does the Newtonian, and in retrospect it seems that the changes in late nineteenth-century and early twentieth-century physics generated a kind of metaphysical wobble that has since rather stabilized itself. Instead of seeing the new physics as a denial of common sense conceptions and certainties, another generation of physicists have quietly made their notion of common sense more accommodating. But if a term like 'relativity' does not really bear the moral and metaphysical burdens often placed on it, this does not reduce – indeed from a cultural historical point of view it rather increases – the interest of such attributions. It seems most likely in fact that the actual content of the new physics is not the cause of changes in world view so much as it is itself assimilated to these; and that when artists used details and metaphors from science or tried to appropriate its general prestige, their underlying metaphysical stance had an independent derivation. Hence if Joyce, Proust, Yeats and Mann are contemporaries of Planck and Einstein in a more than external sense this does not hinge on their understanding, even less transposing, the theoretical content of the new science. I include even Proust here though he is perhaps the trickiest case and owned himself pleased to be compared to Einstein. But the scientificizing aspect of Proust seems to me to belong more to the other side of the large process I have suggested: the modernist emulation of science.

I have remarked that in certain influential interpretations literature and science had exchanged clothes since Wordsworth's time; if science had become more aware of its own creative dimension so literature had sought the scientific model of detachment. The emphasis on detachment, the personal neutrality, of the scientist is the key here and may be distinguished from the general scientific ideal of understanding. Though closely related for the scientist, these ideals may have an independent value in a literary context. Since the French realist novel in the nineteenth century persistently sought analogies with science it is especially helpful in explaining this. Balzac's dedication of *Le Père Goriot* (1834) to the scientist Geoffroi de St Hilaire suggests how his account of man in a specific environment will seek to make use of scientific perceptions. This explanatory conception of the novel on a scientific model was taken to its logical extreme by Zola in his attempt, outlined theoretically in *The Experimental Novel* (1880), to study society and moral behaviour completely within the terms of the scientist. Zola's novels are better and more unpredictable than this theoretical statement might imply, but his theory is a *terminus ad quem* for applying scientific modes of explanation in the novel. Flaubert's *Madame Bovary* (1856) is, in this respect, somewhere between Balzac and Zola but it also represents the crossroad to another possibility. Flaubert constructed his book so that the catastrophe would follow completely from the character, upbringing and environment of Emma Bovary and in this sense he uses the determining causal analysis of Balzac. Yet *Madame Bovary* is close in publication to Baudelaire's *Les Fleurs du Mal* and its contiguity with this influential *symboliste* achievement may alert us to Flaubert's essentially different interest in his material. The explanatory, empirical dimension of *Madame Bovary* is the vehicle for a more inclusive, *a priori* mode of apprehending the story. Unlike Balzac and Zola, who are vibrant with explicit moral passion, Flaubert adopts an Olympian remove. Emma's fate becomes a synecdoche for the essential human condition and the 'scientific' understanding of her is assimilated to an artistic contemplation. Again as with Pater in the English context, there is a close affinity beween the scientific spirit and a purely aesthetic ideal. Thus the explanatory aspect of science, rather than being an end in itself, now serves the neutrality ideal and with Flaubert, in this as in other respects the progenitor of literary modernism, the transition and its hierarchy are apparent.

Hence the artistic purity of literature implies a polarity with science that can also, by its very purity, amount to an identity with the scientific outlook. Furthermore, the ideal of impersonality may chime with the scientific without necessitating any actual identity of content. If, therefore, it is significant that the rise and transcendence of the realist novel are roughly contemporaneous with the rise and transcendence of the Newtonian system, the parallels that have commonly been observed between eighteenth- and nineteenth-century fiction and its contemporary scientific thought do not need to apply in the modern period. The essential spiritual significance of the 'scientific' stance is created in literary rather than scientific terms.

Once again *Ulysses* provides a classic exemplification. Over the course of *Ulysses* the general mood changes to reflect the growing lateness of the hour and the shift of focus on to the older characters rather than Stephen. This psychologically realistic shift in mood is a vehicle through which Joyce enforces a deepening awareness of the impersonal perspective being achieved by the book as a whole. The techniques of the chapters are increasingly impersonalized culminating in the 'scientific' catechism of 'Ithaca'; the chapter immediately preceding the universal 'female' of Molly's final monologue. A couple of observations about 'Ithaca' are pertinent here. While modelled on science, the technique of this chapter is remarkably innocent concerning contemporary scientific developments. It obviously sees science as the neutrally precise description of a world unproblematically open to observation. Secondly, the chapter has, in its context, a curious poetic effectiveness from this technique of question and answer. I am not thinking of such local 'poetic' effects as, 'The heaventree of stars hung with humid nightblue fruit', or the extended comparison of 'woman' with the moon. These are in any case departures from a scientific model. It is rather that the effect of the neutral catechistic manner chimes with the deeper resonances and growing mood of the book to extend the perspective of the painfully achieved 'equanimity' with which Bloom, within this chapter, regards Molly's unfaithfulness. The technique obliges us to consider Bloom's attitude from a cosmic standpoint; it is at once a simple, and yet in the book's terms, complex, state of mind. Bloom's 'philosophical' acceptance, in the popular sense, is given a more complex correlative in the stylistic medium. Once again, scientific detachment provides the model for this quintessential product of the Flaubertian aestheticist spirit in modern literature. The parallel with science is not by virtue of a scientific content, but by a broader affinity arising from the *idea* of science in the literary tradition. And this ideal of scientific impersonality which Joyce inherited most directly from Flaubert was also important to the most influential poet-critics of the time: Ezra Pound and T.S. Eliot. Eliot's account, for example, of the 'impersonality' of poetic emotion in terms of chemical process is a similar conjunction of scientific language and a literary ideal.[17] And Pound constantly holds up scientific method and rigour as the model for criticism.

The general point emerging from this account of literature and science is that there was indeed a literary consciousness of science, but the actual content of the new physics is not reflected in literature. A helpful third term is provided by T.S. Kuhn's *The Structure of Scientific Revolutions* (1962) in which he proposes the notion of the 'paradigm shift'. This means a change in the basic intellectual model by which a given science conducts its research; a change such as has generally occurred only once in hundreds of years. Although he is concerned with science, his term is applicable to other shifts occurring in the late nineteenth and early twentieth centuries such as the development of non-Euclidean geometries and serial technique in music. There was a teasing sense that changes of this magnitude were occurring across the arts and sciences and briefly, before the European war, there seemed to be a kind of renaissance in progress. Though this has in the event proved something of a false dawn, I believe there have been general and permanent changes in outlook of which Kuhn's book is itself a product.

Kuhn's concept of the 'paradigm shift' accommodates the recognition that science, as discussed earlier, does not simply 'progress' towards the understanding of observed reality. While accepting that new paradigms come to oust or comprehend others, and hence espousing an essentially progressive view of scientific knowledge, Kuhn emphasizes the hegemony of the current model and our inability of function without it. Internally science progresses; but we do not say that it is progressing towards reality, only towards range or coherence. There is an awareness that even our apparently most direct intuitions of reality are governed by frames of reference whose arbitrariness it is at any given moment impossible to gauge, let alone correct. Now the traditional musical scale had always been slightly imperfect and Euclid's parallel postulate had always resisted proof. Yet only in the nineteenth and early twentieth centuries were systematic alternatives developed. This suggests a change in attitude as much as knowledge. In this respect, Kuhn is suggestive in describing the difference between Aristotle's and Galileo's accounts of the pendulum by saying that a different intellectual paradigm enabled Galileo to actually *see* something different. This is the precise point of Brecht's 'alienation' technique; to induce for heuristic purposes an unfamiliar perception of the familiar. I believe Kuhn is effectively summarizing an outlook stemming from this period, for the idea of 'paradigm shifts' embodies the recognition that habitual 'common sense' intuitions may hinder as much as help understanding. The ability to step outside the habitual frame of reference has in itself an important heuristic value. It seems to me that the self-conscious mythopoeia of Joyce, Yeats or Mann expresses a cognate recognition. Mental constructions created, like geometries, for their own sake can still be of the highest worth and seriousness. If we necessarily live through myths and models of our world then the conscious exploration and expression of the mythopoeic faculty may well be the fitting basis for a pertinent literature. For all the pain and self-criticism their work encompasses, the philosophical frameworks of these writers allow them time and again a crucial penetration and transcendence of their personal and historical experience.

Language: medium or object

> 'In every case the structural and philosophical rudiments
> were sought out. On all hands a return to first principles was
> witnessed.'   (Wyndham Lewis)[18]

This remark of Wyndham Lewis refers specifically to painting just
before the Great War but it aptly characterizes pervasive modernist
aspirations outlined in the preceding section; the desire in several
fields to re-think not just the detailed practice but the whole frame of
reference. Now, T.S. Kuhn makes the general observation that where
'paradigm shifts' occur there is a corresponding focus of attention on
philosophical first principles. And just as the shift from Newtonian to
modern physics excited a concern for the general status of scientific
theory, so literary artists looked closely at the philosophical nature of
their own medium, language; indeed, this is a sufficiently important
topic to merit separate treatment. Modern literature is not only
conscious of language as its medium of expression, it frequently holds
it up and enjoys it as an object in its own right. This is to some extent
again an aspect of the *symboliste* inheritance. G.A. Lehmann has indicated how the *symboliste* writers had a poetic practice without a
coherent overall theory despite their various attempts to produce
one.[19] Lehmann concludes that the religious and symbolical aspects of
symbolisme were really ways of talking about the emotional and
suggestive properties of language itself. The shift from *symbolisme* to
modernism lies partly in the recognition of this. The modern inheritors of *symbolisme*, when writing or discussing poetry, tend to appeal
to demonstrable qualities of language rather than metaphysical
gesture. Hence the *symboliste* insistence on the autotelic reality of the
poem is still there but with more bearing on the status of language
generally.

Yet once again, this development merges with other independent
fields; particularly, in this case, linguistics and philosophy. The scientific study of language that had grown up over the eighteenth and nineteenth centuries had been primarily historical in emphasis. The nature
of language was investigated through its putative origins in primitive
life. This approach survived in Otto Jesperson's *Language: Its Nature,
Development and Origin* (1922) in which he argues, for example, that
the necessity of pulling a large object would have given rise to commu-
nally agreed sounds. But this historical method was likely to lead to

rather external and piecemeal conclusions, and in the early decades of this century it was increasingly reinforced by the approach, largely associated with de Saussure, of examining the internal structure of language.[20] An avatar of this method still subsists in present-day 'structuralism' and it places greater emphasis on the ordering process of the mind itself as embodied in language. Though we tend to use and think of language as a one for one, referential reflection of objects, ideas and feelings, it is strictly an autotelic system. Its structures, in themselves largely arbitrary, govern our most intimate construction of the world, individually and collectively; and only the more significantly for working at a generally subliminal level.

Philosophy, too, in the Anglo-Saxon tradition turned its attention to language in a comparable way that eventually led, for example, to the movements known as 'linguistic philosophy' and 'logical positivism' extending rather beyond the present period. There seems to be a Lockean strain in the English tradition which, in its modern avatars, came, through Wittgenstein, to see traditional metaphysical problems, such as the existence of God, as linguistic epi-phenomena; as problems of language rather than being. The religious sceptic would not deny that God exists, but that the word 'God' has a meaning. But this really originated in Russell's and Moore's concern with mathematical logic which Wittgenstein then focused more on the nature of language at large.

In a general way, such an analytical awareness of language could hardly fail to have some effect on writers and critics but this could take forms quite different, even opposed, to academic philosophy. Poets and novelists, after all, have a stake in the language that will lead them to keep it out of the hands of scientific philosophers. The Lockean aspect, in so far as it bears on ordinary language, can be naively reductive, having lurking within it Locke's own ideal of an unambiguous, scientific notation of meaning; an ideal that bears little relation to the actual purposes for which language is used. Poets may well share a perception of the primacy of language in conditioning our experience, but they will be likely to understand this through quite different values. Hence while there are fruitful connections between individual figures from literature and philosophy (such as Henry James and his brother, the 'pragmatist', William James; T.S. Eliot and the 'objective idealist', F.H. Bradley, on whom he wrote his Ph.D. thesis; or the Nietzschean aspects of Lawrence and Yeats) there is a representative lesson in the quarrel between Lawrence and Bertrand Russell after their brief attempt to give a joint series of lectures early in the war. Lawrence's portrait of Russell as Joshua Malleson in *Women in Love* indicates how he viewed Russell's intellect as arising from, or at least able to co-exist with, a total lack of responsiveness to life values. Russell's corresponding judgement that Lawrence was fascistic suggests that Lawrence's emotional certainties could only appear arbitrary and dogmatic to him. The disparity is unusually extreme, but it points to a more general difference between the methods and interests of academic philosophers as opposed to poets and novelists. We could, it is true, suggest a counter example in Wittgenstein, a seminal mind in English twentieth-century philosophy, whose sense of language as 'word games' makes him pertinently contemporary to someone like Beckett. Yet Wittgenstein, with his gnomic elusiveness and almost mystical perception of the mystery of meaning, is one of those figures, like Nietzsche, who rather transcend the framework of academic philosophy anyway. Hence, David Holdcroft in his survey of philosophical activity largely charts an area where the interests do not overlap. In so far as philosophy at this time conceived its activity so much in terms of science and logical analysis it had relatively little to say to poets and novelists.

Having offered this general *caveat*, we may consider one area, literary criticism, which does seem to reflect such a philosophical consciousness of language; most clearly and influentially in the critical theorizing of I.A. Richards. Richards had a Coleridgean ambition to understand the literary imagination in a framework of philosophical principle, and shared with Eliot and Pound the perception that literary quality is achieved, and can therefore be demonstrated, in the literary utterance itself and not in the supposed 'ideas' or 'feelings' of the poet. This emphasis on the 'words on the page', at least when its limitations were also digested, was one of the most fruitful perceptions of modern criticism; few serious readers of literature have not gained by the pervasive sharpening of focus on verbal texture that has come to be known under the general heading of 'practical criticism'. Richards, in effect, submitted poetic language to a kind of scientific scrutiny seeking to explain its meaningfulness in psychological terms such as the build-up and release of tension. But 'practical criticism' has become the staple of English literature teaching mainly because it allows for a close and pragmatically disciplined procedure pretty much in isolation from any over-arching theory. It allows for a close scrutiny of language, and is in that sense philosophical, but does not commit you to a particular philosophical view. Hence if there is an impetus from philosophy proper, it is very much transposed into literary critical purposes. Richards, in fact, became a member of the influential Cambridge English school founded in 1917 which was not the first university department studying the vernacular literature, but which did give a new emphasis, in the spirit of Eliot and Pound, to contemporary critical pertinence rather than modelling itself on the historical scholarship of the ancient languages. Eliot declined an invitation to join the Cambridge school though his influence is manifest, even in the very different F.R. Leavis, who responded more to the Arnoldian critical side of Eliot seeking the rigour of close 'scrutiny' without Richards' theoretical superstructure. In sum, the production of modern literature took place in an ambiance encouraging close linguistic analysis; an ambiance partly generated by the two most important poetic innovators, Eliot and Pound, as an intrinsic aspect of their view of poetry.

Hence poets and critics could be said in a broad sense to share the philosopher's concern with language. But even where this seems closest there can be crucial differences of spirit and purpose; the standard of 'accuracy' can be quite different for a poet and an academic philosopher. Indeed, modern criticism has set a high value precisely on the ambiguity of poetic language.[21] When Eliot and Pound sought to fulfil the Mallarméan injunction to 'purify the language of the tribe', they were not concerned to analyse the logical structure of language but to use it at the highest possible levels of intensity. Poetry is language used with economy and control to register a whole experience, ideational and emotional, explicit and subliminal. Reacting against what they saw as the escapist and hypnotic tendency of the Tennysonian manner, Pound and Eliot sought to instate poetry as the completest discipline and attention of consciousness. Hence poetry is better in quality rather than discontinuous in kind from the general body of language. These poets' departure from stanzaic form and Pound's attack on the 'tyranny' of the pentameter in English verse are aspects of this refusal to accord a merely formal, or ready-made, 'poetic' specialness. The concern for excellence in poetry was a concern for the totality of life and expression in their time. This endeavour is a vital and defining centre of literary modernism and relates obliquely to both the scientific, philosophical examination of language and the *symboliste* celebration of language as an autonomous entity. But the *symboliste* impulse lived on in more direct ways too. Despite Eliot's espousal of the Mallarméan aspiration just quoted, the purest inheritance and most characteristic modernist development of *symbolisme* in respect of language is to be seen once again in Joyce.

There is a fascination throughout Joyce's *oeuvre* with the shape and texture of words; a fascination shared by even his youngest characters at the beginning of *Dubliners* and *A Portrait*. This eventually takes over completely in the vast word spinning of *Finnegans Wake* and I must say here that I am one of a large class of readers who find *Finnegans Wake*, despite its lyricism, its humour and the imposing massiveness of its working out, effectively still-born. This does not prevent it being an important landmark in modern literature, however, as it is among other things the terminal point for this reification of language. Its monumental presence gives weight to critical questions underlying Joyce's *oeuvre* generally. At the same time it must be said that Joyce's fascination with language has at its best a richness arising from the intent purity of interest that made *Finnegans Wake* possible. Less directly concerned by the sense of cultural burden animating Pound's or Eliot's interest in the quality of expression in language, Joyce accepted language as a field of mental play, as an intrinsic delight.

One episode of *Ulysses*, 'Oxen of the Sun', makes language its special focus and thus gives a meaning to the Irish exuberance that characterizes the language of *Ulysses* generally. As Bloom sits among the bawdily carousing medical students awaiting the outcome of Mrs Purefoy's labour, Joyce's narrative adopts, in a series of pastiches, an historical succession of English prose styles from Anglo-Saxon to modern American. The pastiche is playful rather than satirical in effect; potential parody of the past is absorbed into a present gusto. Drawing on the whole context of fertility and childbirth, the chapter presents the English language growing organically as an independent vital principle. Language is, in effect, a living thing. Hence it is to be judged not by the Lockean criterion of accuracy, but by its idiosyncratic vitality. Indeed, it is metaphorical but not meaningless to say that a language can die, and the desire for 'accuracy' of a Lockean 'scientific' kind may well be a symptom of its decline. You have only to consider the language of much present-day political or sociological prose, or even literary criticism, the officialese of the 'decision-making process',

o see the mental and emotional deadness Joyce's exuberance resists.
Of course, language only exists in its use by individuals, but these
draw on its general condition as their inheritance. The language of
Shakespeare, so often invoked in *Ulysses*, was not just a personal style
but expressed an especially vibrant moment in the history of English.
The Elizabethan vernacular was still responding to the long hegemony
of French and Latin as the learned and official tongues. Its popular feel,
its fluidity, its coinings and loan-words jostling for acceptance, its very
orthography responsive to the momentary taste of the writer – all
these qualities comprise a medium in which even the normative
expression could be called creative. Joyce seeks to reproduce a comparable condition in the modern tongue with his puns, coinings, loan-
words, portmanteau terms and his prodigious hospitality to foreign
elements.

But the Shakespearean example also enforces a contrast, for, whatever Shakespeare's personal gifts, his language is also the general one,
whereas Joyce's, whatever its ambition, is always threatened by the
isolationism that I feel closes in on *Finnegans Wake*. Joyce, however
archetypal in content and exemplary in significance, is a one-man
show. Just as Flaubert exploited bourgeois clichés to construct a vision
directly opposed to the bourgeois, so Joyce, if more genially, is also
asserting a personal tension against the mainstream, or average, use of
English. There may, indeed, be more at stake here than the individualism of the artist for in *A Portrait* and the early chapters of *Ulysses*,
Stephen ponders the specifically linguistic dilemma of an English
speaking Irish poet. If he uses 'the language of Shakespeare and Ben
Jonson' he is bound by its alien disposition, and the more so as he
recognizes the weight of its historical achievements. On the other
hand, can he now turn to his ancient tongue without a parochial and
antiquarian self-consciousness? Can the English consciousness be shut
out once it is there? The dilemma is representative for the recognition
that a nation's soul lives in its language owes very much to the nineteenth-century exploration of language and folklore a well as to the
spirit of nationalism. Stephen's generation felt the full force of a
dilemma that we are still grappling with in the question of political
devolution'.

Joyce's handling of the English language can be seen, I believe, as
one of the various responses made to this dilemma by Welsh and
Scottish as well as Irish writers who came to maturity within this

growing recognition. Yeats had flirted with the 'Celtic twilight' in th
1880s and 1890s while keeping an inner distance. The Scottish poet
Hugh McDiarmid, produced in the 1920s some magnificent 'Lallans
lyrics after disapproving in principle of such endeavours. In *Finnegan
Wake* Joyce took the English language and used it as a universal Euro
pean tongue spoken by an Irishman. The English reader, reversing th
situation of Stephen with the Dean of Studies in *A Portrait*, is ouste
from his habitually privileged linguistic status. The later case of Dyla
Thomas seems similar in this respect; the English language is take
over from the inside by a Welsh voice. I am not suggesting tha
national self-assertion is the only reason for radical departure from
normal English. The case of Gerard Manley Hopkins, for example
suggests there must be other considerations; though even there Wels
poetry is a part influence. My general point is rather that Joyce'
handling of language is representative of a broad strain in moder
writing but is in tension with the mainstream of English usage. What
ever its motivation, it is a liberation *from* the English language as we
as *of* it.

For the important point here is not the motive, but the result: th
ability to use the language consummately while not being simply *of* it
A brief comparison with Lawrence may help to clarify what I mean b
this. Consider this sentence from 'Oxen of the Sun' next to the endin
of *Sons and Lovers*:

> In ward weary the watcher hearing come that man wild-
> hearted eft rising with swire ywimpled to him her gate wide
> undid.

> He walked towards the faintly humming, glowing town,
> quickly.

Joyce's use of 'ward' and Lawrence's of 'quickly' both exploit olde
meanings latent, but not usually felt, in the modern words. Joyc
places the word at the beginning of the sentence then links it to th
sounds in 'wary' and 'watcher' bringing out the sense of guardianshi
in the etymology of the hospital 'ward'. Lawrence's word comes las
in its sentence and picks up its extra resonance from the contex
already created as well as from its unusually highlighted position
Thus the older meaning of 'alive' is simply an impression arising from
the action itself; the reader sees Paul Morel walk more rapidly an

ntuits his vital resolve. In Joyce's case the etymological sense presents itself more as a pun. Its appropriateness is immediately felt nd the older, stronger meaning flows into the modern word, but it is elt with surprise and a sense of the linguistic cleverness involved. An tymologically unsophisticated reader would miss the effect entirely; if e can imagine such a reader having come so far anyway. Lawrence's sage is, we might say, entirely within the skin of the language; its istory lives within him as part of his present identity. Joyce's unning, while drawing attention to historical linearity, exploits the elt gap. Joyce's cosmopolitanism ranges over the language here istorically as well as spatially.

Now language is not only an intimate expression of the self, it is – e might say, an inherited modality of it. The formative experience of ne past lives in us by the meaningfulness of our community's words. he difference of these two sentences just discussed hence implies a ifferent experience of selfhood. Both writers are concerned with heri- ge but for Lawrence it is a resource to be taken for granted; it exists pontaneously or not at all. The language exists purely as the medium f the inheritance. For Joyce the heritage is indeed felt but it is also en, as it were, from the outside as it might be by a man from another ountry or planet. The 'impersonality' of Joyce, discussed already as a tructural strategy and authorial stance, hence has this stylistic corre- tive too. The self, at least as defined by a local and historical rooting language, is dissolved into an infinite play of verbal possibility. oyce points the way here to the curious transcending of personal nguistic identity, the lateral gliding from one language to another, at is epitomized in Beckett and Nabokov. Nabokov has made his voluntary exile from his native Russian a positive dynamic of his lation to English; and Beckett, even more pertinently, has deliber- tely sought to cut the roots of any spontaneous linguistic identity by riting in French first. Joyce had inherited from the eighteenth- ntury 'man of sensibility' and the nineteenth-century bohemian rtist a myth of the artist as social outsider. In Joyce this figure ecomes the exile; a condition felt most crucially in the domain of nguage. It might be supposed that this whole development is an nfortunate condition imposed by the artist's felt circumstances, but om Rousseau to Beckett the outsider has sought, as well as suffered, is exile. The line from Joyce to Beckett and Nabokov suggests that n inner exile, a detachment from the language one lives in, has

become a positive ideal. Joyce points the way to this ultimate level c
aesthetic withdrawal.

In general, then, modern literature reflects a broader contemporar
awareness of language as a problematic object in its own right. Indeed
if we can detect key metaphors and models running through th
thought of different historical periods, such as the machine or clock i
the eighteenth century and organic life in the nineteenth, the
language itself seems to provide such a model for the twentiet
century. More recently, we have even come to see the act of procrea
tion as using a genetic 'code' and the cooking of food by 'primitive
peoples is interpreted by Claude Lévi-Strauss as a form of symboli
expression. Yet this sophistication about language is also a crisis abou
meaning. Some modern writers have come in their own way to see al
expression as what Wittgenstein saw as 'language games'. Whethe
this is interpreted in a positive or a negative, a Nabokovian or
Beckettian, way, the root perception is the same. Joyce's continua
ventriloquism, his elusively affectionate and satirical use of parody
enables him to straddle the possibilities. At once inside and outside th
language, he can, in the spirit of romantic irony, use it without bein
its victim.

Indeed, the point may be expanded in relation to my broader argu
ments, for this duality of consciousness is a linguistic correlative of th
duality I have defined earlier in aesthetic myth, and it is fraught witl
the same ambivalence. The Joycean/Nabokovian development of
symboliste handling of language accords language an autotelic valu
comparable in some respects to its archaic state. The origin o
language was intimately related to mythic thinking. Words once ha
an intrinsic relation to their objects; to have someone's name was tc
have a means of magical power over him. Historically speaking, th
arbitrariness of words' relations to their objects is a late sophisticatec
recognition and such is the persistent anthropomorphism of language
that the activity of philosophers might largely be described as the
perpetual de-mythologizing of language. But the poet's concern is
more typically to reinvest language with its incantatory and illusionis
power even though he cannot, and generally would not, restore the
archaic mythic conception of it. In Joyce the two extremes touch and
interfuse. Rather than the middle-ground activity of words as arbitrary
counters grappling with the world, there is a magical autonomy exer
cised within the context of 'language games'. Where language a

game' and language as 'magic' meet, it seems to me that the game
element tends to be the more basic. If part of the ambition of modern
writers has been to reinvest language with power, then in the
symboliste tradition as it runs through Joyce the cure seems to me part
of the disease. His linguistic vitality, as it transcends the vitality of any
actual language, is ultimately galvanic rather than organic. If the
language *is* dying, *Finnegans Wake* is surely not its rebirth, but its
dance of death?

Pound and Wyndham Lewis

> ' . . . austere, direct and free from emotional slither.'
> (Ezra Pound on poetry)[22]

The focus of this essay has moved from the philosophical question of
reality to a critical consideration of language and, as I have already
hinted, this provides a context in which to see the poetic revival associated pre-eminently with Ezra Pound. I discuss Lewis with Pound
since they have a common hostility to aspects of the modernist aspiration outlined so far.

Pound came to London in 1908 from America with some interven-
ing time in Italy, as well as in Provence, where he furthered his knowledge of troubadour poetry. The condition of English poetry between
1900 and 1910 must have been about the lowest in its history. C.K.
Stead's *The New Poetic* outlines the milieu in which the schoolboy
heroics of Alfred Noyes and Henry Newbolt were taken seriously as
poetry. At this time, Ford Madox Huefer (later Ford), Editor of the
English Review, collaborator with Conrad and first to publish
Lawrence, was the only person Pound could see with a real interest in
promoting new or good writing. Yet Pound had still to sort out his
own poetic values and find his voice as a poet, which he did partly by
questioning how the modes of Tennyson and Browning could have led
to such a débâcle. Seen with retrospective tidiness, we may say that
Browning includes a great deal of prose, his dramatic monologues
encroach on the area of the novel, while Tennyson suggests a different
danger. His lowest register is not so much prose as what Gerard
Manley Hopkins, who was fighting his own battle with Tennyson in
solitude some decades earlier, called the 'Parnassian' mode. This is a
rhythmic and musical language, clearly in some formal sense poetry,

but which, like a weak solution of blank verse, lulls rather tha[n] invigorates the language. In both cases the poetic element is diffused i[n] its less intensive medium. Pound's early career, therefore, may b[e] seen as an attempt to strip away the inessential and recover the poeti[c] element in its purity.

A key manifestation of this endeavour was his brief association wit[h] the imagist movement around 1912 in which Pound, defining th[e] 'image' as 'a complex of emotion in an instant of time',[23] remove[s] everything extraneous, as in the well known example:

> The apparition of these faces in a crowd,
> Petals on a wet, black bough.

But even at this time the purity of the imagist form was one pole rathe[r] than the summit of his endeavour, for there is also something preciou[s] and limiting about imagism. Its importance historically is that it pr[o]posed an ideal of purity that so many major twentieth-century poets als[o] passed through as a formative phase. But the later careers of Pound[,] Eliot and Carlos Williams, as well as much mid-century America[n] poetry, can be seen as ways of assimilating the isolated intensity of th[e] image to the larger poetic structures necessary to carry any substantia[l] freight. Just as in the novel the modernist revolution was to bring th[e] *symboliste* aesthetic to a new engagement with the world, so the poeti[c] ideal of purity seeks structures that will allow it both intensity an[d] pertinence. In fact, the structural solutions of the fiction have much i[n] common with those of the poetry. I have spoken already of spatial for[m] in *Ulysses* and suggested that Eliot's 'The Love Song of J. Alfre[d] Prufrock' and 'The Waste Land' are comparably spatialized constella[-]tions of image clusters. The individual elements preserve their imagis[t] purity in that they relate to each other not through the linearity [of] argument or narrative but by an equidistant simultaneity. As 'cubist['] constructions suffused by myth, *Ulysses* and 'The Waste Land' hav[e] more in common with each other than either has with any nineteent[h] century work in its own genre. Yet despite these overlappings, th[e] individual artists of the modernist movement are animated by differen[t] personalities and purposes, as becomes more apparent through th[e] hindsight afforded by their later careers. There are respects in whic[h] Pound needs to be sharply distinguished from Joyce, for example.

To speak of modernist literature bringing the *symboliste* stance int[o] a fresh relation with reality is to indicate not a single achievement bu[t]

series of precarious, individual poises of varying method and success.
Where Joyce still worked from the contemplative remove of the
esthete, Pound's insistence on absolute poetic quality is connected
rather with his sense of engagement. Furthermore, he actually had a
first-hand relation to what was going on in music and the plastic arts,
was passionately concerned with the economic structure of society and
even took an interest in the new physics. Hence the shift around 1914
or so from the more aesthetic 'imagism' to the more active, centri-
petal implications of 'vorticism', outlined in Cyril Barrett's essay,
epitomizes the different import of modernism for him. Poetry is the
energizing focus for the whole field of human endeavour. If poetry is
language doing its job without falseness or redundancy, it brings this
standard to bear on all aspects of life and society. His later attacks on
capitalism, or 'usury', are not an economist's argument in a specialized sense. He sees usury, like contraception, as a frustration of
nature. Hence in Canto XIV his condemnation of

> The perverters of language,
> the perverts, who have set money-lust
> Before the pleasures of the senses.

and

> ... Episcopus, waving a condom full of black-beetles.
> Monopolists, obstructors of knowledge,
> Obstructors of distribution.

Around 1914 Pound's outlook might well seem of a piece with that
of the early Joyce whose taut, economical language in *Dubliners*
dissected the sentimentalities of his countrymen. After all, Joyce also
represented a standard of absolute honesty in the emotional as well as
the intellectual sphere and it is this quality in Joyce's prose that Pound
singled out for admiration in his review of *Dubliners*.[24] But Pound's
admiration for Joyce in these terms allowed him subsequently to
recommend ignoring the Homeric parallel in reading *Ulysses*. That
recommendation has its merits, particularly as a corrective to certain
kinds of uncritical exegesis, but it also signals, I think, Pound's lack of
sympathy for the systematizing and self-celebratory aestheticism of
Joyce and the 'Cantos' make a revealing contrast with *Ulysses* in this
respect. Joyce constructs a unified form out of the invocation of
diverse specialisms which are there with a metaphorical, rather than

literal, application. Pound actually engages the problems of history and economics but was never able to complete his vision formally. This is not necessarily to be regretted. Pound had always had an extraordinary effect as a teacher and as a catalyst for the creative activity of others. His work exudes that quality even after his death and the openness of the 'Cantos' is a formal reflection of their being a centre of activity more than an artistically bounded achievement. But what matters here is that Pound's conception of poetry gives modernism a different twist from Joyce's conception of the novel. Courses which run parallel at the watershed can end up far apart. Joyce retires increasingly to an aesthetic remove as Pound becomes more politically embroiled.

This general distinction applies not just with respect to Joyce, but to Eliot and Yeats too. For Eliot and Yeats also prized a timeless spiritual experience and Yeats' mythicizing, like Joyce's, centred on a cyclic model of human experience that gave a comprehensive political and historical import to the mythic transcendence of linear time. Stephen Dedalus' complaint, 'History is a nightmare from which I am trying to awake', strikes a chord sounded frequently in modern literature. And to speak of 'awaking' from history, rather than say 'escaping', is to suggest that history itself is the illusion; that reality lies somewhere beyond everyday life. In this spirit *Ulysses*, like Yeats, goes on to invoke the oriental, mystical notion of time as part of the veil of appearances masking the timelessly real. Mann and Proust also set their political foreground against timeless patterns intuited through art and vision. An important aspect of myth, as I have already pointed out, is its a-temporality, and the aesthetic creation of myth as already discussed above is therefore also a way of transcending the process of history. In effect, these different conceptions of modernism place human action within different frames of historical meaningfulness. Joyce and Proust give the most extreme sense of aesthetic withdrawal. Yeats and Mann suggest the possibility, and indeed the urgency, of individual moral engagement even within their larger historical conceptions. Pound, like Lawrence, seeks to understand the large patterns of history not for contemplation but for responsible change.

That such writers approach the question of history within these comprehensive frameworks, some of them accepting an aesthetic frame by which to escape the juggernaut of history entirely, makes it difficult to relate the content of their writing to the more down to earth

activity of historians. An attack on conventional historical consciousness is what is often at stake. Of course, the fact that key figures in
modern literary consciousness should adopt such a stance is itself of
historical interest. And the fact can be viewed in various ways. A
Marxist critic, such as Georg Lukàcs, would see this as symptomatic of
bad faith in bourgeois sensibility at large. Aestheticism is the recourse
of sensitive intelligence in a situation of political futility. But it can also
be seen as a necessary gesture of spiritual freedom. The impersonal
scale of modern social and political experience means that individuals
are constrained to act with collective emotions and ideas; an aspect of
things most epitomized in Marxism. Yeats, Lawrence and Joyce have
all memorably diagnosed this insidious erosion of selfhood. Hence
their sometimes cranky insistence on seeing contemporary history in
their own terms has an important perception at stake in it.

Of course, these two broad interpretations do not negate each other:
what one admires goes hand in hand with what one deprecates. The
general point, though, is that these writers refract contemporary
history in specialized ways. You must, therefore, determine the angle
of literary mythical refraction in establishing any historical
equations.[25] And it is in this light that we can see a tension between
Pound and other modernist writers with whom he was closely associated. The liberating impulse and techniques of modernism could themselves become a form of spiritual enclosure. From this point of view
Eliot's later Christianity could be as much a case in point as *Finnegans
Wake*. Though Pound has an extensive view of history it is not placed
in such an abstract cyclic framework but is expressed rather in his
concrete handling of historical occasions. To understand this it is
helpful to consider more generally the expression of historical
consciousness in literature.

What is essentially involved here is how the past is felt in, or acts on,
the present and since the inner, or spiritual, history of a given community is contained in its cultural expression, especially its literature, one
practical way in which a poet confronts history is by his response to
the poetic tradition he inherits. Eliot's essay 'Tradition and the Individual Talent' is a *locus classicus* of modernist rumination on the paradox of modernism in this regard. Eliot points out that originality must
be in relation *to* something and the really new work proves in this
sense to be deeply traditional. At the same time, the arrival of a really
new work makes us see the tradition through its eyes and hence in a

new way. The original and the traditional are in a relation of mutual modification that makes the distinction hazy if not meaningless. Such theoretical speculation about the nature of literary tradition matters because it is an aspect of the literature being created. Eliot and Pound conceived of their poetry not as brand new but as the recovery of past poetic energies and values. For *Ulysses*, 'The Waste Land' and the 'Cantos' the tensions of literary history are not only the external conditions of their creation but the very subject matter. The felt presence, or absence, of the cultural past is what these works are largely about. But these writers' ways of evoking the past are different and to discuss them we might posit a kind of sliding scale of accessibility of the past in literature generally.

Walter Scott, as the first substantial expression of the historical consciousness in literature, is the natural point of reference. Scott saw the past as different from the present and therefore as having potentially a dynamic, explanatory relation to it. Life is not fixed but in constant evolution. This historicist awareness can be contrasted with the relative indifference of Shakespeare to historical definition. His Romans, Greeks and ancient Britons are all Elizabethans; which is to say they are simply men. Thus Scott points towards the historically explanatory nature of the novel throughout the nineteenth century. Yet Scott also fathered the 'historical' novel; the popular sub-genre which expresses the soft underside of nineteenth-century historical consciousness: the idealizing of the past. The medievalizing of Keats has its counterpart in pre-Raphaelite painting. Essentially a projection from the present, the past is prized for its very remoteness. History slides from dynamic cause to static pageant and both elements are there in Scott. Hence the historical consciousness can manifest itself in morally opposite ways; as merely escape from the present or as a way of understanding it.

Now Eliot's essay suggests that tradition is a kind of queue in which the most recent comers are in the line but can only relate to their predecessors through the whole. Pound's assumption is rather that he can approach the line sideways on, as it were, having direct access to any single figure in it. Pound, we might say, treats them more as if they were all living at once. The figures are still historically defined but not therefore remote. It is a supra-historical rather than an a-historical stance. Different ways of feeling the presentness of the past are perhaps suggested in the characteristic techniques of Joyce, Eliot and Pound respectively: parody, allusion and imitation. With Joyce's predilection for parody, the past is held in a kind of contemplative suspension within a present-day consciousness. In Eliot's allusions the echoes of the cultural past chime with the pervasively nostalgic emotions of his poems. The past is felt most keenly in its absence. Pound's imitations are rather – and it is a traditional function of imitation – ways of bringing the ancient poets, such as Rihaku or Propertius, into the modern tongue. The sensibility of the original is embodied in present-day terms without any exoticizing gloss such as there is in Browning's period poems. Hence while sharing in a broad sense the aspiration to understand contemporary life through a general historical, and literary historical, perspective Pound's version of this is one that forcefully energizes the past in the present. Again it works by a continuing engagement rather than a mythic, aesthetic structure of withdrawal.

I have suggested these broader implications of Pound's poetic methods to indicate that within the modernist movement there is a radical critique as well as continuance of the *symboliste* tradition. This emphasis comes out even more clearly in Percy Wyndham Lewis who, as an associate of Pound, Eliot and Joyce, knew intimately what they were up to yet spent much energy in the 1920s and 1930s criticizing the direction taken by much of the modernist impulse. A focal point for understanding his objections is that, despite a voluminous written output ranging from novels to polemical essays, he was primarily a painter. His working in a physical rather than a verbal medium was associated in his mind with a greater responsibility towards the actuality of the world. The critical standpoint animating most of his satirical fiction is given explicit formulation in *Time and Western Man* (1927) and the essays later collected under the titles *The Diabolical Principle* (1931), *Men Without Art* (1934) and the more autobiographical *Blasting and Bombadiering* (1937). In *Time and Western Man* he objects, as an artist, to the pervasive de-realizing of the world he detected not only in modern literature but as a general drift of modern thought, equally evident in Einstein and Bergson. Lewis sees all these 'time' philosophies as transposing the solid and familiar world of space into the ghostly medium of time. Proust had argued that we inhabit more time than space, but Lewis would say that we only inhabit time in the less actual modes of memory and projection. As Hugh Kenner has said, Lewis' fiction as a whole 'concerns itself with the unreal, with gradations of unreality'[26] and it is this long-term philosophical

critique that underlies his fiction from the imaginary afterworld of *Th*
Human Age to his satires on contemporary cultural circles such as th
'Bloomsberries'.

Despite local misreadings and misconceptions, his critique c
modernism has an overall cogency and he sees a symptomatic signifi
cance in modernist features I have already discussed. For example, i
his attacks on the Parisian literary review *transition*, Lewis analyse
the spirit of linguistic cosmopolitanism I have discussed in the preced
ing section of this essay. He objects to language losing its context c
national and individual identity to become an autotelic field of play lik
chess or crossword puzzles. So, too, in his book-length polemi
Paleface (1929) Lewis attacked what he saw as a general cult of th
dark races manifest especially in Lawrence and Sherwood Anderson
The superior virtue of pre-civilized life had been a literary motif fron
ancient times down to the 'noble savage' fashion of the late eighteent]
century, but Lewis saw in his own day a more serious and radical abne
gation of civilized mind. This is to some extent a matter of hostil
misreading, but once again there is a fair point, for the primitivis
impulse needs careful control if it is not to be merely sentimental o
worse. Lewis saw it, like the 'time' philosophies, as a kind of spiritua
treason. To seek regression *in* time is another form of withdrawal *fron*
time; both are modes of evasion.

It is not surprising, then, that Lewis attacked cubism on comparabl
grounds. His own style, vorticism, like futurism, has been seen as onl
a variation of the cubist idea. But Lewis was opposed to both and hi
reasons make his own positive values clearer. Lewis saw cubism, mucl
in the spirit of my earlier comparison of it with *Ulysses*, as a
essentially contemplative and hence quietistic mode. It reconstructs it
object but does not criticize it. Futurism is the opposite. Its abstrac
tions are based on an admiration of pure speed and mechanism but it
entire commitment to these values leaves it equally deprived of a
evaluative range. The vortex is between these extremes. It suggests a
equilibrium of forces actually in motion but achieving a near stillnes
of form. Lewis expresses energy and form without worshipping eithe
in isolation. Carrying these painter's terms back into the fiction i
more tricky, but basically Lewis is interested, like Lawrence, in th
play of inhuman energies rather than the 'old-fashioned huma
element'. He does not, however, share Lawrence's compensatin
interest in that human element. Setting himself explicitly, lik

Lawrence's Loerke in *Women in Love*, against anthropomorphic views of life he celebrates neither nature nor man; he observes, and creates, process. This austere vision sometimes comes out in his fiction as an incompleteness of dramatization; he might be taken as the negative case for John Bayley's argument in *The Characters of Love* that an author can only create characters to the extent that he is in some sense capable of loving them. Even Hugh Kenner in his very positive account of Lewis suggests that the human element is an unsolved problem for Lewis down to *The Revenge for Love* (1937).[27] I would add that this seems more than a technical literary problem to me but a close criticism of Lewis is not the main point here. I want only to suggest how he shares the modernist techniques and concerns in a broad sense while interpreting them in a quite different spirit. Whatever the problems of his own *oeuvre*, he, as an insider, detects an insidious undertow to the *avant-garde* currents of his time. Both Pound and Lewis collectively suggest a different, and more negative, interpretation of the modernist achievement represented by Joyce.

James and Conrad

This account of modernism has shifted its focus to a more negative view of the aestheticism underlying the Joycean mode. We may shift the focus further by considering some equally modern and innovatory, if less 'modernist', writers who present a more sombre view of the modern situation at large. Proust, Mann, Joyce, Eliot, Yeats and Lawrence give a bleak analysis of contemporary moral culture, but they find personal solutions (emotional, religious and aesthetic) to set against this. Yet if there is a Thomas Mann to affirm that 'man is lord of the counterpositions'[28] there is equally a Franz Kafka crushed by irresolvable duality. The upward spiralling ironies of the one are matched by the other's destructive ambiguities. In James and Conrad the outlook is also more bleak and their respective treatments of the novel form compare instructively with the pervasive aestheticism already discussed. For picking up James or Conrad after Joyce, their modernity will register as only obliquely related to Joycean modernism and their closer commitment to a traditional realist mode reflects their moral and philosophical outlooks.

Where Joyce stood the novel on its head, James' modernity seems an inner necessity of the traditional form to which he had thoroughly, almost reverentially, submitted himself. He had assimilated the traditions manifest in the moral realism of the English George Eliot, the puritan study of conscience in the American Hawthorne, the aesthetic impersonality and artistic scruple of the French Flaubert, as well as the stoical tenderness of the Flaubert-influenced Russian, Turgeniev. He brought the European realist novel to a consummate achievement and with a lucid consciousness of what he was doing, so that his conception of the novel has since been as influential critically as T.S. Eliot's conception of poetry. Yet, as we have seen, the confident realist handling of self and the world as solid actualities suffered tensions in the modern period and James was in his own way equally responsive to these. Whereas Joyce, taking off from Flaubert, transcends the realist form by accepting it only as an aesthetic *donnée*, James accepts the realist frame in a traditional way and rather makes the subjectivist and aestheticist consciousness part of his subject matter. Hence the importance in James of 'point of view'. His novels are not solipsistic, but their worlds are generally realized through the consciousness of a given character. Subjectivity is thereby handled as part of the material even while the book exploits this subjective viewpoint as its actual containing frame. And the aestheticizing aspect is connected with this. James' novels repeatedly explore and exploit the situation of the detached observer; the person who, however sympathetic, has an essentially vicarious relation to the principal external events. The aestheticist consciousness that encompasses the Flaubertian novel is hence characteristically brought within the frame of the Jamesian novel as part of the material to be tested. Or to put it in more personal terms, the observing consciousness, with its moral comprehension allied to poignant inactivity, embodies the polar possibilities of James' own stance as novelist.

His first novel *Roderick Hudson* (1876) reflects that dichotomy in its basic structure, with Roderick himself on whom the action centres and Rowland Mallett in whose feelings the action is made significant. There is an implied polarity between feeling and action; between living and the understanding or appreciation of life. *The Portrait of a Lady* (1881) takes the pathos of *Roderick Hudson* to a more nearly tragic register exploiting a similar dichotomy. The sympathetic and admiring Ralph Touchett, who dies leaving his father's money to Isabel Archer, proves to be as pernicious an influence in her life as the manipulative adventurer Gilbert Osmond who marries her for her fortune.

The person who most deeply perceives and comprehends is an observer like Ralph, or the later Isabel Archer herself, yet these are removed from the active creation of their own destiny and there is always something in such a stance that can become sterile and manipulative. Where the Flaubert of *Madame Bovary* himself espouses a contemplative remove, in James we see the finest consciousnesses driven to it.

That there is a doubling of Osmond with Ralph and that both express a dimension of the authorial relation to Isabel, suggests that any transcendence of this dichotomy will come not so much from the individual characters as from the complex synthesis of the novel as a whole. The meticulous artistry of the Jamesian novel expresses a beauty and completeness won from, as much as seen in, the life portrayed, and this is a sense in which James must be linked with other modern writers deeply, yet ambivalently, imbued with aestheticist attitudes. Proust, Mann and Joyce as well as James are all implicated in an aestheticist ethos yet have given the most penetrating critique of the sterility it so easily involves. Swann, Stephen Dedalus and Gustav Aschenbach all represent important truths crucial to the works in which they appear yet each is thoroughly criticized within the work itself. It seems that the life to be liberated through art must accept the dallying with anti-life that the aestheticist stance implies, but the aestheticism of these characters does not transcend itself as does their authors'. In James the density of nuanced perception and response is inextricable from life yet tragically extraneous to its purposes. Only in the Jamesian novel, poised midway between a realist and an aestheticist frame, is the dichotomy of life and the fine consciousness brought to an acceptable, if poignant, equilibrium.

The especially controversial part of James' *oeuvre* has always been his late phase, which means in effect the three major novels to appear after 1900: *The Wings of the Dove* (1902), *The Ambassadors* (1903), and *The Golden Bowl* (1904). Argument focuses on the Jamesian style which is a further aspect of the tensions already described. Whether this style is the highest achievement or the final enervation of the Jamesian manner cannot be decided in abstraction from its specific contexts. Broadly speaking, the language of *The Wings of the Dove* seems to me to go hollow because of a fatal emptiness in the figure of Kate Croy who cannot support James' adjectival honorifics. There certainly is a critical problem in the late James. On the other hand, the language of *The Ambassadors* seems to me to embody quite appropriately the poignantly uncertain yet rigorously honest self-scrutiny of Lambert Strether. Once again, he is a Jamesian character for whom emotional understanding occurs in a context of non-fulfilment, and the success of the story hinges on its ability to give Strether's sense of emptiness a felt weight and definition. His highly spiritual perception must have a dramatic density. In this sense the prose is, in its analytic subtlety, enacting a dramatic process. For the objection to James' late prose is its obliqueness; its keeping its object in a state of constant, almost unbearable, plasticity, and attention to what it *does* rather than what it 'says' is vital.

Consider this brief passage from *The Ambassadors* where Strether, torn between loyalty to his native America and excited admiration at arriving in Europe, tours an English town with two Americans who are committed respectively to each of these opposite responses:

> The three strolled and stared and gossiped, or at least the two did; the case yielding for their comrade, if analysed, but the element of stricken silence. This element indeed affected Strether as charged with audible rumblings but he was conscious of the care of taking it explicitly as a sign of peace. He wouldn't appeal too much, for that provoked stiffness; yet he wouldn't be too freely tacit, for that suggested giving up. . . .   (Book I, Chapter III)

James has something of Proust's ability to give an almost physical substance to nuances of mood and perception that might be thought too evanescent or aetherial to be formulated at all. A feeling can be vividly conveyed without being expressly named. Here, James opens with a simple factual statement that could be a complete sentence then, almost wilfully, adds a qualifying clause that throws the apparently straightforward proposition in doubt. Waymarsh's silence thus stands in problematic contrast to the opening impression yet simultaneously derives from that a felt body of its own. And a possible resolution after the semi-colon is frustrated by the interpolated, 'if analysed'. This phrase holds the silence, or the quality of the silence, in an interpretative suspension. The combined effect is that when James goes on to Strether's response to this silence he can treat it simultaneously as a conjectural projection of Strether's own mind and as an oppressive, objective reality. However it works in detail, it is apparent that the comings and goings of the prose; its shifting from act to possibility, from statement to qualification; keep the experience in suspension. For James there seems never to be an achieved truth but a continuing engagement with the flux of perception. The language does not express thoughts so much as the process of thinking. This is the force of T.S. Eliot's comment that James had a mind 'so fine that no idea could violate it'. He did not mean that James resisted false ideas, but that he did not function in terms of ideas at all.

This sense of the mind engaging the world with an ideation not reducible to abstractly formulable ideas echoes what I have said of the mythicizing ironies of Thomas Mann, the 'intuition' of Yeats, and the 'pure' poetry of Pound and Eliot. Hence the similarity between Henry James' prose and the descriptions of mental process in the philosophical writings of his brother William James is not an individual influence but relates to pervasive interrelated ideals of language and thought. The critical point, though, is that James' prose enacts inwardly the dichotomy of understanding and active resolution already discussed. There comes a moment where the desire for complete truth makes it hard to get anything said at all. The infinitely self-qualifying plasticity of the language is at once a minute truthfulness to the flux of experience yet the pursuit of an ideal so pure as to become an end in itself. From within the most intrinsic logic of realist form there emerges an aesthetic stance. James' aestheticism is the more tragic in that it seems remorselessly forced on him.

In Conrad, too, the examination of the moral self within the frame of the realist novel is conducted through juxtapositions of narrative perspective to convey intuitions of evil and vacuity at the heart of the self, yet with a lurking possibility that the technical artistry can become an end in itself. As with James, the subtlety of moral perception brings the novel by its own logic to the awareness of a moral impasse for which the brooding consciousness of the novel itself is the only resolution.

Where James, like Jane Austen, uses a slightly stylized version of upper middle-class life, Conrad finds his moral microcosm most characteristically in the world of seamen. In such a world moral value, even when manifest as individual heroism, is essentially communal. Hence duty has the force of an external and manifest necessity such that its breakdown, individually or collectively, is felt with a corresponding urgency and replication. Conrad felt that the balance of the individual and the social principles in the moral world was shifting towards the former and we may see his perspectivist exploitation of different narrative viewpoints as a reflection of this fact, while his moral occasions insist on the importance of objective moral considerations. The moral self is ideally composed of external loyalties so habitual as to be unquestioning. When they are seriously questioned the potential abyss is already there. The character who has never known the force of these, such as Donkin the dissatisfied sailor in *The Nigger of the Narcissus* (1897), cannot experience their loss but Kurtz and Lord Jim know the vertiginous horror of falling, or leaping, into what they can see to be an abyss. Conrad's perspectivist technique enables us to see both the unreality and the genuineness of this. The delusions of heroism by which Jim judges himself do not make his disgrace less actual and objective. Hence the importance of the author surrogate, Marlow, in these tales, for he has a foot in both worlds. While Kurtz takes the Dostoevskyan leap into the abyss, Conrad himself does not. It is a moral possibility that the self-conscious person must live with in order to avoid and this is the dilemma focused in Marlow. To live with it involves a measure of sympathy and identification, yet that is also its insidious corruption. Hence, while Marlow appears to be struggling to sympathize with Jim, there is a less conscious level at which he is only too readily drawn to do so. Marlow's balancing act is the moral centre of the book even more than the moral ambiguity of Jim. As so often with James too, the final product seems to be a moral knowledge that envelopes but cannot directly sustain the active life.

This refraction by which the events of the novel find their significance more in the observer than in the titular hero points to a quality pervasive in Conrad even when it is not localized in the narrator, Marlow. Even the magisterial political analysis of *Nostromo* (1904) is essentially a brooding upon, rather than an explanation of, the inherent corruption of idealism. There can be no moral action without ideals, yet idealism is a potentially deceptive self-projection. With such a perception of the moral life, there is a danger of Conrad's underlying pessimism becoming an insufficiently self-questioning attitude, a pervasive psychological *donnée*, and a correlative of this is that the narrative technique expressing this becomes an end in itself instead of engaging demonstratively with its material. This self-absorption of technique occurs in *Chance* (1914), I believe, and also I would say in

The Good Soldier (1914) by Conrad's occasional collaborator, Ford Madox Ford. In that book the narrator Dowell is the centre of a dazzlingly professional manipulation of narrative perspectives, but the crucial figure of Ashburnham remains an undetected nullity so that finally the book does not demonstrate a case so much as reflect aspects of Ford's own emotional constitution.

In Conrad, however, this tendency, as with his occasional obfuscatory heightening of rhetoric, is peripheral to the main achievement and this is largely a matter of an integrity of handling and partly related to his attitude towards his art. Conrad saw little hope in the further development of a social evolution that was already weakening communal ties and loyalties, yet neither was he a Primitivist. The *Heart of Darkness* (1902) suggests no such alternative to a rapacious modern economy. This impasse is of a piece with the widespread post-Flaubertian sense of political futility that underlies the making of 'Art' into a supreme value. But while Conrad's novels show the influence of Flaubert in their concern for artistry, their underlying spirit is not Flaubertian. His craftsmanship, I would say, is equally based on the humbler model of the seaman. Conrad's attitude to his craft is consonant with the impersonal duty of his good seaman and storyteller. There is a self-conscious struggle for a kind of naiveté. In sum, the critique of moral idealism in his work is not betrayed by a compensatory idealism of 'Art'. For Conrad, as for James, the logic of his own moral perceptions threatens to drive him into a contemplative remove, but working in the concrete terms of character and action his general pessimism is both qualified and substantiated.

In various ways, then, James and Conrad partake of the broader tendencies of modernist literature yet respond to their world in a manner consonant with the techniques and assumptions of realist fiction. Clearly, at both technical and substantive levels, modernity can have varied, even opposed, implications. There is, however, one feature shared by pretty well all the writers considered so far apart from Lawrence. Despite their crucial impact on English literature, they are not English. This seems not to be accidental and it raises far-reaching questions about the meaningfulness of modernism in the strictly English context. Modernism of the kind considered so far is principally a Franco-American development largely in tension with the native tradition it for some decades overshadowed. It remains now to consider the English situation more closely.

The English and their literature

> 'And a man who is *emotionally* educated is as rare as a
> phoenix.'   (D.H. Lawrence)[29]

It has become increasingly apparent in retrospect that there was
always a polarity between the native literary tradition and the inter
national modernist *avant-garde* that dominated at least the high-brow
range of literary consciousness from about 1914 onwards. This ha
emerged most strikingly as subsequent generations of English poet
have felt for their own voices. To put Auden next to Eliot and Hardy
shows how completely Eliot had created a new mode; Auden's firm
base in contemporary and colloquial idiom along with his difficulty o
surface makes Hardy's deliberate poeticality seem a little quaint. Ye
this same comparison also indicates how far Auden has shifted back to
the directly personal and low-key register that sustains Hardy's poeti
cism. With Philip Larkin, in the post-Second-World-War generation
the recovery of an essentially Hardyesque mode is both complete and
explicit; Larkin records that the discovery of Hardy taught him to shed
the Yeatsian rhetoric of his early verse. And Hardy meanwhile had
not lacked poetic progeny. Hardy himself was writing poetry through
the first two decades of the century and provided models for ironic and
compassionate perception of the Great War by other poets such as
Siegfried Sassoon. His use of the English countryman *persona*, also
successfully deployed by Edward Thomas, was consonant with the
Georgian manner; an avatar of English pastoralism which was turned
to both satiric and elegaic effect in the war poetry of Rupert Brooke
and Wilfred Owen.

That the American Robert Frost had his first popularity in England
is further evidence of this English predilection. Robert Graves, one o
the few soldier poets to survive, also went on to write, albeit with his
own brand of modernist mythopoeia, within a frankly personal, low
key English register. This persistence of an English poetic manner
that is contemporary yet not modernist suggests that English poetry
unlike American, could not get an essential renewal through the
modernist movement. And if one considers the personal manner o
Auden and of Larkin to be self-regarding in a way that Hardy's was
not, then the point has a further thrust to it. English poetry, while
largely resisting the pressure of modernism, also seems to have found
insufficient nourishment from its own resources. Hence if the

levelopment of poetry is suggestive of the English relation to modernism generally, then the questions raised cut both ways. Comparison
with the modernist achievement highlights limitations in the native
tradition but that tradition likewise provides a critique of modernism.
Having devoted the bulk of this essay to some principal aspects of
modernism, I hope we now have a frame of reference through which to
consider the English situation in an economical yet critical way.

I remarked at the outset that D.H. Lawrence is a pertinently
modern writer who opposes root and branch the modernism associated
with Joyce or Proust; we should now add that he is quintessentially
English. This is evident enough in his provincial, working-class, Nonconformist heritage and his thorough assimilation of English romanticism. But Lawrence's own view of English literature put a broader
case. He saw it as a literature pre-eminent in the expression and understanding of (which is different from 'analysis' or 'having ideas about')
the nature and movement of feeling. Lawrence recognized that one
can be highly educated and even very clever while remaining
emotionally uneducated; and he would have added that this was likely
to become increasingly normal with a universal state education
developing primarily abstractive and 'intellectual' abilities. This is not
a 'two cultures' question either. Studying botany in the right spirit
could well enrich the whole man where reading literature badly could
be the most essential corruption. For literature, in which feelings get
expressed and known, is also the medium in which they can get most
insidiously juggled, denied or indulged.

It is from this standpoint that reservations arise concerning modernism as already discussed. The genuine and massive achievements I
have been briefly sketching in this essay hinge time and again on questions of technique with the covert assumption creeping in that the
technical resolution guarantees the spiritual one. The whole question
of 'impersonality', for example, that particularly exercised Joyce and
Eliot, became for them a self-conscious and technical affair sometimes
doing duty for, and even precluding, the actual impersonality of
emotional acceptance that comes through the highly personal voices
of Lawrence, Dostoevsky or Dickens when those writers are actually
doing their job. Or Hemingway could be pondered as a case where
technique acquired from the doyenne of modernism, Gertrude Stein,
could not save him from the emotional indulgence often manifest in
his novels. Particular cases have to be argued, of course, but my

general point is that the emotional subtlety and technical virtuosity of modernist literature can be modes of emotional indulgence and evasion as well as discipline and knowledge, while the aesthetic exclusiveness, the preoccupation with matters of technique and form encourages the assumption that emotional or moral questions of this kind are naive or irrelevant. Hence to Joyce, Lawrence's writing were only naive and perfervid moralizing while Lawrence saw Joyce' as the self-willed imposition of an etiolated cerebrality. Though neither the aesthetic nor the moral extreme actually exists in isolation the general commitments of these two writers are so diametrically opposed as to present us with polar conceptions of literature. This dichotomy pervades criticism too and has led not to mutually invigorating dialogue but to uncommunicating camps. Hence part of the inheritance of this period is a confused and dichotomous vision of the meaning and value of literature at large. It seems to me that the expression and education of feeling is an, if not the, ultimate criterion for judging literature and it is from this viewpoint that it is most pertinent to consider Lawrence and other specifically English writers.

Lawrence combined the artist's, the prophet's and the psychologist's functions in the manner of Blake and, more than any other writer I can think of, the response to him has come to indicate, for both sides, a fundamental register of personality. This is, I believe, an important clue to the nature and significance of his writing. To put it at its broadest, we might say that while the very notion of the self is under threat Lawrence poses a version of the ancient, discomforting question: what does it profit a man if he gain the whole world and suffer the loss of his own soul? The characteristic focus of his works is the man or woman who suddenly faces a hollowness or falsity in the self and tries to get his or her life on to a proper emotional footing; to gain or regain their wholeness. The personal dimension in his writings frequently gets him into trouble and most of his full-length novels have serious flaws and lapses. And when drawing up a list of reservations, we can also include his largely misguided attempts to translate his psychological critique into positive political and social programmes as, for example, in the political 'leadership' phase which culminated in *The Plumed Serpent* (1926) and was then abandoned.

Lawrence's essential quality, though, is an ability to put his finger on emotional falsities and relate them to a larger perception of the stable and permanent elements in emotional life. A minor example is

he relatively early short story 'Odour of Chrysanthemums' – a story
that also demonstrates the highly subjective, lyrical manner in which
he gives himself to his character's feelings. At the end of the story the
miner's wife, who has been mentally abusing her husband, and with
every apparent justification, undergoes something more subtle than a
reversal of feeling when he is brought in dead from a pit accident. She
begins to form the dim consciousness, beneath the flood of immediate
feeling, that she has never really faced death, or her husband, or her
own life before. And at this point what had seemed like a simple
authorial identification with her becomes rather Lawrence's mode of
complete, 'impersonal' acceptance of the women even while turning
the critique against her. This is a brief example, but the emotional
suppleness with which Lawrence moves between levels of the self
gains a larger historical, social and cultural import in his more
complexly representative characters.

The suppleness is what needs stressing as this is, I believe, a principal area of confusion in reading him. Lawrence distinguishes between
the living and the moribund with the same intensity and absoluteness
as Bunyan did between good and evil. And part of the prophetic
dimension of his writing, like Bunyan's, is to see the whole of experience through the overwhelming importance of this polarity. Within
this, however, and again like Bunyan, Lawrence the novelist is
interested in the constantly shifting and deceptive interplay of these
principles. The sort of reader who wants to know the author's 'idea'
or 'view of life' has tended, I believe, to read Lawrence in terms of this
broad polarity and to miss the novelistic suppleness at the centre. The
'Cathedral' chapter of *The Rainbow* is a case in point. Lawrence's
identification here with Will as his sexual feeling for Anna is assimilated to an ecstatic contemplation of the cathedral's upward thrusting
architecture could be seen as the expression of a messily religiose
sexual mysticism on Lawrence's own part. The point of the episode,
though, is to indicate how the genuinely spiritual and artistic impulse
in Will is resulting in a narrowing and distortion of the emotional self.
Lawrence is not approving of Will here but neither is he simply
condemning him. We can only understand Will, let alone form a
judgement of him, dynamically, as it were, against his whole context.
The emotional discriminations in this chapter are subtle and
controlled and when we consider how delicately Lawrence suggests
the balance of the wilful and the unwitting in his characters (partly

because the method is entirely dramatic, not schematic), then we can see how such writing throws the reader on his own resources of emotional intelligence. We are given no general 'ideas' or analysis of feeling; we are obliged to intuit the emotional and judgemental valencies in their actual shifts and flowing.

The importance of Lawrence, therefore, does not hinge on his always being 'right' but on the resources of emotional intelligence he can bring to bear on our sicknesses. I have already remarked, however, that Lawrence's Englishness by his own criterion of such dramatization of feeling did not, unfortunately as I believe, make him the representative English writer of his time. It is difficult to judge how far his pacifism, exacerbated by marriage to a German, was an underlying cause of the banning of *The Rainbow*, ostensibly for obscenity, in 1915. But Lawrence was from then on effectively an outsider to his country in a way that other wartime pacifists were not, and this can be understood better by considering some writers who embodied the more representative literary values within the English context; preeminently the 'Bloomsbury' group.

Some years after the death in 1904 of their father, the Victorian critic Leslie Stephen, his daughters Virginia and Vanessa married and set up households in the rather unfashionable Bloomsbury district of London. Despite their obvious talents, Virginia for writing and Vanessa for painting, the girls had not had the public school and university education of their brother Thoby, but when they married (respectively Leonard Woolf and the art critic, Clive Bell) they attracted to their homes some of the best known people interested in the literary and plastic arts such as E.M. Forster, Lytton Strachey and Roger Fry, as well as the economist J.M. Keynes. Some were acquaintances of Thoby's from Cambridge which in the early years of the century was much influenced by the philosopher G.E. Moore. His *Principia Ethica* (1903), discussed more fully in David Holdcroft's essay, turned a scepticism about general moral principles towards a pragmatic and positive approach to concrete moral situations. Moore is perhaps not an 'influence' so much as a focusing distillation of the English liberal ethos, but this configuration of an underlying scepticism countered by concern for the immediate moral issue, for tolerance, and for individual human relationships as a highest practical value, comes out in the two most substantial writers associated with the Bloomsbury group: Virginia Woolf and E.M. Forster. The values and achievements of these two writers have, therefore, a broader implication for the quality of the liberal culture from which they derive and I wish to consider them now for their symptomatic relation to English liberalism.

Woolf and Forster re-enact something of the larger dichotomy we have seen between Joyce and Lawrence. Forster attacked the English for their failures of emotional spontaneity and Woolf constructed from the random flow of her characters' consciousnesses aesthetic stays against chaos, but the terms in which they each worked are quite distinct from those of Lawrence or Joyce. Though Forster saw Woolf as referring everything to the vague criterion of 'Art' and she saw him as appealing to the opposite, but equally vague, notion of 'Life', the very fact that they could discuss this suggests how much they have in common. What they have in common involves, I believe, not only literary, but social and emotional limitations of a kind not present in Lawrence or Joyce. Let us consider Virginia Woolf first.

Woolf's criticism of conventional novelistic characterization quoted earlier in this essay suggests something of her own positive intention. Out of the random impressions that make up the momentary 'halo' of consciousness she wishes to create emotional structures whose beauty and harmony will reconcile the pain and meaninglessness of experience as lived. Her achievement in this respect is unique and genuine, but I believe her artistic purpose is less pure than Joyce's in a way that makes it at once more poignant and less successful. I say her purpose is less pure because the rehearsal of the randomness of individual consciousness seems to me to have a different, more personal, import than Joyce's. The series of progressive mental breakdowns that dogged her from her mother's death in her early teens till her suicide in 1941 has its impact in her novels, as in moments like the end of 'The Window' section of *To The Lighthouse* (1927): 'She clutched at the blankets as a faller clutches at the turf on the edge of a cliff. Her eyes opened wide. Here she was again, she thought, sitting bolt upright in bed.' The details of Joyce's world have a solid physical presence and he plays serenely at constructing orders out of them. For Woolf and her most typical characters, the very being of the world is more tenuous, evanescent and threatening. Hence, too, the order to be created represents a more urgent psychological investment. It is the unique stay not only against flux but against this terrifying drop into non-being. And so, too, within the book itself Woolf is concerned to test the viability of the aesthetic ordering as an ordering of life. The artist, Lily Briscoe, the subject of the above quotation, is parallelled with the wife and mother, Mrs Ramsey, in such a way that the emotional creativity of the one interpenetrates with the other's artistic achievement. And when Lily finally completes her painting, and her brush-stroke coincides with a moment of family reconciliation such as the now dead Mrs Ramsey would have sought to effect, Woolf is careful to insist on the personal and momentary significance of this achievement for Lily. Though completing the painting coincides with the end of the book, Woolf is always aware how tenuous and provisional is Lily's achievement and her own. This conscious vulnerability of the order achieved within and by the book is quite different from Joyce and gives Woolf a characteristic poignancy.

In this way an aspect of Woolf's writing that hovers on the symptomatic is drawn into its artistic expression, but in other respects the less thoroughgoing aestheticism involves limitations that Joyce escapes. Beneath its structure of imagistic *leitmotifs* played over a tri-partite division of narrative times, the book still rests on something like a story and a moral evaluation of characters, in a traditional way. The trouble is that the logic of Woolf's method of modernist subjectivity does not lead her to explore and test her values in this more traditional dimension of the book, but rather to ride over it. The principal problem here is Mr Ramsey, based on Woolf's own father, who represents the 'male' values of intellectualism, a kind of 'reality principle', as opposed to the emotional intuition and fecundity of the mother. The moment by moment, impressionistic technique of the book is heavily weighted towards the emotional flow of the wife, and the supposed intellectualism of Mr Ramsey is presented in such a notional way that it is hard to gauge how much it may contain of satiric intent. There may even be little or none, for the book preponderates most heavily towards Mrs Ramsey's side precisely at the moments when Woolf, as she genuinely and frequently does, seeks to redress the balance. The pertinent comparison would be George Eliot's handling of Casaubon in *Middlemarch* where the author, in depicting an intellectual failure, manages to render so clearly what an actual intellectual life would be like. And more is at stake here than a failure to 'do' Mr Ramsey. Without him there is no real testing of Mrs Ramsey either but only a cosy acceptance of the authorial values, and, by the same token, the general association of intellect with emotional boorishness remains a sentimental assumption.

There are other works of Virginia Woolf less open to these strictures, but *To the Lighthouse* lets us see, I think, a characteristic problem of her work and some of the reasons for it. Where the more thoroughgoing aestheticism of Joyce found autotelic structures, Woolf's values as embodied in her characters reflect the author's mind without a comparable tension of dramatic objectivity. Her modernist technique of subjectivity, her play with time, her aliveness to other arts, etc., do not always help her to test out her evaluative commitments but rather reinforce the sense of the world as only really existing in minds like her own. It is not the fact of this limitation, but its unwittingness that matters. Jane Austen can restrict her range because she knows she is doing so and what she is leaving out; Woolf gives me the impression rather that there are registers of feeling and being of which she is unaware. If this is so it may reflect not just personal factors but differences in the cultural situations of Austen and Woolf, and to approach this larger question we may consider the case of E.M. Forster too.

Forster is an even more pertinent instance here as he not only embodies a tradition of bourgeois liberal humanism, but he seeks to give it a more explicit political and social testing in his novels. His first four novels may be seen as attempts to find a notation for the emotional spontaneity and corresponding moral vitality that he found lacking in English life. Two of them, *Where Angels Fear to Tread* (1905) and *A Room with a View* (1911) are excellent social comedies, playing on a contrast between emotionally restricted middle-class English characters and emotionally spontaneous Italians. In *The Longest Journey* (1907) he attempts to express the deeper emotional currents through symbolism based on 'Nature', but the effect on the whole is weakly literary. *Howards End* (1910) approaches the English with a story and a symbolism remarkably similar to *To The Lighthouse* and although it is clearly surpassed by *A Passage to India* (1924) I think it provides, like *To The Lighthouse*, a helpful insight into its author generally.

Howards End also focuses on a wisely, all-sympathizing mother who sustains her emotionally crass, but socially successful, husband and whose mantle falls after her death on a younger woman. Again, too, the major dichotomy is between a predominantly male world of external necessities, such as work, and the generally feminine, inner domain of 'personal relations'. The failure of English social life to build the 'rainbow bridge' between these worlds is largely the reason why the culturally aspiring working-man, Leonard Bast, has remained in the 'abyss' of lower-class vulgarity. Despite the scope and worthiness of intention evident even in this outline, as in the novel's motto 'only connect', Forster's deepest admirers have conceded that the treatment of Leonard Bast is hopelessly condescending and precisely because of its worthiness of intent. The more delicate critical issue following from that is its effect on the rest of the novel; as with Mr Ramsey, how do the book's positive values survive? What exactly do we have to connect? It seems to me that what the treatment of Bast most essentially reveals is a limited understanding inherent in Forster's treatment of 'personal relations' and of 'culture' generally.[30] Compare the episode in Chapter VI where Bast and Jacky eat their 'soup square' to the episode in Chapter I of *Sons and Lovers* where Mrs Morel feeds her young son with 'batter pudding and jam'. Forster sees no possibility of vital and complex emotions in his working-class characters except in so far as they have middle-class cultural aspirations. It is not just that the Basts' life is dreary, so is Mrs Morel's, but that Forster should use the external circumstances of working-class life as the sufficient notation of that dreariness. Although quite appropriate for purposes such as social comedy, Forster's seeing things so much in conventional social terms at moments like this defines a limitation that I find throughout his work. It is true even for *A Passage to India* – albeit that it is a much tougher book and represents a personally impressive turn against his own liberal humanism. The essentially religious, metaphysical theme of *A Passage to India* survives, even capitalizes on, a rather external sense of character that shades into caricature. Like 'The Waste Land', *A Passage to India* derives its power from a personal metaphysical crisis rather than from its gestures towards social reference. But in so far as his novels involve a social domain we cannot but be aware, it seems to me, that his emotional intuition into other kinds of life is closely circumscribed.

I am suggesting, then, that Forster has limitations in the range of his social understanding correlative with an unease in the domain of personal feelings, and that in these respects he is close to Virginia Woolf. In fact, I would go further. Their rather hot-house treatment of 'personal relations' has a revealing concomitant, I would say, in their handling of physical sexuality. The impersonal dimension of the erotic, a vitalizing yet also a stabilizing factor in emotional relationships, seems generally a matter of horror to Woolf and incomprehension to Forster. For various biographical reasons each manifests powerful restraints on the emotional life even while affirming its value. But I express my sense of emotional and social limitation in these writers because they seem to me representative of an English moral, social and literary ethos increasingly losing its grip on the life of the time.

The kind of critical case I have outlined against Woolf and Forster has been made, and disputed, many times. Woolf was from the first surprised and hurt by the apparent virulence of adverse criticism while Forster has more slowly become the object of negative revaluation, but in each case the debate has implied the larger issue of their assumed cultural centrality. The virulence properly arises from this larger issue. Now Forster particularly has been a kind of public mentor to many decent and intelligent people especially through the Hitler and Mussolini years. His quiet, self-deprecating humanism provided a positive and personal alternative to the general ideological bullying. It is when Forster is looked at from outside the standpoint of his immediate contemporaries that his worthiness seems to have less of permanent sustenance to it. Jane Austen was part of a particular social nexus but her works stand independently of its passing. I believe that Forster and Woolf, inheritors of the tradition of Jane Austen and George Eliot, do not stand so firmly by themselves, and that this reflects a gap that has widened between the actuality of society and the range of emotional understanding in this literary tradition. It is not, in other words, that one should criticize Woolf or Forster simply, but that one should see them as part of a more general process. It is in the early twentieth century, I believe, as middle-class values become less socially authoritative, that the English bourgeois liberal novel begins to become, in a limiting sense, genteel. This suggests a further dimension to the fate of liberal culture as discussed in Fred Reid's essay.

A suggestive measure of this is to extend the case of Leonard Bast to the general novelistic treatment of working-class people since the 1840s. The several novelists of that decade who considered the 'condition of England' question saw as the vital issue the fact of the 'two nations' formulated in Disraeli's *Sybil*, but they tended to share his optimistic view that knowledge and goodwill on the part of the governing classes could alleviate the lot of their less fortunate brethren. The darkening mid-century vision of Dickens accompanied the recognition that the division was more structural and inherent than accidental to the social order, and by the later decades of the century writers like Gissing give, often unwittingly, a more sinister and distasteful view of the working 'masses'. It is a history of conscious goodwill revealing between the lines a growing fear and estrangement. Even in Aldous Huxley's *Point Counter Point* (1928), Walter Bidlake in the opening chapter notes his actual fear and distaste for working people despite his theoretical sympathy; and although this character is not generally endorsed there does seem to be something of the author's own feeling in the episode. It is worth remarking that Huxley's book came out only a few years after the General Strike and, although its principal concern is with the corruption of contemporary bourgeois culture, in the larger context of the English novel we can see how one nation in its incapacity to connect with the other has itself suffered an increasing sense of moral futility; a division of thought and purpose. Gissing, for all his obliquities of viewpoint, still *cared* but Huxley depicts a weary class stalemate. I don't say which is chicken or egg here, nor do I suggest there was a simple moral or political alternative. Though obviously vulnerable to Marxist critique, the novelists of the 1840s onwards, down to Forster, have been right, I believe, to insist that the 'two nations' question is one of human community as well as economic distribution. But 'cultural' and 'social' are words which have increasingly come to designate two separate things rather than aspects of the same thing as they might, say, in application to the world of Jane Austen. And so, correspondingly, the humanistic 'culture' of Forster and Woolf has become a separate, formally defined domain in which they cannot engage the whole social experience of their time. The positive achievement of these two writers includes their awareness of the tenuousness of their own values in the contemporary context, but it is also part of their historical interest to be symptomatic of this.

If the critical argument over Forster and Woolf involves dispute over basic issues of cultural representativeness then it is complicated by changes in the formation and expression of taste generally. Q.D. Leavis' *Fiction and the Reading Public* (1939) documents a debasing of taste accompanying the rapid growth of a popular daily press, magazines and novels throughout the nineteenth century, but especially in the first decades of the twentieth. And the new medium of film was even more susceptible to purely commercial pressures. This is not to say that film is only commercial and therefore a debasing element. Film developed artistic aspirations of its own and its techniques, in ct, consolidated some of those found in modernist literature. Conrad, or example, is highly filmic with his panoramas, his long shots, his udden close-ups and above all his use of flashback. There are also nore positive ways of looking at popular culture at large, but Mrs Leavis' overall thesis seems to me telling and still sobering. Besides iscussing the prose and presentation of popular journalism of the Northcliffe era, she points out how in this period the now common ivision of high-brow, middle-brow and low-brow writing became stablished; this involving not simply writing of different levels of eriousness and quality, but writing which does not accept the exis- ence of more exacting standards at all.

George Eliot was a writer of the highest seriousness who wrote for veryone, but this social breadth has since been undermined by rocesses larger than the individual writer. There has been in fact a ual process at work. Since Flaubert, serious art has become increas- ngly the possession of an élite; it is no accident that the words 'vulgar' nd 'cliché' in their modern sense date from the nineteenth century. At the same time more popular levels of reading have been taken over y large-scale commercial interests acting not so much cynically as xpressing a lowest common denominator of taste. In between there is he middle-brow, say Hugh Walpole or Somerset Maugham, having either the exactingness of the one nor the possible energy or experi- nce of the other. And where 'serious' and 'popular' culture cease to ave a vital relationship, both are likely to suffer. My remarks so far on he narrowing or loss of grip in the bourgeois novel do not, therefore, mply the possible alternative of a working-class culture. Working- lass writers after Lawrence are effectively the obverse of the bour- geois; whether critical or seeking assimilation they are defined by it. Hence, as 'serious' cultural expression becomes increasingly the acti- ity of an élite and the popular domain is vulgarized, so the relative ecline of the bourgeois liberal tradition of the English novel is ompounded by the absence of a more broadly testing readership. The ssence of the genteel is not to know that it is so and there is eventually o one else to bring this judgement to bear. In sum, it seems to me hat in England the general isolation of serious modern culture is ompounded by the isolation effected by class experience.

Some such sense of general cultural context is helpful in weighing he import of such writers as Galsworthy, Bennett, Kipling, Shaw, Wells and Huxley whom I want now briefly to discuss. For these names include some of a journalistic as much as literary interest and arguments about them, even more than about Woolf or Forster, hinge on larger assumptions about the nature of literature. A writer like Wells addresses himself much more obviously to the issues of the day as the average, intelligent newspaper reader might enumerate them and if the present essay were to have been quantitative rather than qualitative, sociological rather than literary, it would have been Wells and Shaw rather than Joyce who might have had the most emphasis. They worried publicly and explicitly about democracy, technology, urbanization, the emancipation of women and all the other general questions that constitute the proper themes of the historian. On the whole it seems that the writers who most notably address themselves to their contemporary context in this way have not the moral, spiritual and emotional exactingness of the finest modern literature, and they characteristically address, and develop, an audience unaware of, or indifferent to, such criteria. Hence in the following comments I want to suggest their general literary, or sub-literary, kind as well as something of their intrinsic interests and achievements.

John Galsworthy and Arnold Bennett continued to write the nine-teenth-century realist novel; Bennett being the more substantial. Where Galsworthy's *The Forsyte Saga* becomes as flat as it is pano-ramic, Bennett in novels like *Anna of the Five Towns* (1902) or *The Old Wives Tale* (1908) achieves a more satisfying solidity. It was indeed, his relative success in this respect that led Woolf and Lawrence to single him out as their principal whipping boy when attempting to define their own aspirations. But Lawrence's objections touch more than the technique of characterization; he objects to Bennett's emotional fatalism, the narrowness of his moral horizon. In the late nineteenth century the deterministic aspect of Zola's naturalism had its English counterpart in the more suffusive emotional fatalism of Hardy and Gissing. Bennett shares this but in a mode of comparative pathos and indulgence rather than with the tragic and anguished regis-ters of his predecessors. Hence, where Forster and Woolf embody an honourable endeavour of their English liberal culture in the new century, Bennett exemplifies rather its acquiescent emotional drift.

By the 1920s Bennett and Galsworthy seemed distinctly Edwardian, or *passé*, to high-brow critics, and it is revelatory of the cultural developments already described that Bennett was also objected to for making money. Great writers, after all, have always

ritten for money and the objection in Bennett's case points to his
ore insidious relationship with a non high-brow readership. Without
uite the cynicism of the hack or the exactingness of other standards,
Bennett could notionally simulate the mode of Dickens or George
Eliot in which a genuine moral authority was intimately related to
ommercial popularity. For Dickens' desire to please his public was
ot merely commercial, it stemmed from his genuine belief in a
ommon humanity; a belief that was at the centre of his creative intui-
ions. Unlike the great modern writers so far discussed, Bennett seems
ot to have suffered discomfort from the felt divergence of popularity
nd quality and this seems of a piece with the relationship of money-
making and happiness in his novels. In short, his novelistic method
mbodying a confident moral objectivity seems questionable not
imply by contrast with the controlled subjectivity of perspective in
modernist fiction, but because there is no longer a sufficient social
orrelative of the magisterial manner.

Rudyard Kipling, too, is a writer whose interest now lies to a large
xtent in the audience he implies. The revulsion of feeling against
militaristic and colonialist values that set in since the Great War has
meant a corresponding decline in Kipling's reputation. There is some
unfairness in this; not least since he himself expresses unease about
the imperialist venture in 'The White Man's Burden': 'The silent,
ullen peoples / Shall weigh your Gods and you.' And the element of
ure adventurousness that made him something like the official
iterary expression of the Boy Scout Movement (founded in 1908)
often gives him direct access to common feelings and impressions.
One of the sustaining emotions of *Kim* (1901), for example, is the
evident love of India and its peoples. So, too, he has been the nearest
thing to a popular poet in the proper sense as when putting common
eelings into a kind of stylized cockney in his *Barrack Room Ballads*.
Yet, for all that, the generally negative response of the present day
seems justified to me in so far as it represents the questioning of a
arger mythology. The values of *Stalky and Co* (1899), a book admired
incidentally by the egregious 'Bulldog' Drummond, are not only
nadequate for an adult life but, projected on to a political scale, are
ikely to prove actively pernicious.

Unlike these last three writers, George Bernard Shaw offers himself
as distinctly a man of the new age and his conception of modernity is in
revealing contrast to that of the modernist figures discussed earlier.

Shaw was a journalist of great energy, skill and public conscience b
the response to him of the major modern writers is epitomized i
Yeats' vision of him as a sewing machine with incessantly smilin
teeth. I have already remarked how several otherwise different moder
writers have a common hostility to abstractive and ideological mode
of thought. Words, through which we symbolize experience, ca
become substitutes for it, and the growth of a sociological thinking t
cope with the collectivized scale of an industrialized democracy wa
perceived as a spiritual threat. Nineteenth-century working-class an
socialist tradition had included a respect for the concrete local exper
ence of craft and community, an element that emerged strongly i
William Morris, but Shaw's membership of the Fabian Society is
pointer to the way socialist consciousness in the new century shifte
on to a more political and ideological plane. Yeats' remark picks u
the way Shaw is not only a man of ideas, but seems almost entirel
made of them. In this respect, while attacking so much within th
contemporary social order, spiritually he was deeply at one with it.

This quality comes out, I believe, in his preface to the early play *Mr
Warren's Profession* (1894).[31] The play is a brilliant reversal of th
conventional Victorian 'courtesan' convention in which the audienc
enjoyed a sexual thrill contained and neutralized by a sense of super
ority to the 'fallen woman'. Shaw was a part influence on Brecht in hi
recognition that the close, largely unwitting, relation between theatri
cal forms and social attitudes as well as the physical presence of th
audience, made the theatre an especially effective medium for disturb
ing social and political feeling below the level of conscious belief. Th
audience could be literally and spiritually trapped in the theatre. Th
wit of the piece is, therefore, essentially dramatic, not merely verbal
But the preface states as follows one of the moral assumptions b
which the play's trap will be sprung: 'No normal woman would be a
prostitute if she could afford to marry for love.' The way this remar
appeals to the 'normal' woman involves a reification that if you paus
to think about it is surely abstract to the point of untruth. Th
sentence lives by its rhetorical symmetry encouraging us to accept th
word 'normal' here as a convenient counter, but any sense of the way
ward energy of sexual feeling, both positively and negatively, is les
than notional. And yet this abstract generality is not just a convenien
shorthand, it is entirely of a piece with the characterization in the pla
itself. There is something untrue about women not wanting to b

ostitutes or to marry for money just as there is something false about
e endings of *Mrs Warren's Profession* and *Major Barbara*. Shaw's
stractive simplifications, while leaving him space for satiric points
d comic paradox, are in some tangible if ambiguous measure his
tual simplifications as well as formally chosen ones, and it is his
nwittingness, or ambivalence, in this respect that makes him so irri-
tingly coy much of the time. Brilliant as they are as ways of
iticizing the given, even Shaw's best plays reveal emotional blank-
esses when obliged to express a larger sense of life. These remarks are
ally directed more at an inflated evalution of Shaw than at the plays
emselves, for this overrating places an unfair critical burden on
eatrical entertainments designed essentially to smoke out particular
uestions and which, I think, should be produced and enjoyed in that
irit. More to the point, perhaps, in *Heartbreak House* (1921) and *St
an* (1924),[32] his greatest plays, he translates his experience as the
ustrated moral critic and educator directly into symbolic form; the
ilure of Shavian nostrums is perhaps his deepest artistic, if not
ersonal, insight.

It is remarkable that of all the writers considered so far Shaw is the
nly one to have sought expression primarily in the theatre, and the
rama of these decades might very briefly be considered at this point.
espite the great changes in European theatre even before the turn of
e century with Ibsen, Strindberg, Chekhov, Wedekind, etc., the
nglish theatre generally remained the expression of a social
ontinuity within the nineteenth-century 'well-made play' conven-
ons. Even Shaw had to trace the familiar English path of the rebel
ho, after a period of controversy, is tolerated, enjoyed and thus
ssimilated as resident iconoclast; a path many lesser men have
ollowed since. It may be that the collective and commercial aspects of
heatre create special problems in presenting anything radically at
dds with prevailing expectations and it is pertinent that the striking
heatrical energy of the period came with the Irish national conscious-
ess of Shaw's countrymen, Yeats, Synge and O'Casey. A perennial
roblem of dramatists throughout the nineteenth and twentieth centu-
ies has been to give dramatic speech the intensity of poetry while
eeping it natural in feel. Prose and poetry must somehow combine,
ot simply be mixed. One solution found by Synge and O'Casey was
o use a slightly stylized version of the Irish speech where this lends
tself to metaphor, humour, fantasy and a ready religious awareness.

Despite the danger of a stock response this carries with it, particularl
in Synge, they did find a workable medium and the slight stylization i
carried by the aspiration towards a more generally mythic dimensio
in this drama as, more obviously, in Yeats. Some of D.H. Lawrence'
plays, too, only discovered theatrically in the 1960s, used the Nottins
ham dialect, in for example *The Daughter-in-Law* (1912), with les
mythic ambition but with dramatic intensity and emotional firmnes:
Again, however, this was a social and linguistic resource not availabl
to, or having no effect on, the London theatre generally. The Englis.
theatre of these decades was not the *locus* of vital innovation.

Returning to Shaw's activity as publicist of causes brings us to th
other notable journalist of the time with a claim to literary considera
tion: H.G. Wells. Wells presented an even more direct challenge t
the values of modernism than Shaw in that, while frequentl
espousing a collectivized and scientific perspective, he employed in hi
novels a more rounded, or literary, conception of human identity. Hi
early 'scientific romances' are the immediate ancestors of th
twentieth-century sub-genre of science fiction in which the hopes an
fears engendered by science and technology have been given specula
tive expression. On the whole it seems to me that Wells expresses th
romance *of* science as well as creating fables *about* it. His mos
substantial novel of a traditional kind, *Tono-Bungay* (1909), gives
spirited panoramic critique of contemporary British society with it
decaying aristocracy and the fraudulent power of commercial enter
prises, but then, at the end, the Wellsian hero, George Ponderevc
sails away on the new destroyer he has helped to design and whicl
signifies a kind of impersonal, scientific veracity. Like Marinetti an
the futurists, he welcomes the machine here even in its inhuman o
destructive aspects as an alternative to a debased and cloying version c
humanity.

This aspect of Wells helps to explain why at about this time he fel
out with the Fabians, Sidney and Beatrice Webb, while the mor
literary objection to Wells, which relates to this complex of attitudes
is that between the comically sympathetic individualism of, say, M
Polly and the great social historical abstractions, there is relatively littl
sense of a substantial inner life where they can meet. You tend to fli;
from one plane to the other without a technical means or a dramati
forum for creative interaction between them. Yet Wells, who did no
have a genteel background, could deal, indulgently perhaps but no

ondescendingly, with lower social registers in a representative way. He knew something about how many people felt, and he made spirited attempts, as in his science fiction, to translate his perception of contemporary actualities into symbolic and mythic forms; albeit very different forms from the modernist mythopoeia already discussed. He even did well enough to win the reluctant admiration of Henry James. Indeed, until their rupture around 1914, James' attitude to Wells reflected revealingly on them both. James was always quite clear about Wells' 'artlessness' and said so but, as in his essay on Balzac, there is an undercurrent of wistfulness towards an author able to deal so directly and energetically with the world. James could see the dangers of enervation in the scrupulous artistic conscience and thoroughgoing subjectivism of the modern novel even while seeing the impossibility for himself, and perhaps for anyone, of really doing otherwise. In sum, it would be unfair to Wells, as to Shaw, to deny that he achieved more than journalism, but there is in both men an insensibility not only to the more exacting demands of art but to the complexities of the human situation that the highest art reflects. Hence, the figures whom we now recognize as cardinal to modern literature seem to me in this sense right to consider the 'Wellsian' and 'Shavian' spirits not only at variance with their own values and aspirations but as promulgating modes of thought and feeling that, despite the iconoclasm of content, were essentially at one with their time precisely where it was most vital to question or resist it.

All these writers just considered have been controversial because they have offered their own world views as complete and normative, but each at least sees the world pretty consistently within his own terms. Aldoux Huxley differs in turning the most radical scepticism on to his own mind and personality. He had a sincere, if in the nature of things a largely ineffective, desire to escape from his own terms. At once a friend of Lawrence and a grandson of T.H. Huxley, the nineteenth-century scientist and proponent of scientific education, Huxley could see the force of polar positions without finding, like Lawrence, a personal centre or, like Thomas Mann, a structure of ironic mythopoeia, by which to resolve or transcend them. In his most substantial work, *Point Counter Point*, he creates a novel out of the novelist Philip Quarles' inability to overcome these same polarities. The D.H. Lawrence figure, Mark Rampion, is obviously admired but the book's actual structure, reminiscent at times of 'The Waste

Land' in its series of vignettes, does not embody the Lawrentian sense
life. In fact, Quarles constantly laments and ruminates on his ow
restless analytic detachment which incapacitates him for passiona
conviction and emotional rootedness of the Lawrentian kind. And so l
speculates on the possible form of a contemporary fiction that wou
achieve such a unity of experience; a work incorporating the spirit
science as well as mystical illumination and the emotional ordering of
complex musical piece. The inner and outer worlds, the emotional ar
the analytic responses, are to be combined in a literary work if not in h
personality and actual life. The literary ideal, in fact, parallels at mar
points the monumental synthesis of *Ulysses*: '. . . the biologist, tl
chemist, the physicist, the historian. Each sees, professionally, a diffe
ent aspect of the event, a different layer of reality. What I want to do is v
look with all those eyes at once. With religious eyes, scientific eye
economic eyes, homme moyen sensual eyes . . . ' (Chapter XIV). I thir
it is apparent even from this brief quotation that such an externalize
and abstract ideal of completeness is at the opposite pole fro
Lawrence's conception of thought as the 'whole man whol
attending'. It is not surprising that in later life Huxley flipped fror
rationalism to mysticism, for their knife-edge yet polar relation is alwa
apparent. In short, Huxley's significance seems to me that of a very fir
reflector. The spiritual issues engaged in modern literature were fe
with articulate urgency by Huxley as they might present themselves fo
an intelligent, educated and eminently decent contemporary. Thoug
less able than Lawrence or Joyce to make art out of it, Huxley's fe
incompleteness witnesses the spiritual pertinence of these authors.

*

A full discussion of Huxley's satires in the 1920s would lead to a top
he mentions only parenthetically but which I think colours his sense
society and the emotional life more suffusively in the book: the afte
math of the Great War. In fact, my general intention in this section, a
in the essay at large, has been to suggest the nature of the literar
medium through which contemporary life and ideas have been refra
ted, rather than to survey ideas and social developments in then
selves. Before concluding this sketch of the English ambianc
however, I want partly to reverse the emphasis and consider, as a
example, how the largest single complex of external events, th
European war, can be seen refracted in literature.

Writing from the perspective of the 1930s, Wyndham Lewis divided the period psychologically into the pre-war, the war and the post-war; ending fairly abruptly around 1926, the year of the General Strike. As he himself recognizes, this is a retrospective, even mythic, vision but it does seem to reflect some shifts and fashions of feeling at the time. The pre-war world later acquired an Edenic value epitomized in the long summer of 1914 preceding the hostilities of the winter. As Fred Reid's essay makes clear this world was not actually untroubled. We have already seen in *Tono-Bungay*, for example, a radical and universal condemnation of the social order. And the novel's ending using the destroyer may be associated with other artists' more explicit and positive anticipation of war as a destruction of the *status quo*. Yet the very fact that the war, assumed to be short-lived, adventurous and a kind of moral purgative rather than a physical blood-letting, could be anticipated in this way suggests a worldly, if not Edenic, innocence. Even without subscribing to the jingoistic feeling that accompanied the end of the Boer War, there was no foreseeing the relentles horror of the trenches. It is not surprising, then, that much of the literature concerned directly with the war itself plays repeatedly on contrasts: the present and the past; the front and at home; technological horror and the beauty of nature. Wells would not have used his destroyer in that way now. On this general topic I cannot do better than refer the reader to Paul Fussell's *The Great War and Modern Memory* (1975) which documents in detail the varieties of response within these basic patterns and emphasizes the widespread literateness of the British soldiery and their recourse to literary tradition, such as *The Pilgrim's Progress* and English pastoralism, as ways of transcending or morally taming the experience of the front.

As his title suggests, though, Fussell is also concerned with the more suffusive ways in which the war subsequently shaped and coloured men's minds. Though questionable in detail, his account of this is well worth reading in full. In the present context, I will only add that the 1920s, when satire was the predominant vein, seem time and again to depict an emotional deadness not only in the object of the satire but within the satirist himself. Apart from 'Hugh Selwyn Mauberley', the post-war decade soon saw in *Women in Love* and 'The Waste Land' two major works which did not concern themselves directly with the war yet seem, in imagery and feeling, to be saturated with its presence. Hence these works could act as emotional bridges

connecting the war to a more general definition of contempora:
experience; for such a definition is clearly what these works were take
to offer. The war, in other words, helped to define the forms of feelir
even outside of specifically war literature. And this might shed furth
light on authors already discussed. Virginia Woolf's embodiment
the destructiveness of time in the central section of *To the Lighthou*
is a synecdochic use of the war years, and the liberal humanism
E.M. Forster's pre-war years is seen as hollow in *A Passage to Indi*
In both cases there are independent and personal reasons for the mor
cast of the work, but the configuration of a post-war mood is al:
traceable. I even wonder about Fielding's stand against jingoist
hysteria in *A Passage to India* and the sinister, searchlight effect of tl
lighthouse beam in Woolf's novel.

Towards the end of the twenties came *Lady Chatterley's Lov*
(1928) and *Point Counter Point* both of which use war cripples
symbols of general emotional blight. Again, these novels are not *abo*
the war but its constant use as a moral shorthand suggests its mo:
suffusive emotional presence behind them. The flapper aspect of tl
1920s, the restless pleasure-seeking, is, it seems, the concomitant
an underlying emotional blankness, and in this respect the emotion
dualism of *Lady Chatterley's Lover* as Connie moves from one plane '
the other is very much of its time. Yet these books seem to signal tl
end of the 'post-war' as do, more evidently perhaps, R.C. Sherrif
Journey's End and Edmund Blunden's *Undertones of War* both
which imply a more retrospective response than literature produce
straight from the front. By the late 1920s, the 'post-war' seems to I
over and with the General Strike and economic collapse attentio
turns, as throughout the 1930s, to social and political concerns of tl
moment. Lewis pointed out that this was also the end of the moderni
movement which had been characterized by a dedication to art abo
social or didactic purpose. In retrospect, he seems to have been rig!
for the social concerns of Auden, MacNiece or Orwell in the 1930s (
seem to signal the end of the classic phase of modernism, even thoug
some of its big documents, like *Finnegans Wake* and *Joseph and l*
Brothers, were still to be completed.

The fact that we can so readily isolate this phase of modernis:
points to broader critical issues that his brief survey of native Engli
writing has attempted to highlight. As a kind of latter-day Renaissan
with implications for the whole range of culture and society, tl

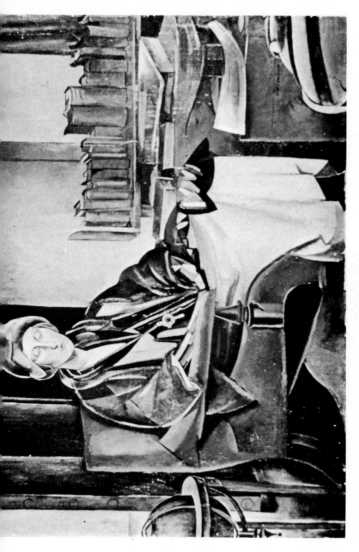

3 *Edith Sitwell* (1923-35) by Wyndham Lewis (The Tate Gallery, London; © Mrs G.A. Wyndham Lewis, by permission)

4   *Les Demoiselles d'Avignon* (1907) by Pablo Picasso (Collection, The Museum of Modern Art New York; The Lillie P. Bliss Bequest; Oil on canvass 8' x 7'8'')

5   (on facing page) *Nude Descending a Staircase* (1912) by Marcel Duchamp (Philadelphia Museum of Art: The Louise and Walter Arensberg Collection)

7 *Leben und Treiben in Universal City um 12 Uhr 5 mittags* (1919) by John Heartfield and George Grosz (Akademie der Künste der Deutschen Demokratischen Republik; © Mrs Gertrud Heartfield, by permission)

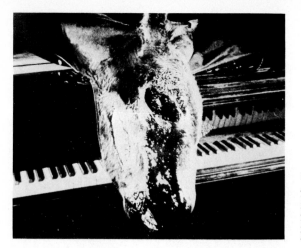

8 Still from *Un Chien Andalou* (1928) by Luis Buñuel (Courtesy of National Film Archive/Still Library; © Contemporary Films Ltd)

9 *Ecce Homo* (1921) by George Grosz (Galerie Nierendorf, Berlin; © Estate of George Grosz, Princeton, NJ, by permission)

modernist movement must surely be seen, despite the distinction of its individual achievements, as very largely abortive. And to the extent that this is so a teasing ambivalence hangs over it: was it dispersed by the war, fascism and other cultural developments or did it rather collapse under its own intrinsic logic? These are not exclusive alternatives, of course, but it matters how internally coherent and stable we see it to have been; how much human experience it could really accommodate. This kind of question was raised at the end of the period by Edmund Wilson in *Axel's Castle* (1932). As the title suggests, Wilson follows the modernist movement from its origins in French *symbolisme* to suggest that the element of autotelic self-preoccupation carried the danger of an ultimately trivializing remove from the felt concerns of human beings. However elegant and imposing it may be, such literature is becoming a game. Subsequently in Nabokov and Beckett, for example, we can see the modernist synthesis divided into its self-celebratory and its nihilistic possibilities but in each case entirely autotelic; a game played in a void. In the Marxist view, forcefully put by Georg Lukàcs, this literature is the spiritual correlative of the moral bankruptcy and bad faith of bourgeois society. It is the illicit emotional enclave of fine sensibilities seeking to transcend, without leaving, the bourgeois world view. I have already remarked that such literature seems to me to be fighting to preserve the individual spirit against the forces ranged against it as much by Marxist ideology as by the bourgeois and capitalist world, but there is no doubt that the social and spiritual ramifications are of this order.

And there is a further difficulty in coming to terms with such questions in that we are ourselves part of the problematic situation. Even at an everyday pedagogical level, the great works of modern literature are now part of an accepted canon in a way that probably makes it harder rather than easier to digest them. The very familiarity of *Ulysses*, 'The Waste Land' or the Byzantium poems as fields of exegetical manoeuvre has given them an artificial accessibility that undercuts the slower, circling formation of judgement. Is there a 'common reader' of *Ulysses* and what does he make of it? And where, on the other hand, a serious critical engagement is attempted it tends to fall into one or other of the camps inherited from the modern period. Compare, for example, F.R. Leavis' *New Bearings in English Poetry* and *D.H. Lawrence: Novelist* to Hugh Kenner's *The Pound Era*. There is no dialogue possible. Leavis would dismiss *Ulysses* and Proust while

Kenner has only contempt for Lawrence. Even their language reflec
this; Leavis adapting the flexibility of James' prose to Lawrence
moral conviction and Kenner using the ranging ellipses of Pound.

Hence any sense of how literature in these decades reflects the li
around it will hinge on what literature, and what view of literature,
chosen. It seems to me that a spiritual cartography of the time mu
include the modernism of Joyce, Proust and Mann whose aesthet
mythopoeia synthesizes, however precariously, visions of huma
completeness from the very materials of dissolution and disbelief. Bu
it is difficult to transpose these into terms of the reader's own life; a
least, without losing the exactingness of the original. Their myth
orderings may amount, in effect, to a highly sophisticated endors
ment of the present-day vulgar relativism that offers a sceptical,
sympathetic, tolerance as the highest value; even, it seems, i
religious education. If Thomas Mann, as Erich Heller says, 'huma
izes the state of doubt', has he also given moral blankness a goc
name? Mann's own record of political conscience is, of course, admi
able, and the question bears on the long-term implications of h
literary mode, not on his personal life. But Mann himself made
pertinent statement in a letter written very late in his career:

> . . . when I hear myself being called the 'foremost novelist of
> the age' I want to hide my head. Nonsense! I am no such
> thing; Joseph Conrad was, as people ought to know. I could
> never have written *Nostromo*, nor the magnificent *Lord
> Jim*; and if he in turn could not have written *The Magic
> Mountain* or *Doktor Faustus*, the account balances out very
> much in his favour.
>
> (Letter to Irita Van Doren, 28 August 1951)

I believe the kind of distinction Mann draws here to be vital. He see
the density of emotional dramatization in a novelist like Conrad, w
might simply say in a novelist, to be something requiring a differen
and more complete order of moral intelligence. To take this as
normative definition of literature might save us the anguished parado
posed by George Steiner and others who ask whether concentratio
camp guards reveal the hollowness of culture because they rea
Goethe and played Mozart. Culture is not what you know about, bu
what you *are*. Unfortunately, it seems to me, the whole ethos o
modernism and the criticism it has engendered has, very muc

ontrary to its own best intentions, tended to exacerbate this exter-
alization of culture. The kind of complexity and sophistication exer-
sed in Joyce and Proust can survive their self-indulgences in a way
at is not true of Conrad or Lawrence. When these latter slip into
dulgent or obfuscatory rhetoric this signals something awry in what
ey are doing; whereas in Joyce or Proust the criticism one might
ake of their emotional assumptions is perforce aimed at a level
terior to the work – the work itself having a magnificently tight and
mprehensive structure within its own terms. In sum, if the great
odernist writers provide a spiritual map of the time, there are others
whom we will turn to find out how to live in that terrain.

otes

1 Quoted by Wylie Sypher, *Rococo to Cubism in Art and Literature*, New
York 1960, p.288.

2 As the texts discussed are generally available in several editions, I give
chapter rather than page references.

3 Letter to Edward Garnett, 5 June 1914.

4 'Modern Fiction', written April 1919.

5 In *The Widening Gyre: Crisis and Mastery in Modern Literature*, New
Brunswick, NJ 1963.

6 *Rococo to Cubism in Art and Literature*, op. cit.

7 Cf. Sergei Eisenstein, *The Film Sense*, translated by Jay Leyda, London
1943.

8 '...denn im Leben der Menschheit stellt das Mythische zwar eine frühe
und primitive Stufe dar, im Leben des einzelnen aber eine späte und reife.'
Adel des Geistes, Stockholm 1945, p.592.

9 Cf. *Primitivism*, London 1972, pp. 18-20 and 32-8.

10 *Joseph and his Brothers*, translated by H.T. Lowe-Porter, New York
1934.

11 The ensuing discussion of Yeats is largely adapted from my essay 'The
Assimilation of Doubt in Yeats' Visionary Poems', in *Queen's Quarterly*,
LXXX, 1973, pp. 383-97, by permission of the Editors.

12 *The Renaissance*, London 1920, p.237.

13 *Essays and Introductions*, New York 1961, p.viii.

14 ibid., p.164.

15 *Yeats*, New York 1970, p.439.

16 *Art and Illusion*, New York 1960, p.285.

17 'Tradition and the Individual Talent', in *Selected Essays*, London 1951,
p.18. First published in 1917.

18 *Blasting and Bombadiering*, London 1937, p.251.

19 *The Symboliste Aesthetic in France, 1885-1895*, Oxford 1968.

20 *Cours de Linguistique Générale*. Course given 1906-7, 1908-9, 1910-1].
    Published in Geneva in 1916.
21 Pre-eminently in William Empson, *Seven Types of Ambiguity*, Londo
    1930. The book is dedicated to I.A. Richards.
22 'A Retrospect', in *Literary Essays of Ezra Pound*, New York 1918, p.1.
23 'A Few Don'ts', *Poetry*, I, 6, 1913. Reprinted in *Literary Essays*, op. c
24 Cf. *The Egoist*, I, 14, 1914. Reprinted in *Literary Essays*, op. cit.
25 Such a distinction has a crucial bearing on the charge of fascism sometime
    directed at, say, Lawrence or Yeats. These writers, I believe, explored an
    understood authoritarian values and conservative feelings often incompre
    hensible to the liberal progressive cast of mind, but precisely because the
    conceived such issues in spiritual and psychological terms they would ne
    have condoned the imposition of a fascist state. In retrospect they can k
    charged with complicity in contributing to a generalized fascistic myth
    logy, but it may be that the real failure was a more general one in no
    recognizing and harnessing in a politically positive way the complexes
    value they represented. The issue, clearly, is a delicate one but the
    supra-historical systems are an attempt to hold rival orders of value i
    simultaneous and testing focus without merely flipping to the fascistic.
26 *Wyndham Lewis*, New York and London 1954, p.131.
27 ibid., p.27.
28 *The Magic Mountain*, translated by H.T. Lowe-Porter, New York 192
    p.496.
29 'John Galsworthy' in *Phoenix I*, London 1936, p.539.
30 For a thorough exposition of this case cf. Duke Maskell, 'Mr. Forster
    Fine Feelings', *The Cambridge Quarterly*, V, 3, 1971, pp.222-35.
31 Date of composition. First performed privately in 1902 and publicly i
    1925.
32 Dates of first London performances.

Select bibliography

Barzun, J. *The Use and Abuse of Art*, Princeton, NJ 1974.
Bantock, G.H. 'The Social and Intellectual Background', in *The Moder
    Age*, ed. B. Ford, London 1961.
Bradbury, M. *The Social Context of Modern English Literature*, Oxfor
    1971.
Bradbury, M. and McFarlane, J. (eds), *Modernism 1890-1920*, Harmond
    worth, Middlx 1976.
Chapple, J.A.V. *History and Literature: Documentary and Imaginatit
    Literature 1880-1920*, London 1970.
Chiari, J. *The Aesthetics of Modernism*, London 1970.
Cox, C.B. and Dyson, A.E. *The Twentieth Century Mind*, vols I and I
    Oxford 1972.
Eisenstein, S. *The Film Sense*, transl. and ed. J. Leyda, London 1943.

Eliot, T.S. *Selected Essays*, London 1951.

Ellman, R. and Feidelson, C. (eds), *The Modern Tradition*, Oxford 1965.

Frank, J. 'Spatial Form in Modern Literature', in *The Widening Gyre*, New Brunswick, NJ 1963.

Frye, N. *The Modern Century*, Oxford 1967.

Fussell, P. *The Great War and Modern Memory*, Oxford 1975.

Gillie, C. *Movements in English Literature 1900-1940*, Cambridge 1975.

Hartman, G. *Beyond Formalism: Literary Essays 1958-1970*, New Haven, CT 1970.

Heisenberg, W. *The Physicist's Conception of Nature*, Westport, CT 1958.

Hauser, A. *The Social History of Art*, vol. IV: *Naturalism to the Film Age*, London 1962.

Howe, I. Introduction to *The Idea of the Modern in Literature and the Arts*, ed. Howe, New York 1976.

Josipovici, G. *The World and the Book: A Study of Modern Fiction*, London 1971.

Kazin, A. 'The Background of Modern Literature', in *Contemporaries*, London 1963.

Kenner, H. *The Pound Era*, Berkeley, CA 1973.

Kline, M. *Mathematical Thought from Ancient to Modern Times*, New York 1972.

Leavis, F.R. *New Bearings in English Poetry*, London 1950.

Leavis, Q.D. *Fiction and the Reading Public*, London 1932.

Lukàcs, G. 'The Ideology of Modernism', in *The Meaning of Contemporary Realism*, transl. J.N. Mander, London 1963.

Meyer, L.B. *Music, the Arts and Ideas: Patterns and Predictions in Twentieth Century Culture*, Chicago, IL 1967.

Orwell, G. *Inside the Whale and Other Essays*, Harmondsworth, Middx 1962.

Pound, E. *Literary Essays of Ezra Pound*, London 1954.

Spears, M.K. *Dionysus and the City: Modernism in Twentieth Century Poetry*, Oxford 1970.

Stead, C.K. *The New Poetic*, London 1964.

Stein, G. *Lectures in America*, New York 1975.

—— *Picasso*, London 1978.

Steiner, G. *Extraterritorial: Papers on Literature and the Language Revolution*, London 1972.

Sypher, W. *Rococo to Cubism in Art and Literature*, New York 1960.

Weightman, J. *The Concept of the Avant-garde: Explorations in Modernism*, London 1973.

Whitehead, A.N. *Science and the Modern World*, Cambridge 1926.

Wilson, E. *Axel's Castle*, London 1961.

2 The disintegration of Liberalism, 1895-1931

FRED REID

Introduction

The preceding essay has indicated the difficulty for the liberal tradition of English literature in encountering the social world of the twentieth century. The present essay complements that account by tracing the fortunes of liberalism as a formal political movement in the same period. The history of liberalism in Britain has a central significance since the movement was pioneered in Britain between 1846 and 1885, and remained of major political significance there longer than in any other country. What precisely happened to English liberalism and when it happened have long been preoccupations of historians. George Dangerfield, writing in America in the 1930s, was confident that liberalism was dead; killed between 1910 and 1914 by the revolt of diehard peers, patriotic Unionists, militant suffragettes and syndicalist workers against its principles of compromise and respectability. 'For it was in 1910 that fires long smouldering in the English spirit suddenly flared up, so that by the end of 1913 Liberal England was reduced to ashes. From these ashes, a new England seems to have emerged.'[1] Since liberalism was dead before 1914, the British Liberal party was also doomed. Everything that it stood for – 'free trade, a majority in parliament, the ten commandments, and the illusion of progress'[2] – was being challenged and judged inadequate. The First World War simply administered the *coup de grâce* to an exhausted and bankrupt party.

Many recent historians have refused to accept so pessimistic a view of liberalism or of the pre-1914 Liberal party. Dangerfield, they argue as too ready to dismiss the 'new liberalism' of the period 1908-14, ioneered by Beveridge, Winston Churchill and Lloyd George.[3] Far rom exhausted in 1914, the Liberal party was committed to progress nd teeming with new ideas for the improvement of Britain. The war illed it, to be sure, but as a bus knocks down and kills a healthy pedescrian.[4] Moreover, if the First World War and its aftermath destroyed he Liberal party, it did not destroy the appeal of liberal ideals. There emained a recognizable affinity between pre-1914 liberalism and ost-1945 labourism. 'New liberalism' envisaged not only the Velfare State (which Beveridge survived to help develop after 1945) ut also the 'mixed economy' of private enterprise supported by ationalized undertakings. In short the belief that the British Liberal arty was viable before 1914 leads such historians to emphasize what as forward-looking and vital in it: the increasing preoccupation with ocial reform; the ability to contain the challenge of the Labour party or the allegiance of working-class voters; and the failure of rival creeds o undermine support for parliamentary government between 910-21 when this challenge commanded so much public attention. And since, according to this view, it still represents the best hope for he survival of liberal values in a world of dictatorships and bureaucracy, the assessment of liberalism as a political creed has a bearing ven for the present day.

There is undoubtedly a strong element of truth in this view, yet too xclusive a preoccupation with the resources for survival of liberalism nay have the effect of rendering unintelligible the doubts, anxieties nd pessimism in so much of the intellectual culture of the period 900-31. Contemporaries did not have the benefit of hindsight and vere often impressed by facts which, in the optimistic perspective, liminish almost to vanishing point. An economic historian studying ate-Victorian and Edwardian Britain, for example, may consider the American invasion'[5] to have been given highly exaggerated significance by a press prematurely alarmed by economic decline. Yet to the tudent of Henry James, reactions to the penetration of Europe by American finance and capital may be an important aspect of the 'international theme'. And novelists, playwrights and poets were not alone in believing that old moral certainties were breaking down before a growing tide of economic exploitation, imperialism and anti-democratic reaction. They lived in a world where these issues were constantly raised n the realm of practical affairs. With their contemporaries, they often

wavered ambiguously between anxiety and optimism and their mood
cannot readily be understood within an historical framework which
heavily emphasizes stability and smoothes out crises. Indeed, unless
we bear in mind the turmoil and struggle of the period, we may even
be tempted to think the fears and anxieties were themselves the
figment of a literary imagination, over-heated by pessimistic trends in
the realms of philosophy and science. Such trends did exist and the
events of political and economic history can never provide a sufficient
explanation of them. But to ignore the history of an anxious epoch
would be to misapprehend the reality underlying even those imagined
worlds apparently most distanced from it.

Hence the purpose of this essay is informative. It provides an introduction to the historical study of the period and assesses the different
views of the crisis of English liberalism. The aim is to show why, at
least until 1929, it was possible to take a hopeful or a pessimistic view
of liberalism and progress in Britain; or indeed to stand in an intermediate position of inquiry and doubt.

Free trade and the second industrial revolution

The twentieth century opened with Britain in a mood of doubt and
self-criticism. It had been made clear for at least two decades that the
high hopes of a wide free-trade order automatically working to
Britain's advantage would not be realized. The world had become an
arena of economic struggle for industrial markets 'that served to
separate the strong from the weak, to discourage some and toughen
others'.[6] Other countries, most notably Germany and the United
States, had begun rapid industrialization in the 1860s. By 1890, the
USA had passed Britain as the world's largest producer of steel, with
Germany surpassing her also in 1893, and in the same decade these
countries greatly increased their tariffs in order to protect their new
industrial systems from foreign competition. Thus, in the 1890s
Britain's exports virtually ceased to expand[7] while her dependence on
imports was increasing – mainly because it was cheaper to import
cereals, beef and mutton from North and South America and
Australia than to grow these commodities at home. As a result, the
size of the 'trade gap' – excess of imported goods over exported –
trebled between 1870 and 1900.[8]

This deterioration in Britain's trading position did not lead her

Conservative government in 1900 to abandon the policy of free trade. From the standpoint of the economy as a whole, there was nothing to worry about. Britain paid for her huge imports with the interest she earned on capital exported abroad in the days of her industrial leadership in the mid-nineteenth century. She also had the world's largest merchant fleet and acted as the world's banker and the income earned from these services also contributed to her strong balance of payments position. She continued to lend abroad in growing amounts, with a preference for the less developed areas of the world – South Africa and Argentina, for example – and this stimulated demand for British exports.

Yet for all these comforting reassurances, pointed out by successive Chancellors of the Exchequer of both parties, there was a growing body of opinion which publicly questioned the state of 'national efficiency'.[9] By comparison with Germany and the United States, the British industrial system was beginning to look old-fashioned and run down. New scientific inventions, some of them pioneered in British laboratories, were being applied there at a much faster rate than in Britain. America was striding into the new age of mass production of consumer goods', first with the sewing machine and, later, with the automobile. Germany was pioneering the production of artificial dyes and man-made fibres and, by 1900, had the first 'grid' in Europe for the long-distance transmission of high-voltage electricity for industrial power. Britain was not wholly without new developments of this kind, but her main efforts were still in the traditional 'staple' industries, textiles, coal, iron and steel, and these were already being forced out of European and North American markets into the developing areas of the British Empire, South America and the Far East. Moreover, even where new developments did take place in Britain, they seemed to be undertaken by foreign firms. American electrical-engineering firms undertook the electrification of the London Underground and a number of urban tramway systems in the 1890s, while the British chemical industry was reinvigorated by the foreign immigrants Brunner and Mond. 'The American invasion' dominated press headlines in the 1890s alongside growing lamentations concerning the increasing familiarity of the label 'Made in Germany'. The growing significance of New York as a rival financial centre to London was already apparent while the arrival of the American banking house of Morgan in the City of London itself was noted in conjunction with the

collapse, in 1890, of Barings, the last purely British-owned merchan
bank.[10]

Those who sounded these alarms in the name of 'national eff
ciency' were a varied group who emphasized different diagnoses an
solutions. Some wanted to see a national system of secondary educa
tion introduced, so that Britain could give her children an adequat
scientific training for the new age. Others were concerned with th
'land question', doubting whether it was a wise policy to run dow
British agriculture and depopulate English villages at a time when, a
Seebohm Rowntree and Charles Booth were demonstrating, one-thir
of the urban population already lived in slums and could not obtai
enough work and wages to keep it in a minumum standard of physic
efficiency.[11] Finally, there were the Fabian Socialists, Sidney an
Beatrice Webb, who had made a special study of the growing trade
union movement of the 1890s and the increasing scale of strikes. I
1900 the trade unions had set up the nucleus for their own politic
party, in the Labour Representation Committee, led by two Scottis
Socialists, James Ramsay MacDonald and James Keir Hardie. Th
Webbs did not think much of the new party, but they argued that th
heat could never be taken out of class conflict, industrial or politica
until the State undertook to provide a minimum standard of living fo
all its citizens.[12]

Imperialist rivalries

However if the changing balance of economic power was underminin
faith in liberalism, so also was the changing balance of military powe
and the growth of imperialist rivalries between the great powers in th
1890s. Liberalism had stood for peace ever since John Bright ha
campaigned against the Crimean War. With his equally famou
partner Richard Cobden, Bright had argued that war was inimical t
trade, served only the interests of the old militarist aristocracy, an
was justifiable only for purposes of national defence in face of th
clearest aggression.[13] Now 'little Englandism', as it came to be called
was like all political slogans, ambiguous. It could justify imposin
colonial rule on India, provided it was regarded as a temporary evil fo
the purpose of civilizing India and opening it up to free trade. It coul
also justify the maintenance by Britain of the strongest navy in th
world in order to protect her large and peaceful commerce. Lor

almerston used it in the 1860s, when he wanted to justify a policy of olation from European entanglements. England he asserted had no ternal allies and no eternal enemies. Only her interests were eternal.

Isolation was often taken to be a triumph of the principles of Cobden nd Bright, but was really based on a hard-headed calculation of Britain's strategic position in the world and on the advantages gained nder the Treaty of Paris, which ended the Crimean War in 1856. Jnder the Treaty, the Russian fleet was excluded from the Mediter-anean by the neutralization of the Black Sea and the closing of the Bosphorus to Russian warships. In the Mediterranean itself France, Britain's other naval rival, was neutralized by the presence of a British leet and in this way the short route to India through the Suez Canal vas kept open for British trade.

This 'Crimean system', as it has been called,[14] began to break lown after 1870. Russia took advantage of German support during he Franco-Prussian War to repudiate the Black Sea clauses of the Treaty of Paris. She began to work again for the break-up of the Turkish Empire, by encouraging the nationalism of the Slav peoples f South-Eastern Europe. Disraeli suspected her of trying to capture he Bosphorus, but when, in 1877, he threatened her with war to prevent this, Gladstone worked up opposition to his policy and swept ack into power in 1880 on the slogan, 'Peace, Retrenchment and Reform'.

Gladstone's campaign fostered the belief that there were no funda-mental divisions of interest between the great powers which should give rise to the use of force. International relations could be regulated by the 'Public Law of Nations', administered by the 'Concert of Europe' meeting in regular congress. His Home Rule policy for Ireland lso encouraged the belief that small nations rightly struggling to be ree could be given local self-government in more or less formal connection with Britain. But his occupation of Egypt in 1882 demon-trated the limits which British statesmen placed on the application of hese high-sounding principles. Egypt had to be occupied to protect the hort route to India when the government of the Khediv collapsed before the semi-nationalist revolt of Arabi Pasha. As in India, the mposition of British colonial rule on Egypt was held to be temporary, pending the restoration of 'good' government, but its consequence was o exacerbate rivalry with the great powers.[15] France, who regarded North Africa as territory in which she could find compensation for the lost provinces of Alsace-Lorraine (taken from her by Germany in 1870), now regarded Britain as an interloper. She not only demanded British withdrawal from Egypt, but sought to extend her own West African empire by taking over Sudan and Morocco. In 1894 she entered into the dual alliance with Russia.

Russia was meanwhile coming into conflict with the British Empire in the Far East. The extension of her railway network into Asia increased her pressure on the weak states which surrounded India – Afghanistan, Tibet and Persia. Her search for a warm-water port on the Pacific as a terminus for the Trans-Siberian Railway led her to seek the partition of China.

Britain had long had informal control of the Yangtse Valley and wanted to see her commerce extended throughout the Chinese Empire. She was, therefore, opposed to a partition policy, but found it impossible to take a tough line with the Russians. The Admiralty pointed out that the Royal Navy was not large enough to take on the French and Russian fleets simultaneously in the Mediterranean. Moreover, between 1899 and 1902, Britain became embroiled in a war in South Africa against the Boer Republics. The British wanted the Boers to grant citizen rights to immigrants who had come in to work in the gold mines on the Rand. By this means, they hoped to swamp the Afrikaner population of South Africa and so bring the whole sub-continent within the British Empire. This would guarantee to them the security of the long Cape route to India and the naval position in the Indian Ocean. The Boers, who nursed an inveterate hatred of blacks and British alike, refused to acknowledge any formal British suzereinty in South Africa and, fearing that Britain intended to subjugate them by force, invaded the British Cape Colony.

Britain found it no easy matter to conquer the tiny Boer Republics. She suffered serious defeats in the field. Her armies were badly led by an incompetent High Command. New recruits to replace defeated troops were often found to be unfit for military service, on account of their bad living conditions in working-class slums.

Meanwhile, Britain's isolation began to appear dangerous. Russia proceeded to annex Manchuria in China and the French government, busy extending their influence in Morocco, discussed plans for an invasion of Britain. The Prime Minister, Lord Salisbury, might describe this isolation as 'splendid', but there were many in high places who had come to regard it as dangerous and to insist that

Britain must have allies who, if not eternal, could at least help to contain the threat from Russia and France.

The Colonial Secretary, Joseph Chamberlain, advocated openly an alliance with Germany. An ex-Liberal Minister, who had left Gladstone's government and party in 1886 in protest against Home Rule for Ireland, Chamberlain never had much time for Liberal sacred cows such as *laissez-faire* and 'little Englandism'. He had come to see foreign affairs as a relentless Darwinian struggle between the great powers for economic exploitation of the 'uncivilized' areas of the world. Unless Britain was prepared, he argued, to throw herself wholeheartedly into that struggle alongside her brother-Teutons of Germany, success would go to the Slavs or the Latins. But Germany had no desire to go to war with Russia over some quarrel between her and Britain in the Far East, while Britain had no interest in becoming involved in a war to protect Germany, or her ally Austria-Hungary, from Russian expansion in Central and South-Eastern Europe. Despite frequent negotiations between 1899 and 1902, therefore, no alliance with Germany proved possible.

The failure of these negotiations had a bad effect on British 'Germanophobia'. Germany's economic success had, as we have seen, stimulated resentment in Britain. To this had been added, during the 1890s, commercial rivalries in Africa and elsewhere. Robert Louis Stevenson and others sought to arouse British opinion against the 'barbarism' of German colonial administrators.[16] The Kaiser's '*welt politik*', moreover, played on anti-British feeling in Germany and seemed to take a more practical form when, in 1900, Germany began building a navy which, it was claimed, would be large enough to challenge the Royal Navy.[17] The Admiralty began to press for enlargement of the fleet. The new mass-circulation newspapers, the *Daily Mail* and the *Daily Express* took up the cry of the German peril. A Navy League was formed to campaign for a strong fleet, while Lord Roberts, disgusted at the inadequacy of British military performance in South Africa, formed a National Service League to campaign for military conscription. Naval expenditure grew by over one-third between 1900 and 1904. In 1902, Britain entered into an alliance with Japan to ensure herself of naval support in the Far East if relations there with Russia should lead to war with the dual alliance. The liberal ideal of peace, retrenchment and reform now seemed under attack by demands for increased armaments, a standing army and military alliances.

Revolt in the Conservative party

The British Conservative party had been led in Parliament by repre
sentatives of 'the landed interest' since its restoration to politica
power in 1867. Disraeli is merely the exception who proves the rule
for the ruling oligarchy of great landowners and country gentlemer
was always willing to recruit talent from among the intelligentsia and
even from trade, if the recruits were in their turn willing to conform to
the style and tone of country-house life. By refraining from any funda
mental challenge to free trade, established since 1846, the Conserva
tives had successfully wrested from the Liberal party after 1886 the
claim to be the natural guardians of the national interest.

They represented themselves as defenders of property against the
radicals in the Liberal party, who called for increased taxation of the
rich to pay for smallholdings for the rural poor. Again, they were the
defenders of the Union against Irish Nationalists whose demands for
Home Rule seemed to endanger Britain's security by placing Ireland's
Atlantic seaboard (potentially at least) outside the control of London.
Finally Lord Salisbury and the Conservative party represented a firm
policy which would keep Britain's enemies at a respectful distance
while maintaining 'peace with honour' whenever possible.[18] Thus
Conservatives had attracted to their support many businessmen who
had formally supported Palmerston, but who found Gladstone weak in
foreign affairs and dangerously radical at home. This formed the basis
of what has been called the 'Unionist hegemony' in politics, which
lasted from the election of the first government of Salisbury in 1886 to
the defeat of his nephew, Arthur Balfour, in 1905.[19]

By 1900 however the fundamental compromise over free trade was
beginning to be challenged within the Conservative party and with it
the political leadership of the 'Hotel Cecil', as the family connection of
Salisbury and Balfour was known. They hoped to ensure Britain's
position in the changing world by a cautious adaptation of traditional
nineteenth-century policies. On the domestic front, they allowed
Joseph Chamberlain to take the first tentative steps towards social
reform, with his Workmen's Compensation Act of 1897 and his
Royal Commission on Old Age Pensions of 1898. Their Education
Act of 1902 allowed local authorities to begin developing secondary
education (though it bitterly offended Nonconformists by putting
Church schools 'on the rates'). In foreign policy, they aimed at

reating a good understanding with the other great powers. Success
ame with France in 1904, when France agreed to recognize Britain's
osition in Egypt in return for British support of her Moroccan pene-
ration.[20] Understandings with Russia and Germany proved elusive
ut in 1902, a treaty with Japan ensured a naval ally in the Far East
gainst Russia.

Efforts were made to achieve military and naval improvements with
he minimum possible expenditure. A Committee of Imperial Defence
vas set up to plan strategy. John Fisher, an outspoken young admiral
vith reforming views, was made First Sea Lord in 1904. By 1906 he
ıad begun the concentration of ships in Home Waters and embarked
•n a programme of scrapping obsolete ships and replacing them with
arger, faster and more heavily armed battleships of the Dreadnaught
·lass.[21] Despite two major inquiries, army reform proved harder to
levise and this question was still under discussion when Balfour's
government fell in 1905.

These reforms did nothing to allay the fundamental discontent with
ree trade on the part of many of the businessmen recruited into the
»arty since the 1860s. West Midlands metal trades, Scots ironmasters
ınd the like saw their traditional markets invaded by German
:ommerce and wanted some form of protection to defend their
nterests. Landowners, hard pressed by the long fall in agricultural
orices, also began to turn against the great aristocrats who used their
entier incomes from banking and commerce to shore up their social
ınd political influence.[22] Although mutual suspicion had long kept
hese two groups apart, resentment had begun to build up against the
lomination of the Conservative party by the Cecils and, in 1903 they
obtained for the first time a spokesman in the highest levels of the
oarty: Joseph Chamberlain.

Chamberlain had long been convinced that the unification of the
British Empire into a self-contained super-state was a major step in
strengthening Britain's position against Russia and Germany. The
failure to obtain a German alliance by 1902 convinced him of the
urgency of the question. Yet he believed that free-trade interests inside
the Conservative party would prevent Balfour from taking the first
step of giving the White Dominions a preference in the British market
for their agricultural produce. In 1903 therefore, he resigned from
Balfour's government to begin a campaign for imperial preference. A

Tariff Reform League was formed, which quickly had a majority of the Conservative MPs on its side.[23] Not all were convinced imperialists in Chamberlain's sense. Some wanted protection against industrial exports from Germany and the United States, as well as preference for colonial foodstuffs. Others were attracted by the idea that tariffs might finance social reform; thus avoiding the higher death duties and increased income tax favoured by Socialists and some Radicals. Some were simply old-style agricultural protectionists. But the significance of the Tariff Reform campaign is twofold. It challenged the compromise with free trade in the Conservative party and the Cecil group of aristocrats, bankers and others who supported it. It also gave the Conservative party a new ideological colouring, imperialistic, patriotic and anti-democratic. The Conservatives had always exploited such opinions for electoral purposes, but the tariff reformers heightened these subdued tones into the brilliant hues of ideological rhetoric.

The Liberal revival

This heightening of party conflict was in part the consequence of a Liberal revival, which Chamberlain's campaign provoked. The previous Liberal government of 1893-5 had been weak and short. Thereafter, the party split into warring factions, divided over imperialism, Ireland and social reform. 'Little Englanders' and 'Pro-Boers' opposed the conduct of the war in South Africa. 'Liberal-imperialists', following the ex-premier Lord Rosebery, supported the Conservative government until victory over the Boer armies was achieved. But Chamberlain's imperialism held few attractions for the 'Liberal-imperialists'. Unwilling to allow Boers or Irish nationalism, or Cobdenite sentiment against colonialism, to endanger the vital interests of British commerce and security, they had no liking for an imperial policy which struck at the basic Liberal doctrine of free trade. The party relied heavily on support from economic interests which did well under the free-trade system. Great coal-mining magnates throve on supplying the coal which fuelled British merchant ships round the world. Great shipowners had an identical interest in free trade so that their ships could carry as much as possible. City bankers prospered from the export of capital. Countries which borrowed it used it to build up their own industries and export their commodities back to Britain. Tariff reform was thus a god-sent opportunity for the Liberals, rallying the support of powerful property interests at a time when mounting pressure for social reform within the party might have accelerated the flight of property away from it.

After 1903, therefore, Campbell-Bannerman, who had won a leading position as a critic of the Conservative government's 'methods of barbarism' in South Africa, was able to unite the warring factions of the party around the defence of free trade. He was carefully tender of Gladstonian sentiments, refusing to allow Home Rule for Ireland to be dropped from the party's programme, and pledging it to repeal the Conservative's education and licencing Acts which had so outraged the Nonconformist conscience.[24] He was conciliatory towards labour, pledging that the party would do something to restore the legal position of trade unions which had recently been undermined by the Taff Vale case in the House of Lords. In 1903, therefore, he permitted his Chief Whip, Herbert Gladstone, to enter into a secret understanding with the Labour Representation Committee, whereby Labour was promised a straight fight against the Conservatives in thirty-five constituencies where it had a good chance of winning in the absence of a Liberal candidate. In return Ramsay MacDonald, for Labour, promised to do all in his power to discourage LRC candidates from running against Liberals elsewhere.[25]

Nor did Campbell-Bannerman do anything to resist the growing idea that social reform was the key to future 'progress'. Many Liberal party candidates now accepted the view of Booth and Rowntree that poverty was often due to economic factors rather than personal short-comings, and this 'new liberalism' gave rise to demands for the early introduction of old age pensions, measures to curb 'sweating' and State provision of smallholdings to keep the agricultural labourer on the land. The 'new Liberals' argued that social reform could be financed by cutting arms expenditure and imposing heavier taxation on landed property.[26] Thus 'new Liberals' often came into conflict with 'Liberal-imperialists', who wanted to see a strong navy and a reform of the army.

Campbell-Bannerman hoped to reconcile these differences. Fisher's reorganization of the navy was already producing economies in naval expenditure. An international peace conference was scheduled to be held at The Hague in 1906, at which he hoped to achieve an agreement with the Germans on naval disarmament. The task was made easier in 1905 by the defeat of Russia at the hands of the Japanese fleet. For some years to come, Russia would pose no naval threat in Asia or Europe. Nevertheless, the leading Liberal-imperialists in the party – Asquith, Grey and Haldane – remained suspicious. They made an agreement among themselves not to serve in a Campbell-Bannerman ministry. But when Balfour resigned in 1905, 'C.-B.' was able to overcome their resistance by offering them the key posts of the Exchequer, Foreign and War Offices. Britain's last Liberal governments thus came to power under a committed Gladstonian Prime Minister, who brought imperialist ministers into the heart of his Cabinet.

Balfour himself found great difficulty in keeping his own party from splitting into warring factions over Tariff Reform. Free-trade ministers had resigned from his Cabinet as well as Chamberlain, and his own willingness to entertain the idea of a tariff as a means of retaliating against industrial countries which protected their markets against British goods, was far from acceptable to the Tariff Reform League. He resigned, therefore, hoping that the Campbell-Bannerman ministry would split up over imperialism. Instead, it drew closer together and, in 1906, won a landslide victory at the polls. The Conservatives had lost their hegemony. The 'Hotel Cecil' had lost its domination within the party. Subsequent by-election victories were to increase the strength of tariff reformers at the expense of the Balfourites. The Conservative compromise with liberalism was at an end. The party no longer accepted the liberal assumptions about progress and the breach was marked by the general assumption of the title 'Unionist', emphasizing fundamental opposition to the Liberal party on the Irish question.

Liberals and Unionists

The Liberal government, returned in such triumph in 1906, soon ran into all the difficulties which had beset its predecessors, but in a more critical form. Its hopes of achieving dramatic economies in armaments expenditure were dashed when disarmament talks at The Hague broke down. Germany brushed aside with contempt the suggestion that the strongest naval power in the world should talk to weaker powers about reducing the size of their navies – 'the colossus asking the pygmy to disarm'[27] as Tirpitz put it. Germany's attempt to drive the French out of their colonial position in Morocco in 1905-6 strengthened anti-German opinion in Britain. Germany was seen as aiming at the kind of Continental domination that Napoleon had once gained and from which he had been toppled only by British sea power and participation in Continental warfare. Accordingly, in 1906, Grey, the Foreign Secretary, was authorized by Campbell-Bannerman to set up secret talks between the British and French General Staffs, who agreed that, should France be attacked by Germany, a British army would take up its position on the left of the French line of battle. This agreement changed the *entente* of 1904 into an informal alliance and decisively ended the nineteenth-century policy of isolation. So grave was its consequences for liberalism, that the arrangement had to be kept secret from Parliament and, indeed, from most of the Cabinet. In 1906 Grey took a further step towards building a Continental bloc against German power by entering into an *entente* with Russia, now weakened by the war with Japan. Britain secured by this agreement the approaches to India. Russia undertook not to penetrate into Afghanistan or Tibet and was allowed to occupy Northern Persia in return for recognition of the British route to India on the Persian Gulf.

From the German standpoint these arrangements looked like dangerous encirclement. Fisher's naval reorganization, moreover, seemed to present them with overwhelming force in the North Sea. In 1908 Germany began to accelerate her naval building programme to meet the challenge of the Dreadnaught. The British Admiralty proposed to reply by building four new Dreadnaughts each year. This brought a storm of protest from Radicals in the Liberal party and from the Labour party who were urging the early introduction of old age pensions. Anti-German civil servants, Unionist politicians and press magnates became alarmed that radical resistance would cut the naval programme. Balfour, Harmsworth and Fisher's rival in the navy, Lord Charles Beresford, whipped up Germanophobia in support of an annual rate of six Dreadnaughts. 'The nation gave no mandate to weaken its navy for the sole purpose of providing . . . doles to the Socialists', said a *Daily Mail* leader.[28] Asquith, who had succeeded Campbell-Bannerman as Prime Minister on the latter's retirement in 1908, proposed as a compromise to build four Dreadnaughts immediately and four additional ones if the German rate of building warranted it. The 'big navy' campaign responded with the slogan 'We want eight and we won't wait', and the government finally accepted eight.

The government seemed to have collapsed before an irrational wave of public opinion whipped up by the press. Novels and plays appeared about the peril of Germany; powerful armament firms supplied the press and the government with alarming reports concerning German capacity for arms manufacture.[29] A government, elected to further peace and retrenchment, seemed to be in the hands of the men who controlled the organs of mass-communication and who were allied with the Unionist party. As Balfour put it, it was the intention of the Unionists 'to control, whether in power or in opposition, the destinies of this great Empire'.

Meanwhile old and new liberal causes languished. The Unionist leaders used the House of Lords to obstruct the passage of liberal education, licensing and land legislation, while the government hesitated over social reform. Campbell-Bannerman and Asquith both feared the 'socialist' implications of State provision of work for the unemployed, regulation of the hours of labour and the demand for a minimum wage. Yet there was mounting evidence that further delay would be dangerous for the Liberal party. Unemployment was rising fast in 1906-8. The tariff reformers were winning by-elections everywhere. The Labour party was mounting strong pressure for its 'right to work' Bill. The Government's own Radical supporters were increasing their pressure. Some Radical MPs regularly voted with the Labour party on social reform questions, while Lloyd George and Winston Churchill (Chancellor of the Exchequer and President of the Board of Trade) were campaigning openly for more social reform and less armament expenditure. There was thus a real danger that, unless the government could smooth the path of progress for 'new liberal' measures, it would be defeated in Parliament and the way would be opened for another election on Tariff Reform under far less favourable circumstances than in 1906.

The major obstacle to social reform was that it implied progressive taxation; an anathema to industrial interests in the Conservative and Liberal parties alike. Yet some new basis of taxation was becoming inescapable. Armaments were producing budget deficits. Indirect taxation was already too heavy and nothing more could be got out of local authority rates. For the budget of 1909, therefore, Asquith and Lloyd George looked back to the 'new liberal' proposals of 1895-1905. While making income tax a little more progressive, they proposed to introduce a range of new taxes on land values, urban as well as rural, and a tax on mineral royalties. These new taxes, they claimed, would provide a basis for raising expenditure for the foreseeable future, while leaving the profits of industry untouched. It had always been a fundamental liberal belief that rent from land was 'unearned', and 'new Liberals' argued that the element of rent from land could be taxed away leaving the profits of industry to fructify in the pockets of those who made them.

The 'People's Budget' of 1909 seemed therefore to put progress and liberalism on a new basis, without violating its fundamental principles. It enchanted Radicals and Labour representatives by attacking their old enemy, the landed aristocracy – the upkeep of a single duke cost the equivalent of two Dreadnaughts, Lloyd George claimed. It reconciled Radicals to the government's foreign and naval policy. When, in 1911, Germany again intervened in Morocco, Lloyd George publicly warned that England would not stand by and see France destroyed as a great power. He and Churchill were eventually drawn into the inner circle of ministers who controlled foreign policy without reference to the rest of the Cabinet. Under its guidance, the arrangements with France were drawn tighter by the transfer of the British Mediterranean fleet to the North Sea and of the French Channel fleet to the Mediterranean. This was an implicit commitment on the part of the British to defend the French coast against bombardment by the German navy.

The budget had the further advantage that it was difficult for the Unionists to oppose. They themselves had pressed for the higher expenditure on armaments which made it necessary and their tariff alternative would raise the cost of living. Nor could the Unionists readily fall back on their position in the House of Lords. By convention, the Upper House never interfered with the government's financial legislation.

Yet the People's Budget represented everything that the Unionists most hated. It proposed to tax the country gentry, whose rent rolls had been reduced by years of agricultural depression. It opened the door to 'socialist' taxation (for the Unionists rightly understood that there was no clear way in which rent from land and profits from industry could be separated for fiscal purposes). Finally, the land taxes could not be raised without an extensive national survey of land values, and the clauses empowering this survey had been included in the Finance Bill. This the Unionists took to be a machiavellian and unconstitutional device for preventing the House of Lords from discussing the principle of taxation policy.

On this narrow and rather specious issue, Balfour and the Unionist leaders determined to advise the Lords to reject the budget. The government responded by calling a general election in January 1910. Party conflict, which had been intensifying since the 'naval scare' of 1908, now rose to new heights. The government rallied its followers to a new crusade against 'the stupid party'. Tariff Reform, anti-socialism and Germanophobia glared from the headlines of the Unionist press. The Liberals lost heavily, especially in the English rural constituencies, and they had to depend for support on eighty-two Irish Nationalists and forty Labour members. Labour suffered in the reaction against liberalism. Moreover the Osborne judgement of the House of Lords in 1910 had prohibited trade unions from imposing a political levy on their members in support of the Labour party, and its leaders were therefore unable to drive a better bargain with the Liberals than they had done in 1903. The real gainers from all this were the Irish Nationalists, who now held the balance of power. They were prepared to support a Liberal government in office, but only on condition that it introduced a Home Rule measure for Ireland and, in addition, abolished the veto power of the House of Lords, in order to ensure its passage. Asquith reluctantly agreed to their terms.

The Unionists were now confronted with the spectre of Irish Home Rule. Nationalist ideas had grown in Ireland under the stimulus of the Gaelic revival and the propaganda of the new Sinn Fein party.[30] Many Irish Nationalists would no longer be content with Home Rule or devolution. They wanted an independent republic, entirely free from the British connection. Unionist imperialists were made frantic by the renewed possibility of Home Rule under these new conditions. The Liberal government had just created a new Union of South Africa, in which domestic power had been entirely handed over to the Afrikaners. All the 'sacrifices' of the Boer War seemed to have been in vain. Now Ireland was to be placed at the mercy of the enemies of England. The very possibility roused them to a fever-pitch of opposition.

Their first line of resistance was to oppose the Parliament Bill which the Liberals now presented in 1910 for limiting the Lords' power of veto. Any Bill carried three times by the House of Commons would become law, whether or not accepted by the Lords. The Upper House rejected it and, after unsuccessful negotiations between the parties, the Liberals summoned another general election in December 1910. The results were virtually identical to those of January, but Asquith now disclosed that he had obtained the consent of the King to create enough Liberal peers to overwhelm the Unionists' majority in the House of Lords. Faced with this choice, the Lords gave way and passed the Parliament Bill.

With the Parliament Act passed, the Liberal government now proceeded to honour its commitment to the Irish National party in Parliament. Its Home Rule Bill for 1912 was a cautious measure, aimed at conceding the minimum to the Irish Nationalists and preserving as much of the British connection as possible. Defence, and the retention of forty-two Irish MPs in the Westminster Parliament, were intended to preserve it. Even so, it proved too much for Protestant opinion in Ulster to swallow. Mostly of Presbyterian Scottish descent, they believed as strongly as they had in 1886 that 'Home Rule means Rome Rule', and began drilling in order to resist the Bill by force should the government try to force it upon them. Their actions presented the British Unionist party with an opportunity to wreck the Home Rule Bill without the aid of the House of Lords. They had just rid themselves of Balfour as leader and elected the Scots-Canadian ironmaster Bonar Law. His social origins and his harsh platform style could not have been more symbolic of the transformation of the party since the days of the 'Hotel Cecil'. Law and Carson, leader of the Ulster Unionists, introduced an amendment demanding the exclusion of Ulster from the Home Rule Bill. They believed that this would wreck its chances because Redmond, leader of the Irish National party, would never be able to accept it. His followers believed that Ireland was one and indivisible. Equally, Carson and Law believed that the Union was one and indivisible, and had no desire whatever to see Home Rule prevail in the south of Ireland. And Carson formed the Irish 'Covenant' movement, which hinted at resistance to Home Rule by force.

How far Carson and the self-styled Ulster volunteers would have gone in resistance can never be certainly known.[31] If Asquith had been in a position to offer them the complete exclusion of Ulster, Carson might have been willing to accept, rather than plunge Ireland into civil war at a time of growing international danger. Asquith, however, could not do better than offer exclusion of Ulster for six years, which

Carson rejected, and the apparent impasse led to serious alarms and excursions. Lord Milner, the ex-Governor-General of South Africa and an extreme imperialist, put himself at the head of a British 'Covenant' movement which he, for one, hoped would use force if the government tried to compel Ulster to accept Home Rule. In 1914, a general and fifty-seven officers stationed with the British Army in Dublin resigned, rather than obey an order to proceed to Ulster to guard military installations there. This 'Curragh mutiny' heightened the impression that the Liberal government could not count on the loyalty of the army.

The Irish embroglio contributed to the government's difficulties in another direction. The suffragettes' campaign of window-breaking, arson and hunger strikes was acutely embarrassing to a government which was supposed to stand for individual liberty. They were demanding the vote on the same terms as men, that is, household suffrage. But Liberal and Labour supporters of female suffrage were unwilling to support a demand which would have enfranchized only single, elderly, propertied and therefore Conservative women. By 1913, Asquith was willing to grant government support to a women's suffrage amendment to the new manhood suffrage Bill then before Parliament, but the Unionists would have used their suspensory veto to block it for three years unless the government accepted a measure for the redistribution of seats. Such a measure would have cut down Irish representation at Westminster, and this the Irish Nationalists were not prepared to accept until Home Rule was carried. The life of Parliament was too short for the government to use the Parliament Act to carry adult suffrage and the whole question was therefore set aside. Not, however, by the women; for the militant suffragettes, led by Christabel Pankhurst and her mother, were enraged by the widespread male prejudice of Edwardian England.[32] Peaceful demonstrations were often met with considerable violence on the part of the police or counter-demonstrations of young louts. Women had their breasts pinched, their clothes torn off and other indignities forced upon them.[33] The determination to confront male oppression with unflinching courage led the suffragette leaders into a political impasse from which they could not escape.

Diehard peers, Ulster volunteers, 'Curragh mutineers', suffragette militants – all these alarms took place against a background of mass excursions by organized labour. The low level of unemployment

etween 1910 and 1914 produced a great explosion of trade-union
membership, especially among unskilled labourers in the transport
industries. Workers reacted, often unofficially, against the long fall in
their standard of living which had taken place since the turn of the
century. Unskilled workers had no scarcity value with which to
bargain, and sought to enforce the closed shop by means of mass
picketing; which frequently caused rioting and clashes with blacklegs
organized *en masse* by their employers. There were serious riots in
South Wales in 1910. The government sent troops to the strike areas
to help the police keep order. Shooting occurred and two strikers were
killed at Liverpool and two more at Llanelli in 1911. In 1912 there
was a national coal strike for a minimum wage and later that year the
Port of London was closed by a lock-out. In 1914, the three trade
unions principally involved, the National Union of Railwaymen, the
Transport Worker's Federation and the Miner's Federation formed a
triple alliance', under which they agreed to present their wage
demands simultaneously.

Britain seemed to many observers to be subsiding into class war.
There was a good deal of revolutionary rhetoric flying around.
Theories of 'direct action' and syndicalism were being popularized by
the new workers' paper, the *Daily Herald*, and workers' leaders
frequently asked why, if the diehard peers could defy parliamentary
government, they could not. There is no evidence of a widespread
syndicalist revolt against Parliament and the trade-union leaders at
least had no intention of using a general strike as an instrument of
political action.[34] But industrial relations were difficult to manage and
the government was unpopular because its national insurance legislation of 1911, by levying contributions, imposed a new form of taxation on the workers, and because it was slow to introduce legislation to
reverse the Osborne judgement.

On top of these troubles came, in 1913, the strange affair of the
Marconi scandal. Two ministers, Lloyd George (nominally a Welsh
Nonconformist) and Rufus Isaacs (a Jew) were discovered to hold
shares in the American Marconi company, whose separate but related
English Company was in competition for a government contract to
link the Empire by a chain of wireless stations. The ministers had
purchased the shares at the suggestion of Godfrey Isaacs, brother of
Rufus and managing director of the English Marconi Company. They
had profited considerably from the speculation in Marconi shares,

which took place while the contract was known to be under protracted negotiation. The government was then trying to steer through Parliament a Bill for the disestablishment of the Anglican Church in Wales, a measure to which the High Anglican wing of the Unionist party, led by Lord Hugh Cecil and supported by G.K. Chesterton, took violent exception. They denounced the Bill as a conspiracy on the part of Nonconformists and Jews to disestablish the Church in England itself, and Chesterton's brother, Cecil, alleged in his newspaper that the ministers had corruptly used their private knowledge and power to make profit out of the Marconi speculation. England, it was alleged, was being undermined by a government involved with corrupt Jewish financiers and equally corrupt Celtic Nationalists. The Unionist leaders took up the cry in the hope of defeating Asquith's government. A Select Committee of the House of Commons cleared the ministers of corruption, but split along party lines on the question of whether they had deceived Parliament by not declaring their interest in the American Marconi Company. This attempt to create something like a Dreyfus case in Britain thus fell rather flat, but Lloyd George suffered a considerable setback in his political career and was saved from resignation only by Asquith, who insisted that he be given Liberal party backing.[35]

By 1914, therefore, the Liberal government was badly buffeted by a series of critical problems which had thrown the whole country into a state of agitation and some danger. Dangerfield was undoubtedly right to see that the issues raised from 1910 onwards were the beginning of a long crisis which was to stretch from the First World War to the great crash of 1931, a crisis which would ruin the Liberal party. Few historians would deny this. What is hotly debated is whether the Liberal party was already doomed before the war broke out. Dangerfield, and more recently, Shannon and Pelling,[36] argue that it was because its position on the left was being overtaken by the Labour party. Other historians suggest it would have been capable of adjusting to its problems but for the accident of the war.[37]

Of course historians really have no means of knowing whether the Liberal party was or was not in a fatal decline before the outbreak of the war. The evidence remains conflicting and difficult to interpret. Apologists for the party sometimes seem to exaggerate its position by ignoring or playing down facts which tell against their case. It is by no means clear that business interests in the party would have gone along with Lloyd George's bold plans.[38] The Labour party, halted in its advance by the Osborne judgement, was consolidating its position after the passing of the Trades Disputes and Trade Union Act in 1913. It was again planning to finance more candidatures and, if it could not defeat the Liberals on a wide front, could at any rate make sure that they could not obtain a parliamentary majority.[39] Nor could the Liberals be sure that tariffs would remain unpopular for ever. Protection in some form or other would be needed if Britain's tiny car industry were ever to be established on a thriving, modern footing.[40] Lloyd George was far from confident that his party could face up to these tasks and, in 1910, had secretly proposed a coalition with the Unionists to concentrate on a programme of modernization. Finally, the Liberals had shown no capacity to rid themselves of the deep obses- sion with national security which plagued all European nations in those terrible years of approaching war. None wanted war, yet none seemed capable of the constructive statesmanship which could alone have avoided it. By turning the *entente* with France into an informal military and naval alliance, and by giving way to Unionist pressures for a big navy, the Liberal party played its part, along with the other nations of Europe, in raising the level of international tension. In this sense, therefore, the crisis of war which befell it between 1914 and 1916 was no accident, but the outcome of events which the Liberal government had itself helped to shape.

The Liberals and the war

The Liberal government entered the war united in defence of the inte- grity of Belgium and the independence of France on 5 August 1914.[41] By December 1916, Asquith had been deposed and the Liberal party shattered into two fragments which made war upon each other with increasing bitterness and hostility. The years from 1916 until the first Labour government of 1924 are the years of the party's death agonies. Never again would Britain see a Liberal government.

Many reasons can be given for the break-up of the party and historians, given their disagreements about its pre-war potential, are still uncertain of the weight to be given to each cause. One reason was the continuing force of old party issues. Many Liberals were unwilling to enter a coalition with the Unionists, fearing that it must lead to protectionism, military conscription and the end of *laissez-faire*. Those

Unionists, on the other hand, who had regarded the government c
the hated 'Squiff'[42] as the greatest misfortune for England since th
civil war, exploited the military failures (which were really unavoid
able) to damage the prestige of the government. The Liberals, now in
weaker position, faced the same hostile combination of generals, pres
magnates and anti-German Unionists who had been striving for thei
downfall since 1906.

Asquith had to resist the demands of back-bench Unionists and
growing number of Liberals that the State should take over the direc
tion of the economy for the duration of the war. This was by no mean
as simple a matter as it sounds, involving hostility from *laissez-fair*
Liberals and delicate negotiations with the trade unions. The charge
levelled against him of 'drift' were not always fair. But his handling o
the political situation was clumsy. He lost the support of Redmond an
the Irish Nationalists by making too many concessions to the Ulste
men, and permitted Sinn Fein to profit from the rash uprising i
Dublin at Easter 1916.

Finally, he underestimated Lloyd George. The Welshman's succes
after May 1916, in organizing the production of munitions, pointed t
him as an alternative Prime Minister who, with Unionists' backing
could organize the war effort. He had also attracted the support o
important Liberal businessmen. There were great capitalists, like Si
Alfred Mond, who had always hankered after State direction of
modernizing economy. There were also great shipowners, who stoo
to gain from guaranteed profits against the shipping losses which th
U-boats caused. And there were an indefinite number of inefficien
firms in engineering and textiles, who had everything to gain from th
total destruction of their pre-war competitors in Germany.[43]

And last but not least, there was the Labour party. Most of them
wanted victory over Germany as much as did the employers, and fo
much the same reasons. But they also wanted some of the rewards a
well as the sacrifices: protection against the soaring cost of living an
conscription of riches to curb the profiteering of businessmen.[44] Afte
much hesitation, they agreed to give Lloyd George a chance to prov
that he was the real friend of the people he had always professed to b
and, on 5 December 1916, Arthur Henderson, the leader of th
Labour party,[45] joined Lloyd George's War Cabinet along with thre
Unionist ministers.

In helping to form the coalition of 1916, Lloyd George may no ave been consciously intent on breaking up the pre-war progressive lliance of Liberals, Labour and Irish, but events in 1917-18 certainly onspired to ensure this. Unlimited submarine warfare and the heavy asualties on the Western Front imposed great sacrifices on British vorkers. A wave of unofficial strikes spread through the cities. The tussian Revolution in February 1917, and the withdrawal of Russia rom the war brought popularity for the first time to the peace propaanda carried on by Ramsay MacDonald, the Independent Labour arty and a small handful of Radicals. Arthur Henderson, who supporsed the holding of a peace conference of European socialist parties at tockholm, had to be dismissed from the War Cabinet. Deeply offenled, and sensing the possibilities of building on the new strength of rganization which the war had brought to trade unions, he declared ublicly that he would never again serve in any government in which abour did not have the controlling interest. By the end of 1917, abour had adopted war aims very like those propounded by MacDonald and the 'pacifists'. In 1918 it adopted a new party constiution which would give disciplined cohesion, a dominant voice to the rade unions, and, in the famous clause four, a declared socialist objecive which served to differentiate the party clearly from the Liberals.[46]

In 1918, the long-delayed breach between the Liberal party and rish nationalism came to a head. Lloyd George attempted to impose conscription on Ireland. The Irish in the south rallied to Sinn Fein and he Irish National party withdrew from Westminster. A provisional arliament was set up in Dublin and, shortly afterwards, the Irish Republican Army was formed, to wrest Ulster, and with it complete Republican independence, from Britain

Finally, the rupture between Lloyd George Liberals and the Asquithites was embittered by the Maurice debate in May 1918, vhen Asquith sought to censure Lloyd George for allegedly starving he Western Front of troops. Lloyd George began to see that his oolitical future must lie in continuing coalition with the Unionists. The idea had had its attractions, as we have seen, since 1910. It now seemed to make even more sense. Everything that the pre-war Liberal oarty had stood for seemed to have been swept away by the war. Asquith's own Chancellor, McKenna, had introduced tariffs (albeit for revenue rather than protectionist purposes) which it would be difficult to remove after the war. *Laissez-faire* had been swept away beneath a vast system of controls over industry. Victorious British armies in the Middle East were adding new colonial territories to the British Empire and the old dream of imperial unity seemed to be drawing near. Dominion armies fought alongside British; and Jan Smuts, the Boer Prime Minister of South Africa, sat in the War Cabinet. Those landowners and capitalists who had once stood in the way of his 'new liberalism' now seemed, in the light of bolshevism and the Labour party's clause four, to be essential pillars of economic liberty. The future task of the 'Nationalist-Socialist' (as he now privately described himself) would be to strike a balance, in the interests of the Empire, between State intervention and economic individualism as against the forces of international proletarian revolution.

Accordingly, in 1917, Lloyd George began to develop plans for post-war reconstruction, aiming at the modernization of public undertakings such as railways, the encouragement of new industries, and the rationalization of old ones. He also put forward a series of proposals aimed at reconciling the workers to a sense of corporate involvement in capitalism. An Act was passed to give the vote to all men at twenty-one and to women at thirty. An education Act provided for secondary education to the age of fourteen for all children. 'Homes fit for heroes' were promised by a new housing programme. Bonar Law, the Unionist party leader, seeing the opportunity to capitalize on Lloyd George's prestige as the victorious war leader, agreed to prolong the coalition by a secret arrangement whereby Lloyd George's supporters were guaranteed some one hundred and fifty seats in the House of Commons. On the morrow of the German surrender, in December 1918, with the German navy interned at Scapa Flow, and German armies withdrawn from Belgium and France, Lloyd George was also victorious at the polls and the coalition was returned with a massive majority. Asquith's followers were decimated, returning some thirty strong. The Labour party, though it polled a large vote, obtained only fifty-seven seats and went into opposition against the coalition. Sinn Fein swept the board in Ireland and refused to sit at Westminster. The pre-war Liberal party was dead. Socialism had been rejected. It was up to Lloyd George to show how victory could be turned to account for the British Empire.

The post-war world

The pre-war leaders of the Unionist party saw Lloyd George as their hief hope of retaining working-class support against the rising tide of ocialism and Labour party policies. For a brief space in 1919-20 they vere even prepared to discuss the fusion of their party with the Lloyd George Liberals.[47] But grass-roots Unionism was not so enamoured vith the wizard of Wales as their leaders appeared to be. They saw his econstruction plans and his prolonging of wartime controls as a half-vay house to socialism. They wanted no nationalization of industry by he State. Rather, they wanted to be freed from State control to make s much profit as they could while German industry lay helpless and xhausted at their feet. Heavy public expenditure on Lloyd George's educational, housing and national insurance reforms they regarded as waste'. Pressure therefore mounted steadily against the coalition rom within the Unionist party, denouncing the 'corruption' of Lloyd George's method of government, his flagrant sale of honours, his lisregard of Parliament and the traditions of Cabinet government.[48]

Their hostility was checked in 1919-20 by the danger of a general trike. The pre-war triple alliance had been revived and the Miner's Federation was demanding that it force a general election by 'direct action' on the question of nationalizing the mines. Lloyd George nanoeuvred carefully through the danger, buying off the railwaymen vith a substantial concession and the dockers with a royal commis-ion.

In 1921 and 1922, however, the 'anti-waste' campaign rose to a climax. Lloyd George was forced to cut public expenditure drastically, and to abandon his education, housing and industrial modernization plans. Railways and mines were decontrolled and schemes for their modernization abandoned, while the miners were left to fight a bitter and unsuccessful struggle against wage-cuts in 1921.

This victory for retrenchment and *laissez-faire* was due, in the main, o the world depression, which began in 1921. World prices for Britain's staple exports slumped. A severe fall in agricultural prices ruined the value of markets in the Empire and the 'underdeveloped' world. Britain's new industries – cars, aeroplanes, petro-chemicals – were, as yet, too small to replace these lost exports.

The Bank of England no longer enjoyed the massive pre-war gold reserves which had enabled it to act as the world's banker. Currency flowed in and out of London as business confidence rose and fell, creating the twentieth-century balance of payments problem. In the export staple industries, firms met the crisis by trying to drive down

wages. Labour responded with waves of defensive strikes and a stron
upsurge of voting for the Labour party in municipal and by-election:
Lloyd George's main attraction for the Unionists had gone.

In 1921-2 he further intensified Unionist opposition by his deviou
negotiations with Sinn Fein, which led to the setting-up of the Iris
Free State and the retention of Ulster within the United Kingdom
Unionists were outraged, not only by this apparent surrender to th
IRA 'murder gang', but also by Lloyd George's apparent willingnes
during the negotiations to buy Sinn Fein compliance with a promis
that Ulster would be kept weak in order to force it eventually into th
Free State. At the same time, the Prime Minister's foreign policy
which he conducted personally in semi-presidential style, ran agains
Unionist traditions with its appeasement towards Germany an
Bolshevik Russia, and its support of Greece against Turkey, the ol
guardian of the Bosphorus.

By 1922 Unionists were reasoning that the old game of holdin
back Labour and 'Bolshevism' through Lloyd George was up. If clas
politics there had to be, better to face them squarely and straigh
forwardly through a revived Conservative party than be dragged, the
knew not whither, by the 'terrible dynamic force' (as Stanley Baldwi:
called him) of Lloyd George.

The Coalition broke up at a famous meeting of the Conservativ
party at the Carlton Club on 19 October 1922. Lloyd George resigne
and a general election followed. He called on the voters to return a
many 'coalitionists' as possible, to build up the centre against Tor
and socialist extremism. His plea fell on deaf ears. The coal field
deserted him as he had deserted them in 1921. Labour reaped th
harvest. Asquith's Liberals enjoyed a minor revival. The Conserva
tives returned to power, first under Bonar Law, who died after si
months in office, and then under the rising star, Stanley Baldwin.

The collapse of the coalition in 1922 represented the end of a
attempts to deal with Britain's problems of decline by radical policie
of modernization. Lloyd George's attempt to build a progressiv
government on the basis of his own personal popularity and the finan
cial backing of powerful interest groups in industry, finance and th
press had failed. Yet none of the old party nostrums of pre-war Britai:
seemed to meet the problem. Tariff Reform and imperial unity were c
little appeal at a time when dominions and colonies were too depresse
to offer a market for British exports. Baldwin failed to win an electio:

on Tariff Reform in 1923 and his attempt allowed the Labour party to form a short-lived minority government in 1924. Yet the Labour alternative fared no better. Social reform and rapprochements with Russia, Germany and the League of Nations frightened the electorate. Both parties, after the experience of short-lived governments in 1923-4, turned away from radical policies to 'safety first'. In effect, this meant clinging to the old liberalism of free trade, *laissez-faire* and the gold standard. The Bank of England kept interest rates high in order to prevent problems with the balance of payments. 'Dear money' meant retardation of industrial development. Unemployment remained at 10 per cent and over throughout the inter-war period. Only the export of American capital to Germany and Central Europe between 1923 and 1928 brought some recovery in world trade. But the financial collapse of the American stock market in 1929 dragged down these economies also. In 1931 Britain was forced by a major balance of payments crisis to leave the gold standard. It was the end of a liberal era whose creation Britain had pioneered between 1846 and 1885; whose achievement had been but imperfectly realized, and whose destruction by imperialist rivalries had long been foreseen.

Doubt and anxiety had been growing in the 1920s and the sense of a world order in dissolution pervades its literature and its politics. The alternative world-systems pressed from left and right seemed alike unacceptable to the liberal tradition. Liberals rejected the propaganda of the extreme left for colonial liberation by revolution, for intensification of the British class struggle by means of a general strike and for an outright socialist economy as a means of abolishing unemployment and mass poverty. These demands seemed to them to point only to the servile State, attacked by Hilaire Belloc before 1914. Liberals also rejected the propaganda of the extreme right, still demanding imperial consolidation, a tough line with nationalists in India and Egypt and with trade unionists at home.

Yet both extremes seemed to be making headway between 1921 and 1931. The period up to 1926 saw the growth of the left in the trade unions and the Labour party. In 1920 the TUC strengthened its central administration by the formation of the General Council, to which many left-wing militants were elected. The ILP grew in membership until 1927, producing plans and blueprints for 'socialism in our time', against which the orthodox economic policies of Phillip Snowden and Ramsay MacDonald seemed out-of-date and unconstructive.

On the right, Stanley Baldwin's policy of a *de facto* co-operation with moderate Labour leaders was severely jolted by the events of the General Strike in 1926. Under pressure from Winston Churchill and certain press magnates, the Conservative party took a swing to the right. Trade unions were once again prohibited by law from levying contributions to the Labour party from their regular membership (1927). During the panic years, 1931-2, cuts in unemployment benefit were enforced as part of a policy of reducing public expenditure. Meanwhile, Baldwin was challenged for the Conservative leadership because he favoured negotiating with Gandhi and the Indian Nationalists.

Yet the conflict element in British politics between 1921 and 1931 should not be exaggerated. Compared to her Continental neighbours, Italy, Germany and France, Britain was a stable society. The social bases of parliamentary democracy were not swept away. The middle classes did not collapse. Their standards of living were maintained by falling food prices. Their ranks were enlarged by the growth of professional employments, both in the public sector and in the great new industrial corporations such as ICI (formed 1926). Correspondingly there was no uniform immiseration of the British working class. If South Wales, Lancashire and the West of Scotland became distressed areas, with unemployment rates reaching as high as 75 per cent in some communities, the Midlands and the South-East, on the other hand, saw the emergence of modern industry. Lloyd George' National Insurance Act of 1920, though modified by subsequent Conservative governments, provided a makeshift safety net and diverted the unemployed from socialism to demands for adequate benefit.

Extremist politics, as a result, never became dominant in either of the major political parties. The search for solutions to domestic and international conflict in terms of collaboration and compromise continued. Big business and the TUC held talks on industrial relations in 1927 and Conservatives such as Harold Macmillan showed a growing interest in the new economics of J.M. Keynes, involving the use of public enterprise to stimulate investment and reduce unemployment. In imperial affairs, Baldwin was able to rout his opponents and carry the Government of India Act in 1935, which extended local government by Indians.

Writers of the 1920s, therefore, had no need to turn away from politics in despair. Rather, they could see themselves as part of a truggle to salvage the essentials of the liberal tradition in an age of lissolution. The suburban living of the middle classes could be seen as a wasteland'; the post-war generation of middle-class youth as cyni-ally hedonistic in 'a brave new world'. Between Britons and Indians here seemed to be no 'passage' for common human understanding. Yet it is possible to argue that such representations reflect not the writers' despair so much as their view of a world which needed to be aved for culture. As Raymond Williams has pointed out, the idea of 'ulture was often condescending to the popular taste, but in this it was lso typical of the rational élitism of the liberal tradition.[49] For all their ense of being adrift on a storm-tossed sea, they never doubted that heir cultural tradition represented 'the lighthouse' where rescue and helter could be found.

Notes

1 G. Dangerfield, *The Strange Death of Liberal England*, London 1936, p.vii.

2 ibid., p.viii.

3 K.O. Morgan, *Age of Lloyd George*, London 1971, pp. 50-2.

4 T. Wilson, *The Downfall of the Liberal Party 1914-1935*, London 1966, pp.15-19.

5 *See below*, p.97.

6 D.S. Landes, *The Unbound Prometheus*, Cambridge 1969 pp.231ff.

7 D.H. Aldcroft and H.W. Richardson, *The British Economy, 1870-1939,* London 1969, p.65.

8 B.R. Mitchell and P. Deane, *Abstract of British Historical Statistics*, Cambridge 1962, p.333.

9 G.R. Searle, *Quest for National Efficiency*, Oxford 1971, pp.54ff.

10 E.J. Hobsbawm, *Industry and Empire*, London 1968, pp.151ff; S.B. Saul, *Studies in British Overseas Trade, 1870-1914*, Liverpool 1960, pp.116ff; S.B. Saul, 'The Impact of America on British Industry, 1895-1914', *Business History*, III, 1960-1, p.31; C.P. Kindleberger, *The Formation of Financial Centres*, Princeton, NJ 1974, pp.12ff.

11 Charles Booth, *Life and Labour of the People of London,* vols I-IV, 1902 edn, pp.131ff, reprinted New York 1969; B.S. Rowntree, *Poverty, A Study in Town Life,* 1902, pp.32ff.

12 H. Pelling, *Origins of the Labour Party, 1880-1900*, Oxford 1966, pp.211-15; F. Reid, *Keir Hardie*, London 1978, *passim*; K.O. Morgan, *Keir Hardie*, London 1975, *passim.*

13 A.J.P. Taylor, *The Troublemakers*, London 1957, pp.40ff.

14 R. Shannon, *Crisis of Imperialism*, London 1974, pp.114ff.

15 R. Robinson and J. Gallagher, *Africa and the Victorians*, London 1961 Chapter IV.

16 K. MacKenzie, 'Some British Reactions to German Colonial Methods 1885-1907', *Historical Journal*, XVII, 1974, pp.165-75; O.J. Hale *Publicity and Diplomacy*, New York 1940, pp.13-291; Z. Steiner, *The Foreign Office and Foreign Policy, 1898-1914*, Cambridge 1969 pp.75ff.

17 V.R. Berghahn, *Germany and the Approach of War in 1914*, London 1973, pp.25-64.

18 R. Blake, *The Conservative Party from Peel to Churchill*, London 1970 pp.97ff.

19 E.J. Feuchtwanger, *Disraeli, Democracy and the Tory Party*, Oxford 1968, *passim*.

20 G. Monger, *End of Isolation*, London 1963, pp.21-331.

21 G.H.C. Jordan, 'Pensions not Dreadnoughts', in *Edwardian Radicalism, 1914*, ed. A.J.A. Morris, London 1974, p.162.

22 N. Blewett, 'Free Fooders, Balfourites, Whole Hoggers', *Historical Journal*, XI, 1968, pp.95-124.

23 Chamberlain was able to represent his proposals as 'tariff reform' because the government had introduced a duty of 3d per cwt on imported corn This duty was not intended as a permanent deviation from free trade. It was a device to pay for the South African war, but, as Ensor remarked, 'it possibilities in connexion with imperial preference were obvious to most people except its author'. R.C.K. Ensor, *England, 1870-1914*, Oxford 1936, p.349.

24 Balfour's Licensing Act of 1904 outraged the Nonconformist conscience by providing for the compensation of publicans whose licences were withdrawn as a matter of public policy.

25 F. Bealey and H. Pelling, *Labour and Politics, 1900-06*, London 1958. Chapter V.

26 H.V. Emy, *Liberals, Radicals and Social Politics, 1882-1914*, Cambridge 1973, pp.142ff.

27 Quoted by Jordan in *Edwardian Radicalism*, op. cit., p.171.

28 ibid.

29 Hale, *Publicity and Diplomacy*, op. cit., pp.326ff.

30 F.S.L. Lyons, *Ireland since the Famine*, London 1971, pp.224ff.

31 A. Gollin, *Pro-Consul in Politics*, London 1964, pp.172-223.

32 H. Pelling, *Popular Politics and Society in late-Victorian Britain*, London 1968, pp.147ff; D. Morgan, *Suffragists and Liberals*, Oxford 1975, *passim*; B. Harrison, *Separate Spheres*, London 1978, pp.55-91.

33 A. Rosen, *Rise Up, Women!*, London 1974, p.176.

34 Pelling, *Popular Politics*, op. cit., pp.147ff; cf. W. Kendall, *The Revolutionary Movement in Britain, 1900-21*, London 1969.

35 F. Donaldson, *The Marconi Scandal*, London 1963, *passim*.

36 Shannon, *Crisis of Imperialism*, op. cit, pp.383ff; Pelling, *Popular Politics*, op. cit., pp.101ff.

37 P.F. Clarke, *Lancashire and the New Liberalism*, Cambridge 1971, pp.312ff; cf. his 'The Electoral Position of the Liberal and Labour Parties, 1910-14', *English Historical Review*, XC, 1975, pp.828-36.

38 Emy, *Liberals, Radicals and Social Politics*, op. cit., pp.226ff.

39 R.I. McKibbin, 'James Ramsay MacDonald and the Problem of the Independence of the Labour Party, 1910-14', *Journal of Modern History*, XLII, 1970, p.216.

40 S.B. Saul, 'The Motor Industry in Britain to 1914', *Business History*, V, 1962-3, pp.22-44.

41 Hazlehurst has argued that for most Liberals the German violation of Belgian neutrality was only a convenient pretext for doing what they had always believed it would be necessary to do: defend France in the interests of British security in Europe. C. Hazlehurst, *Politicians at War, July 1914 to May 1915*, London 1971, pp.25ff.

42 Their name for Asquith.

43 A.J.P. Taylor, *English History, 1914-45*, Harmondsworth, Middx 1970, pp.104ff; cf. Morgan, *Age of Lloyd George*, op. cit., pp.55ff.

44 R. Harrison, 'The War Emergency Worker's National Committee, 1914-20' in *Essays in Labour History*, ed. A. Briggs and J. Saville, London 1971, pp.211ff; J. Winter, *Socialism and the Challenge of War*, London 1974, pp.234ff.

45 Ramsay MacDonald had resigned in 1914 in order to oppose the war.

46 R. McKibbin, *Evolution of the Labour Party*, Oxford, 1974, pp.88ff.

47 M. Cowling, *Impact of Labour, 1920-24*, Cambridge 1971, pp.60-128.

48 K.O. Morgan, 'Lloyd George's Premiership', *Historical Journal*, XIII, 1970.

49 R. Williams, *Culture and Society*, London 1958, pp.7-27.

Select bibliography

Most of the following works give good and extensive guides to further reading.

Dangerfield, G. *The Strange Death of Liberal England*, London 1936.

Ensor, R.C.K. *England, 1870-1914*, Oxford 1936.

Hobsbawm, E.J. *Industry and Empire*, London 1968.

Morgan, K.O. *Age of Lloyd George*, London 1971.

Shannon, R. *Crisis of Imperialism*, London 1974.

Taylor, A.J.P. *English History, 1914-1945*, Harmondsworth, Middx 1970.

3 From the one to the many: philosophy 1900-30

DAVID HOLDCROFT

The essay on literature emphasized the importance of the differing views of reality, implicit and explicit, which may be involved in changes of literary forms. The principal concern of this essay is with philosophical ideas during the same period, and an assessment of their relative importance. However, those philosophical ideas which have significantly influenced literature, or for which parallels can be found in literature, are not necessarily the most important from a philosophical point of view. If Russell is arguably the most important philosopher of the period, his impact on literature would seem to be limited to that of providing material for a character in a novel by Lawrence and a poem by Eliot.[1] Whilst Bradley and McTaggart, though much less important figures in the history of philosophy, undeniably have influences on Eliot and Yeats respectively. There is the further problem that often discernible influences on literature are not by contemporary authors at all; a good example in point would be the influence of Nietzsche during our period.[2] So in order to keep a clear perspective this essay is written primarily from the point of view of a philosopher, attempting at the same time to pick out a number of specific connections with literature, and to provide footnotes for further reading. There remains the possibility of deep structural parallels between the literature and the philosophy of the period, and a brief attempt to consider what these might be is made in the final section.

I

'There is nothing which, to speak properly, is individual or
perfect except only the Absolute.'   (F.H. Bradley)[3]

In 1900 the number of professional philosophers in Britain was still
very small, and by far the biggest concentration was in Oxford and
Cambridge. Many of their papers appeared in the journal *Mind*. A
glance at the numbers in the early years of the century reveals a small
number of contributors whose names recur with considerable
frequency, and none greater than that of the Oxford philosopher F.H.
Bradley who had fourteen papers published between 1900 and 1910.
Bradley was the foremost representative of the dominant philosophical
movement of the time, idealism. The version of idealism which he
developed is known as absolute idealism. A central tenet of idealism is
that reality is dependent on or determined by experience; Berkeley, for
instance, had argued that to be is to be perceived.[4] Bradley went even
further and maintained that reality and experience are one and the
same thing: 'Sentient experience in short is reality, and what is not
this is not real' (*Appearance and Reality*, p.127). Obscure though this
position is, it is one which many contemporary idealists would have
accepted. What, however, made many of them baulk was Bradley's
monism, i.e., his claim that reality is one and indivisible, and does not
consist of a number of particular things related to each other. For to
deny the existence of all particulars is to deny the existence of the self
and of God, and seemingly, in so doing, the presuppositions of
morality and Christian theology.

The key to Bradley's position is his denial of the reality of relations,
'...our experience when relational is not true'. Bradley deploys
many arguments in support of his contention. For example, if a relation related two things, the question would arise, 'what relates it to
each of them?' We could answer it by positing two further relations,
but the original question arises about each of them: 'The links are
united by a link; and this bond of union is a link which also has two
ends; and these require each a fresh link to connect them with the old'
(p.28). But if relations are not real, then neither is anything which
involves relations. So neither space, time, causality, nor individual
things, can be real. For time to exist, for instance, some events would
have to take place before other events, but this is obviously impossible
if events cannot be related to each other.

However, if reality, the Absolute, is one and undivided, it would seem that our thoughts about it must be false. Thought necessarily involves the use of discrete concepts; but to use a concept is to classify and particularize, and thereby falsify. But how can we have any notion of the Absolute in that case, and is not Bradley trying to say what, given his own premises, cannot be said? Bradley's answer seems to have been that it is immediate experience which provides us with a clue to the nature of the Absolute:

> In the beginning there is nothing beyond what is presented, what is and is felt, or rather is felt simply. There is no memory or imagination or hope or fear or will, and no perception of difference or likeness. There are, in short, no relations and no feelings, only feeling.[5]

So it is not immediate experience, but thought and language, which misleads us about the nature of the Absolute.

One of Bradley's central tenets is that one cannot distinguish me from what I experience, it and I are really part of one non-relational whole. Another, as we have just seen is the superiority of experience over thought. Eliot, we know, wrote a dissertation for Harvard University about Bradley between 1911 and 1915, admired him very much indeed, and arguably, at least, found that Bradley articulated for him views about the self and the value of experience as opposed to abstruse thought which he found immensely congenial.[6] Since Eliot was working on 'Prufrock' in 1911, any attempt to look for a direct Bradleyan influence on the poem is perhaps misguided. But the lack of definition of Prufrock himself, the haziness of the borderline between him and his world, certainly make it plausible that 'he' is a Bradleyan subject in no way determinately marked off from the objects of his experience. And though, for example, Eliot's remark in another context that 'Language in a healthy state presents the object, is so close to the object that the two are identified' represents from Bradley's point of view an impossible ideal, it is nevertheless one to be applauded and approximated to. Here indeed is perhaps the most important and interesting parallelism between a mode of philosophical thought and a poet in our period.

The most radical departure from Bradley, that of G.E. Moore and Bertrand Russell, rejected both idealism and monism. But there were less drastic departures; one which was popular rejected monism, but retained idealism. The result, known as personal idealism, had influential

dherents in both Oxford and Cambridge. A third tendency hostile to
nonism, but arguably ambiguous about idealism, was pragmatism.
The leading pragmatists, Peirce, Dewey, and William James (the
brother of Henry James[7]), were Americans, but the movement had
ne prolific and combative protagonist in Britain, F.C.S. Schiller. The
estruction of Bradleyan idealism is usually attributed to Moore and
Russell. But if his own articles are anything to go by, the enemy he
ecognized at the time was not them but the Personal Idealists and the
pragmatists.

II

'To search for ''unity'' and ''system'' at the expense of
truth, is not I take it, the proper business of philosophy . . . '
(G.E. Moore)[8]

Russell tells us that it was towards the end of 1898 that, at Cambridge,
he and Moore rebelled 'against both Kant and Hegel. Moore led the
way, but I followed closely in his footsteps.'[9] The paper which marks
the outbreak of the rebellion, 'The Nature of Judgment', Moore must
have thought a poor one since he did not include it in his collected
papers, but it undoubtedly had a big influence on Russell, and is for
that reason, if no other, an important one. Its thesis is uncompromis-
ngly realist. Idealism, we saw, maintains that what we experience is
dependent on our experience of it. Realism maintains, in opposition,
the independence of the object of an experience from the experience of
it. One would, therefore, expect a Realist to argue that the object of a
judgement is not dependent on it; and Moore does not disappoint this
expectation.

He begins by agreeing with Bradley's criticism of those (e.g., Mill)
who had treated the judgement as a mental state, but criticizes Bradley
for not going far enough. Eschewing the word 'idea' because of its
psychological associations, he uses 'concept' instead, and argues that
the concept involved in a judgement is not a *mental* fact nor any part
thereof. A judgement is built up out of concepts, and asserts a specific
connection between them. To assert 'the chimera has three heads' is
to assert that there exists a certain connection between concepts, and
what is said is false because 'such a conjunction of concepts is not to be
found among existents'. Unlike an idea, the nature of a concept is not
dependent on thought. Concepts are 'incapable of change; and the

relation into which they enter with the knowing subject implies n
action or reaction.' Further, and most strikingly, it is necessary 't
regard the world as formed of concepts'. Thus things, as well as judge
ments, are composed of concepts; and concepts cannot be regarded a
abstractions from things, since things are formed from them.

Since there are many concepts, Moore's position embraced plura
ism (as opposed to monism) as well as realism. His account of th
nature of judgement clearly involves a bold hypothesis about th
nature of reality, and an equally striking one about the relation of tru
judgements to that reality. In claiming that the objects of though
constitute a mind-independent realm of timeless entities, he claime
no more than various contemporary philosophers of an ant
psychologistic persuasion did, Frege, Meinong and Brentano, fc
instance. But there is an additional boldness in identifying thos
objects of thought with the ultimate constituents of things. If this is sc
then the constituents of a true judgement will be identical with thos
of some fact about the world, and the way in which they are related i
reality will be as the judgement asserts them to be. The ideas tha
reality has a plurality of ultimate constituents, which can also b
constituents of judgements, and that a judgement is true when it
constituents are related as they are in reality, are amongst the leadin
ideas of logical atomism. So that if Russell and Wittgenstein are th
most distinguished of the Logical Atomists, Moore has a good claim t
be the first.

Moore went on to publish a steady stream of papers, on a wide rang
of topics, a number of which, 'The Refutation of Idealism' (1903)
'The Conception of Reality' (1917), and 'External and Internal Rela
tions' (1919), contained important criticisms of idealist positions. The
first of these Moore later thought was very confused. Confused or not
it is a powerfully argued paper. Its target is the dictum that to be is t
be perceived, a claim which Moore thought all versions of idealism ar
committed to, so that to refute it is to refute idealism. The dictum, h
argues, rests on a confusion of the object of an experience with ou
experience of it. When I am aware of blue my awareness is one thing
the blue of which I am aware another, and the latter is in no sense par
of the content of my experience. 'There is, therefore, no question o
how we are to ''get outside the circle of our own ideas an
sensations''. Merely to have a sensation is already to be outside of tha
circle.'[10]

Moore's publications during our period also included two books on ethics, of which the first, *Principia Ethica* made a great impact. Moore was deeply convinced that most ethical systems were vitiated by confusing quite distinct questions, and there are three questions which he insisted should be sharply distinguished: how is 'good' to be defined?; what is meant by calling an action right, or a duty?; and, thirdly, what things are of intrinsic value, that is, ought to exist simply for their own sakes?

His answer to the first of these questions was that the property *good*, which he called a 'non-natural' property because it cannot be studied by any of the natural sciences, is simple and indefinable. Proposed definitions all commit what he called the 'naturalistic fallacy', so called because many attempts at definition identified the property *good* with a natural property, such as *pleasure*, which can be studied by one of the natural sciences. But the same fallacy is involved if *good* is identified with a transcendental property, such as *being willed by God*. Perhaps the most cogent of Moore's arguments is that 'whatever definition be offered, it may always be asked, with significance, of the complex so defined, whether it itself is good' (*Principia Ethica*, p.15). Thus, the fact that we can significantly ask whether what is more evolved is good, seems to show that the proposal that *good* may be defined as *more evolved* is in error.

Turning to the second question, Moore maintained that to say that an action is right is to say that it will produce the greatest possible amount of good. Hence, what it is right for me to do on a given occasion will have better consequences than anything else I could have done. It follows that no moral law that one ought *always* to perform a certain action can be self-evident since it is unlikely that any action will always have better consequences than its alternatives. Moreover, even if it did, we could not know that it did, since the consequences stretch on indefinitely into the future. The most we can do is to show that certain actions will generally have better consequences than any alternatives. Actions of this sort are ones which tend to preserve the existence of civilized society, without which few, if any, goods can be obtained. Rules which can be justified in this way are ones which prohibit violence against persons and property, and enjoin one to keep promises, to be industrious and temperate. Such rules should always be followed, but in other cases one 'should rather judge of the probable results in his particular case, guided by a correct conception of what things are intrinsically good or bad' (p.181).

If what is right is what produces the most good, to act correctly on must know what things are intrinsically good, and what not. To disco ver what intrinsic value some thing has one should ask what value 'w should attach to it, if it existed in absolute isolation, stripped of all it usual accompaniments' (p.91). Pursuing this method we see, Moor argues, that the fundamental tenet of hedonism, that the only thin which is good is pleasure, is false. If hedonism were true then pleasur would be good whether or not someone was conscious of it, wherea 'some consciousness at least must be included with it as a veritabl part of that end' (p.89). Consciousness of pleasure is an example c what Moore called an 'organic whole'. It may be that consciousnes *per se* is of small, or no value, but consciousness of pleasure is of mucl greater value than pleasure on its own. It follows that the value of whole is not, or anyway need not be, equal to the sum of the values c its parts.

The part of *Principia* which most influenced Keynes and hi contemporaries was the final chapter, 'The Ideal', in which Moor tells us which things are intrinsically good. His fundamental intuitior was that, 'By far the most valuable things which we can know o imagine, are certain states of consciousness, which may be roughly described as the pleasures of human intercourse and the enjoyment o beautiful objects' (p.188). These constitute the *raison d'être* of virtue and the only criterion of social progress. The constituents of an aesthe tic enjoyment are an appropriate aesthetic emotion, a cognition of beautiful object, and a true belief. The latter is perhaps a surprising addition to the list, but Moore argues that *ceteris paribus* an aesthetic experience which involves a true belief about the object of the experi ence is better than one which involves a false belief. The pleasures o personal affection also involve an appropriate emotion towards, and a true belief about, a beautiful object, though an account of them is complicated, Moore thinks, by the fact that that object is itself good This complication arises in all cases in which what is admired is a mental quality of a person, though in these cases our experience is even more valuable when these qualities have an 'appropriate *corporeal* expression'. And since admirable mental qualities largely consist of a contemplation of beautiful objects, when we admire some one's mental qualities we contemplate such contemplation. But though 'the love of love, is by far the most valuable good we know' (p.204), this is so only if it is understood to include the love of beauty.

On this there is no better comment than Keynes': 'The New Testament is a handbook for politicians compared with the unworldliness of Moore's chapter on "The Ideal". I know no equal to it in literature since Plato. And it is better than Plato because it is quite free from fancy.'[11]

Keynes was, of course a member of the Bloomsbury group, and he said in 1938 of Moore's *Principia* that 'its effect on *us*, and the talk which preceded it, dominated, and perhaps still dominate everything else.'[12] Quite who he meant to refer to by 'us' is disputable; but it seems clear that at least Desmond MacCarthy, Clive Bell, Leonard Woolf, Lytton Strachey, and Saxon Sydney Turner, should be included. So that if the *Principia* and its author was not *the* major influence on Bloomsbury, it was undoubtedly *a* major influence.[13] The effect of *Principia*, in Keynes' view, was not altogether what Moore had intended. His view that certain states of mind are much the most valuable things there are – what Keynes called 'Moore's religion' – was accepted. But his view of the nature of right action was largely ignored. This gave Bloomsbury a moral point of view which was not utilitarian, and which emphasized the life of contemplation at the expense of that of action. Such a point of view, Keynes admits, ignores much that is important, and he confesses to a feeling that Lawrence may have been right in saying that they were 'done for'.[14] Yet arguably Keynes underestimates the extent to which Bloomsbury took a stand on matters of 'action', such as feminism and the First World War. After all, one conclusion one could derive from Moore's writings was that there is a very considerable degree of judgement involved in disputes about what is right. And it was precisely its judgement which Bloomsbury was prepared to exercise in an independent and critical way.

III

'Whatever may be an object of thought, or may occur in any true or false proposition, or can be counted as *one*, I call a *term*.'
(B. Russell)[15]

In his autobiography Moore wrote that the main motive for his philosophical writings was provided by things other philosophers had said. By contrast, Russell's interest in many philosophical problems arose from his concern with mathematics. As an undergraduate a Cambridge he read mathematics, and though he says he gave it up i disgust on graduation, he clearly remained keenly interested in mathe matical issues. In 1900 he heard the Italian mathematician Pean lecture at an international conference. He was greatly impressed b the rigour of Peano's work, and learnt from him how it was possible t construct a deductive system adequate for the whole of mathematics which rested on a small number of definitions and postulates. Bu what is the status of the postulates of such a system, and of the unde fined terms they contain? Russell formulated the thesis (known a logicism) that Peano's postulates could be proved by logical means and that the undefined terms they contain can be defined in purel logical terms. As he put it, 'when once the apparatus of logic has bee accepted, all mathematics necessarily follows'.[16] This thesis had unknown to Russell, been independently formulated by the Germa mathematician Frege, with whose work, however, he soon becam acquainted. Detailed substantiation of the thesis was to occupy Russel for a decade. Its immediate fruit, however, was the production of th first draft of *The Principles of Mathematics* only five months afte meeting Peano. Since the book when published was some 500 page long, and packed with argument on highly technical topics, th production of a draft in so short a time testifies to the immense inven tive ingenuity of Russell.

Before he published the final version, however, Russell discovered a serious flaw which threatened to undermine his programme. A key notion was that of a class, since Russell defined a number as a class of classes which are similar to each other. Similarity Russell explains as follows: 'Two classes are similar if there is a way of coupling their terms one to one. For example, in a monogamous country, you can know that the number of married men is the same as the number of married women, without having to know how many there are of either (I am excluding widows and widowers).'[17] Now since we can establish that two classes are similar without knowing what the number of either is, then, since similar classes have the same number of members, we can define a number, without circularity, as a class of similar classes. Clearly, this definition of number can be no clearer than the notion of a class, and in 1902 Russell discovered a paradox which brought the whole notion into question, by showing that a fundamental assump- tion about the nature of classes is mistaken. The assumption is that one can specify the members of a class by specifying the property which a thing must have to be a member of it. The class of men, for instance, is that class which contains all and only those things which have the property of being a man. But if the assumption is correct, then the property *is not a member of itself* must determine a class, i.e., one each member of which has the property of not being a member of itself. Consider then the class of all those classes which are not members of themselves; this must either be a member of itself or not. But neither alternative can be maintained, for if the class is a member of itself it is not, and if it is not, it is. Russell sketched a solution of the paradox in an appendix to the *Principles*, but the detailed elaboration of it and of other problems was to prove most difficult.

In his preface to the *Principles* Russell wrote that on 'fundamental questions of philosophy, my position, in all its chief features, is derived from Mr G.E. Moore'. Certainly, Russell's views about the nature of judgements and propositions have a number of marked similarities to those expressed in 'The Nature of Judgment'. Russell's account of propositions is, like Moore's, resolutely non-psychological: 'a proposition, unless it happens to be linguistic, does not itself contain words: it contains the entities indicated by the words' (*The Principles of Mathematics*, p.47). There are many such mind-independent entities, and whatever may be an object of thought he calls a 'term'. All terms have being, and 'A man, a moment, a number, a class, a relation, a chimaera, or anything else that can be mentioned, is sure to be a term . . .' (p.43). Thus Russell's realist theory of the proposition leads to a rather reckless positing of entities. Moreover, there are various points at which the general theory comes under great strain. One concerns the analysis of so-called denoting expressions, 'a man', 'some man', 'all men', 'some men', etc., the analysis of which is essential to the development of a branch of logic known as predicate calculus. According to the general theory there ought to be an entity corresponding to each of these expressions, and Russell did indeed conclude that 'There is, then, a definite something, different in each of the five cases, which must, in a sense, be an object, but is characterised as a set of terms combined in a certain way . . .' (p.62). Russell described these objects as paradoxical, and one can see why. The object denoted by 'a man', for instance, would have to be a disjunction of Fred, or Bill, or Peter, etc., i.e., be that 'object' consisting of either Fred, or Bill, or Peter, etc.; clearly a disjunctive object is a very odd object indeed.

Definite descriptions also posed problems; what, for instance, doe
'the golden mountain' denote?

Russell was to abandon this theory of denoting in 1905, and came
to think it desirable to avoid many of the commitments of the *Prin
ciples* to the existence of certain sorts of objects – points and instants
for instance. However, though his realism became more moderate, he
never abandoned realism. The philosophy of Moore and Russell is
often seen as a return to the traditions of British empiricism, i.e., to
the work of Locke, Berkeley, and Hume. This, however, is a most
misleading picture of their work in the early years of this century
which was profoundly anti-psychologistic. They avoided the Empiri
cists' key term, 'idea', and insisted that they were not analysing the
contents of minds, but describing mind-independent entities. Admit
tedly, their work on the philosophy of perception has affinities with the
writings of the Empiricists, but this granted, no self-respecting Empiri
cist would have countenanced non-natural properties (see p.131), or
half the objects acknowledged by Russell in the *Principles*.

IV

'If our conclusions are correct, the universe consists of
selves, . . . whose whole content consists in their perceptions
of themselves and of each other. . . . '

(J.E. McTaggart)[18]

Personal idealism was of the nature of an internal revolt by those who
accepted idealism, but objected to the implications of absolute idealism
for the notion of personality. The conclusion that persons are no more
ultimately real than are other apparently real entities such as chairs
and tables was repugnant. The consequences for morality, and even
more clearly for religion, seemed to many to be totally unacceptable. In
1902 there appeared a volume edited by Henry Sturt entitled *Personal
Idealism*, which consisted of eight essays by members of the University
of Oxford. They were not all Idealists, and some were not philosophers, but they were united, according to Sturt in his preface, in
defending personality from the twin attacks of naturalism and absolute
idealism. It is somewhat ironical that a variety of idealism should have
been linked, with naturalism, as a threat to the existence of persons
and of God, since the first great Idealist, Berkeley, had been a resolute

pponent of naturalism, and had thought that only an idealist philo-
ophy could combat atheism. Interestingly, therefore, one of the
ontributors to the volume, Hastings Rashdall, argued for a position
ot at all unlike Berkeley's. The Absolute he interpreted as a commu-
ity of souls which has a presiding soul, God. Reality thus consists of
God and the other souls, together with their experiences. Each soul
ther than God is created by God, and so is not eternal. But God is not
n the theological sense infinite, since he is limited by the souls he
reated. Rashdall went on to become a distinguished theologian, and
he contributors to *Personal Idealism* were, anyway, too loosely-knit a
group to constitute a sustained threat to absolute idealism, so that the
hallenge petered out.

Much the most distinguished Personal Idealist, J.E. McTaggart,
was to be found, however, not in Oxford, but in Cambridge, where he
was lecturer in philosophy at Trinity College whilst Moore and
Russell were undergraduates there.[19] McTaggart was a sympathetic
nterpreter of Hegel, and the culmination of his own work, *The
Nature of Existence* (1921, 1927) is uncompromisingly metaphysi-
al, and extremely closely argued. He tries to show that time, space,
hange, and matter, are all unreal, and that what exists is a commu-
ity of independent spirits, none of which is supreme (so that there is
o God), and which are related to each other by love. McTaggart
distinguishes carefully those conclusions which he thinks he can
establish conclusively from those which he cannot. Starting with only
wo empirical premises, 'something exists', and 'what exists has
roperties', he claims to prove that reality consists of a group of
ubstances each of which is infinitely divisible. Moreover, the fact that
each substance is infinitely divisible would lead to an absurdity unless
a certain relation, which McTaggart calls 'determining correspondence', holds between some description of each substance and all its
parts. McTaggart then turns to the second part of his inquiry, the aim
of which is to see what can satisfy the *a priori* requirements established
in the first part, i.e., to see what substances could actually be related by
the relation of determining correspondence. At this point complete
proof ceases to be possible. We can show that no relation of determining correspondence can hold between matter and its parts, or sense
data and their parts. Moreover, it *could* be the case that perception is a
relation of determining correspondence, so that spirits, since they
perceive, could be the substances McTaggart is trying to identify.

Certainly, of the three sorts of substances that we apparently have experience of only spirits satisfy the condition of determining correspondence. What, however, stands in the way of a *strict* proof that the are the substances which constitute reality is the possibility that ther are other substances of which we have no experience, and that thes may also satisfy the condition of determining correspondence. 'Bu although we have no absolute demonstration, we have, I think, goo reason to believe that all reality is spiritual'.[20] The selves which consti tute reality are, McTaggart goes on to argue, related to each other b love, and are in a certain sense immortal.

Though McTaggart's arguments are at times of great intricacy, hi style is very lucid and unrhetorical, unlike that of many other Idealists He combined great inventiveness with considerable analytical skill and his proof of the unreality of time, for instance, exhibits this skill t a high degree.

One of the contributors to *Personal Idealism* who went on to publis prolifically was F.C.S. Schiller. He was not in fact an Idealist, but Pragmatist, indeed the only British Pragmatist of any stature in ou period. Pragmatism was primarily an American movement, and th American Pragmatist with whom Schiller had the closest affinities wa William James. Schiller was a humanist who insisted that we mus never lose sight of the fact that human beings act with certain ends i view, and that their actions are well or badly chosen as means to thos ends. This is as true of theories and beliefs as it is of actions in general They are adopted to further certain human purposes, and should b assessed in relation to them. To lose sight of this fact is to be guilty o intellectualism, to drive a wedge between theory and practice, an results only in empty abstractions. One result of this tendency ha been, Schiller argues, the separation of psychology from logic – an that they should be separated is something which Bradley, Moore, an Russell were united in maintaining – to the impoverishment of bot sciences. A judgement is something made by a certain person, at certain time, with certain ends in view, and its meaning is constitute by the intentions of its author. By contrast, the judgement studied b formal logicians is dehumanized and depersonalized. In consequence formal logic has ceased to be, as it should be, a study of inquiry, an has become one of the 'verbal implications of "dictionary meanings"' (*Contemporary British Philosophy*, I, p.392).

The formal logician might argue that his interest is in universa alidity and absolute truth, and that this entitles him to abstract from he contexts of particular judgements. But Schiller's reply was that he notion of absolute truth is chimerical, and that truth, like theory, has to be seen in relation to human purposes. Faced with certain problems we adopt hypotheses 'which are not idle, but are meant to be used. Their *value* is *tested* by their *working*, and to survive they have to be *verified*' (p.401). If the consequences predicted occur, then the hypothesis is confirmed, but we can never obtain complete confirmation. Hence, our hypothesis can never be conclusively established. The most that can be claimed is that it is the '*best and truest up to date*'. It follows that 'no truth is eternal; every truth has its day'.

The pragmatist theory of truth caused a stir, and Bradley, Moore and Russell, were united in attacking it. What disturbed many critics is the idea that truth is what works, and that it is mutable. Certainly, Schiller's account of the notion of working leaves much to be desired. In the case of scientific truth what is true works in the sense that it can be verified; though this does not seem to have the consequence, as Schiller somewhat rhetorically claims, that every truth has its day. But when one leaves the sphere of science for that of morals and aesthetics, etc., one seems not to have an analogue of verification, so that it becomes extremely obscure what working is. In these cases it seems that what works is what one wants to. Aware of the problem, Schiller resorted to talk of 'survival value'; in biology 'there is a sort of working, which, while wholly devoid of any rational appeal, yet exercises a far-reaching influence on our beliefs . . . ' (p.406).

Schiller seems to have had little enduring influence. This is perhaps not surprising, since it is not at all unusual. What is perhaps more surprising is that, with the characteristic exception of Russell, the same can be said of pragmatism in general, which, in this country, provoked refutations galore, but failed to win over a sizeable body of adherents. Why latter-day Pragmatists should have fared differently is a puzzling question.

V

'What made it the more annoying was that the contradictions were trivial, and that my time was spent in considering matters that seemed unworthy of serious attention.'

(B. Russell)[21]

The contradiction of the class of all those classes that are not member of themselves, discovered in 1902, was one of a family of paradoxes, to which belongs the well-known one about Epimenides the Cretan who said that all Cretans are liars. The logicist programme of reducing arithmetic to logic could not be carried out until a solution to the paradoxes could be found, but Russell reports that it was not until 1906 that he found one. In 1902 he started to collaborate with the Cambridge mathematician A.N. Whitehead in working out the logicist thesis in rigorous detail. The result of their collaboration, the monumental *Principia Mathematica*, was published in three volumes between 1910 and 1913. Ironically, they were not only not paid for it but had to contribute £100 towards the cost of publishing: 'We thus earned minus £50 each by ten years work. This beats the record of *Paradise Lost*.'[22] *Principia Mathematica* was of immense logical importance, though it is generally agreed now that logicism is false. Moreover, a number of theories developed whilst writing it had a very big impact indeed on the practice of philosophy.

The most influential of these, the theory of descriptions, first appeared in a paper called 'On Denoting' (1905). It marked a radical break with the theory of denoting phrases (i.e., such phrases as 'all men', 'a man', 'the present king of France') developed in the *Principles of Mathematics* where, it will be recalled, Russell had argued that to each such expression there corresponds an object – though one of a rather 'paradoxical' kind. This has the implausible consequence that the present king of France must in some sense *be* because 'the present king of France is bald' is significant, though false.

Russell's new theory made a decisive break with the idea that there corresponds an object to each denoting expression. In this respect denoting expressions are, in Russell's view, unlike proper names. If 'John' really is a name, then there is some thing, John, which it names, and 'John walked home' makes an assertion about that thing. But, Russell argued, 'a man' is not the name of some peculiar, indeterminate, sort of object, and so 'a man walked home' does not assert something about an object in the way in which 'John walked home' does.

The key to Russell's new theory is his notion of a propositional function. One can obtain a propositional function by taking a sentence and omitting the proper name(s) it contains; e.g., to 'John walked home' there corresponds the function 'x walked home'. Now if it is rue of John that he walked home, but false of Peter that he did, then we can say that the propositional function '*x* walked home' is sometimes true – because true of some persons, but not of others. Russell goes on to argue that 'a man walked home' may be analysed as 'the propositional function "*x* walked home" is sometimes true'. Thus 'a man walked home' is essentially a proposition about a propositional function, and there is no need to worry about the sort of object which is denoted by 'a man', since there is no such object. Perhaps the best way of seeing what Russell is driving at is to construe 'a man walked home' as being about what '*x* walked home' symbolizes, viz. the concept *having walked home*. What is asserted then is simply that the concept *having walked home* has instances.

Russell argued that all denoting expressions can be analysed in a similar way, including definite descriptions. For 'the present king of France is bald' is equivalent to the conjunction: (i) someone is a present king of France, (ii) at most one person is a present king of France, and (iii) whoever is a present king of France is bald. Each of these, as analysed by Russell, is about a propositional function. Thus the analysis shows that 'the present king of France is bald' is equivalent to a conjunction of propositions about propositional functions, and hence that the fact that it makes sense to say that the present king is bald does not mean that he has in some sense to *be*; all that has to exist are the relevant propositional functions. The very real merits of Russell's proposals can be seen by considering 'the present king of France does not exist'. According to the old theory the king would have in some sense to *be*, in order that we can say that he does not exist. But on the new theory there is no such problem; what is asserted is 'the function "*x* is a present king of France" has no instances'.

There are at least three reasons why Russell's theory was important. Firstly, it showed that it is not necessary to assume that to every nominal expression there corresponds an object. Connectedly, it showed how analysis could enable one to prune the over-generous ontology of the *Principles of Mathematics*. Thirdly, it showed that the grammatical form of a sentence may be a poor guide to its logical form. Grammatically, 'John went home' and 'a man went home' are very similar, but logically they are quite different.

The idea that as well as our ordinary grammar there is a deeper logical grammar received further impetus from the theory of types, which was Russell's solution to the paradoxes. Technically the theory is complicated, but the essential idea is that the paradoxes all involve an illegitimate totality. Epimenides' statement that all Cretans are liars is paradoxical only because he is a Cretan, so that what he says applies to his own statement, with the result that if it is assumed to be true it must be false. If Epimenides' statement is construed so that it is about a set of Cretan statements not including his own, then no paradox arises. Russell, therefore, proposed the rule that, 'Whatever involves *all* of a collection must not be one of the collection'.[23] So the class of *all* classes that are not members of themselves cannot itself be another member of the totality. To avoid the creation of illegitimate totalities, Russell proposed the existence of a hierarchy of types. The basic type consists of individual things, the next of functions of individual things, the next of functions of functions of them, etc. The thesis then is that what can be said of objects of a given type cannot be said of ones of a higher type. For instance, 'John is human' makes sense, but 'humanity is human' does not. The theory implies that though from a grammatical point of view 'the class of all classes which are not members of themselves is a member of itself' is unobjectionable, from a logical point of view it is meaningless. We can speak only of all classes of a given *type*, and the class which has classes of that type as its members will not itself be of that type. So, it seems, ordinary grammar once again proves a poor guide to logical structure.

VI

'One purpose that has run through all that I have said, has been the justification of analysis, i.e., the justification of logical atomism, of the theory that you can get down in theory, if not in practice to ultimate simples. . . .'

(B. Russell)[24]

When *Principia Mathematica* was completed Russell turned increasingly to problems in metaphysics and epistemology; but though the problems were different his approach to them was profoundly influenced by his work on the philosophy of mathematics. In the *Philosophy of Logical Atomism* (1918) he said that the sort of philosophy he wished to advocate 'is one which has forced itself upon me in the course of thinking about the philosophy of mathematics'.[25] Whilst

n *Our Knowledge of The External World* (1914) he went so far as to
say that every philosophical problem is 'in the sense in which we are
using the word, logical'.[26]

Perhaps the most important idea drawn from his work on the philosophy of mathematics which Russell applied to problems in other areas
was that of a logical construction: 'The supreme maxim in scientific
philosophising is this: Wherever possible, logical constructions are to
be substituted for inferred entities.'[27] An example of a logical
construction is the definition of a number as a class of classes similar to
each other, a definition which shows how to systematiclly translate all
talk about numbers into talk about classes of classes, so that if we
countenance the existence of classes, we have no need to countenance
that of numbers as a separate and irreducible category. The definition
of number thus not only shows how numbers may be analysed, but
also how we may avoid commitment to their existence as an irreducible category, and commit ourselves only to the existence of the
entities out of which they are constructed. In general, a logical
construction shows how to analyse entities of one kind A into another
B, and, at the same time, how to avoid commitment to entities of the
kind A as an irreducible category. The main advantage of treating
something as a logical construction, Russell argues, is that it
diminishes the risk of error. The fewer types of entity one commits
oneself to, the less chance there is of going wrong.

It is easy to see how if one treats whatever is complex, e.g.,
numbers, physical objects, persons, etc., as a logical construction, one
will be led to the idea of ultimate simples, for unless there are such
simples the whole process of analysis involved in logical constructions
will have no terminus, and hence no direction. However, logic cannot
tell us what is ultimately simple once we leave the field of logic, yet to
apply the idea of a logical construction to problems in metaphysics we
must have some view of what is simple and most fundamental.

At this point Russell's empiricism — which was not much in
evidence when he wrote the *Principles* — comes to the fore. As an
Empiricist he maintained that what are given to us in sense perception
are sense data not physical objects, and sense data were for him one
type of 'logical atom'. In the *Problems of Philosophy* (1910) he
argued that when we look at a table, for instance, what each one of us
immediately sees is different, if only slightly so. So if an immediate
perception is one which involves no interpretation of what is

perceived, and a sense datum is defined as the object of an immediate perception, no two persons' sense data are identical. Moreover, Russell argued, it would be an unwarranted favouritism to identify my sense datum of the table with the real table at the expense of the sense data which others have. The real table cannot be identified with my sense datum of it, nor with anyone else's, but is an inference from it. Russell was soon to abandon the view that the real table is an inference from sense data. But he continued to maintain that the objects of immediate perception are sense data, and to cite them as examples of 'logical atoms'. They are not, however, the only kind of logical atom for they are particulars, and Russell was convinced that the existence of universals, i.e., of properties and relations, cannot be reduced to that of particulars. The universal *yellow* is not a particular thing, but something which can be possessed by particular things. The recognition of universals makes Russell's empiricism an oddly qualified one, but what is characteristic of such works as *Our Knowledge of the External World, Mysticism and Logic*, and the *Philosophy of Logical Atomism* is the application of ideas developed when working on *Principia Mathematica*, particularly that of a logical construction, to general philosophical problems within a broadly empiricist framework.

In line with his general position Russell treated physical objects as logical constructions. But logical constructions out of what? If we restricted ourselves to sense data the result would be 'gappy'. A sense datum presupposes an observer, so that there would be no sense data at times at which no one was observing. Moreover would not the resulting construction be idealist in spirit, since sense data are mental entities? Russell's response to these difficulties was characteristically bold. Sense data, he argued, are physical entities, not mental ones, having a causal but not logical dependence on observers. To solve the problem of non-continuous observation, he introduced the notion of sensible which has 'the same metaphysical and physical status' (*Mysticism and Logic*, p.148) as a sense datum, except that it need not be sensed. Moreover, just as my sense data belong to a different perspective from yours when we both look at a penny, since we look at it from different points of view, we can, in a similar fashion, think of sensibilia as belonging to perspectives. And perspectives can obviously be ordered; in some, for example, the penny will look circular, in others it will look elliptical, and so on. Now, 'We may collect together all those perspectives in which the appearance of the penny is circular

hese we will place on one straight line, ordering them in a series by
ᵗe variations in the apparent size of the penny' (p.153). Similarly,
ᵗose perspectives in which the penny appears as a certain sort of
ᵗlipse can be ordered in terms of apparent size, and so on. 'By such
ᵗeans, all those perspectives in which the penny presents a visual
ᵗpearance can be arranged in a three dimensional order' (p.154). The
ᵗnny then is to be identified with the set of its perspectives ordered in
ᵗis way – a rough analogue would be a cubist painting. The construc-
ᵗon is ingenious, and though it seems to have convinced no one,
ᵗussell retains large elements of it in his account of his present view of
ᵗe world in Chapter II of *My Philosophical Development.*[28]

The culmination of Russell's work at this time was the *Philosophy
ᶠ Logical Atomism*. Characteristically, he wrote that he was mainly
ᵒncerned with explaining 'certain ideas which I learnt from my friend
ᵗnd former pupil Ludwig Wittgenstein'. But since many of the ideas
ᵗre plainly Russell's, this influence is not readily discernible. It is
ᵗerhaps to be seen in the emphasis which Russell places on the notion
ᵗ a fact, and on the importance of symbolism, since 'Some of the
ᵗotions that have been thought absolutely fundamental in philosophy
ᵗave arisen, I believe, entirely through mistakes as to symbolism . . .'
ᵗhilosophy of Logical Atomism*, p.186).[29]

Russell's fundamental contention was that there exist facts 'which
ᵗelong to the objective world. They are not created by our thought or
ᵗelief except in special cases' (p.183). Facts have constituents, and the
ᵒnstituents of the most fundamental kind of fact – which Russell calls
ᵗatomic facts' – constitute the 'logical atoms' of the theory in that
ᵗhey are themselves incapable of further analysis. These atoms are
ᵗither particulars, such as little colour patches, or universals, i.e.,
ᵗroperties and relations. As well as facts there are propositions. They
ᵗo have constituents; a proposition is a complex symbol whose parts
ᵗre symbols. With certain exceptions, each of these constituent
ᵗymbols has a meaning, and its meaning is literally identical with that
ᶠ a constituent of a fact (p.196). For example, if 'this is white' is
ᵗsserted of a sense datum, then the meaning of 'this' is literally the
ᵗense datum in question, and that of 'white' is the universal white.
ᵗoreover, if 'this is white' is true, then the meanings of its compo-
ᵗents will be constituents of the *fact* that this is white. So the truth of
ᵗhe proposition will consist in correspondence with a fact, and in an
ᵗntelligible sense the proposition will have the same structure as that

fact. In other words, the structure of a proposition mirrors that of possible fact.

It follows that a catalogue of the structures of possible facts is *eo ips* one of the possible types of propositions there are; and to specify a possible types of propositions would, of course, be to specify all th possible kinds of things that can be thought or asserted. So the que tion what kinds of fact there are is an interesting one. Atomic fact Russell maintains, are the most basic kind of fact. They are such fac as this is white, this is to the left of that, i.e., facts which contain onl particulars and properties or relations.

However, when one considers what facts there might be other tha atomic facts a doubt about Russell's programme arises. For if tru propositions correspond to the facts, then ought there not to be th disjunctive fact that Socrates is dead or alive, and the negative fact tha Socrates is not alive? And what sorts of facts are these? As far as th first sort of fact goes Russell sees no need to posit its existenc 'Socrates is dead or alive' is true if *either* it is a fact that he is dead, *or* is a fact that he is alive – there is no need to introduce a further fac the fact that he-is-either-dead-or-alive. However, Russell argued tha for various reasons it is necessary to suppose that there are negativ facts – a view which he says nearly produced a riot at Harvard. Bu many have found the existence of such facts very difficult to swallow Moreover, he was able to offer only a very tentative analysis of suc psychological facts as that Othello believes that Desdemona love Cassio, so that his programme of trying to relate what it is possible t say to the types of facts there are, remained incomplete, and clearl threw up a number of extremely contentious issues.

VII

'There are indeed things that cannot be put into words. They *make themselves manifest*. They are what is mystical.'
(Wittgenstein)[30]

Russell described his philosophy as logical atomism, and the only bool Wittgenstein published in his lifetime, the *Tractatus Logico Philosophicus* (1921) may also be so described. But though there ar similarities between Russell's philosophy at that time and Wittgen stein's, in that both accept that complexes can be analysed int mples, and that the meaning of a simple symbol is the object for hich it stands, there are profound differences. Wittgenstein's logical omism is much more uncompromising. What facts there are is etermined by the atomic facts, so that there are no additional irreducle categories of facts, such as negative facts. There is, moreover, no ace of empiricism in Wittgenstein's work, so that whatever his mples are – and notoriously he does not give a single example – they re not sense data. By contrast, his doctrine of the mystical is much nfluenced by the transcendental idealism of Schopenhauer, which was uite alien to Russell.

Born of a wealthy and artistic Jewish family in Vienna in 1899, Vittgenstein came to the University of Manchester in 1908 to study ngineering. Becoming interested in problems in the philosophy of nathematics, he went to Cambridge in 1912 to work under Russell nd spent five terms there. In 1914 he enlisted in the Austrian army, erved on the Eastern Front, and was decorated several times. During ne war he jotted his philosophical thoughts down in a series of noteooks, three of which have survived, and the *Tractatus*, finished in 918, grew out of these notebooks.

The *Tractatus* consists of a series of numbered propositions, some of vhich are extremely cryptic; for instance, 5.632 says 'The subject oes not belong to the world: rather it is a limit of the world'. It deals, ometimes very briefly with a large number of problems. There is an ccount of the nature of logical propositions; a criticism of Russell's heory of types; a theory of meaning; a metaphysics which makes the xistence of facts, not of things, of central importance; a theory of the ature of philosophy; a discussion of the nature of the soul and of the nystical; and so on.

The ontology of the *Tractatus* is one of facts, as the opening propoitions make clear:

1   The world is all that is the case.
1.1 The world is the totality of facts, not of things.

Moreover, what is a fact is that there exist atomic facts. No example of n atomic fact is given, but we are told that what constitutes an atomic act is a configuration of simple objects, which fit into one another like inks in a chain. The objects themselves, which form the substance of he world, 'are unalterable and subsistent; their configuration is what s changing and unstable' (2.0271). The way in which objects hang

together in a particular atomic fact constitutes its structure; but the
is nothing about any one such fact which can be deduced from a
other, since they are independent of one another (2.061). This la
point effectively precludes a Russellian interpretation of Wittgenstein
atomic facts, since a fact about the colour of a sense datum does n
have the requisite independence from other facts. However, t
puzzling question remains why Wittgenstein thought there must
atomic facts, and, hence, why simple objects, whose configuratio
constitute them, also must exist, since he cannot give an example
either.

It seems that he was convinced of their existence on *a prio*
grounds. Two points combine to form his argument. One is that t
sense of a sentence is something *definite*. The other is that the sense
a sentence, e.g., 'on Wednesday it will rain', is something one ca
grasp in total ignorance of its truth. Now this is possible, Wittgenste
thought, because the sense of a sentence is complex, and is constru
ted out of the senses of its constituent signs. These might, in turn,
complex, but ultimately if we are not to have an infinite regress the
must be simple signs whose sense is not constructed out of that
other signs. These simple signs, names, stand for objects, and t
object *is* the meaning of the name (3.203). The object, moreover, h
to be simple, since if it was not, to attach a name to an object would n
be to give that name a definite sense. 'The demand for the possibilit
of simple signs is the demand for the definiteness of sense' (3.23).

Thus considerations to do with the nature of language at least part
underpin Wittgenstein's metaphysics; and it is perhaps not surprisin
that his theory of language – the so-called picture theory – shou
have attracted more attention than any other part of his book. H
developed both a general theory about the nature of pictures, and
specific theory to the effect that propositions are pictures of a speci
sort. The detailed elaboration of the theory is extremely subtle, b
perhaps the key idea is that the propositional sign is, like a fac
complex, and has a structure. Thus, 'this precedes that' consists of
least two simple signs, or names, arranged in a definite order which
itself plainly significant, since 'this precedes that' does not say th
same as 'that precedes this'. The way in which the names are relate
is the propositional sign's structure; and it also has a form, which
the possibility of its having that structure.

Now a propositional sign can have the same form as a fact, an cause this is so it can present that fact: 'If a fact is to be a picture, it ust have something in common with what it depicts' (2.16). But it is ot only necessary that the propositional sign should have the same rm as the fact it presents, it must also be the case that the names it ontains have been correlated with the objects which constitute the ct. Then the fact that the names belonging to the propositional sign e related in a certain way says that the objects with which they are orrelated are also so related. Hence, the fact that 'this' and 'that' are lated in a certain way in 'this precedes that' says that the object orrelated with 'this' precedes the one correlated with 'that'.

It will be recalled that according to Russell the task of philosophy is classify the logical forms of propositions. But according to the cture theory this is not possible. What a proposition has in common ith what it presents, its form, cannot itself be described – forms nnot be pictured. 'In order to be able to represent logical form, we ould have to be able to station ourselves with propositions some- here outside logic, that is to say outside the world' (4.12). The only ings that can be represented are possible states of affairs, and the ly propositions are the propositions of natural science – 'The tality of true propositions is the whole of natural science . . . ' (4.11).

It follows that there are no philosophical propositions; and this ems to justify a positivist interpretation of the *Tractatus*, a conclu- on which is lent support by some things Wittgenstein says about the ature of philosophy. The fact that our language uses the same word symbolize logically distinct functions produces the most funda- ental confusions of which philosophy is full: 'Most of the proposi- ons and questions to be found in philosophical works are not false but nsensical . . . (and) arise from our failure to understand the logic of ar language' (4.003). A more positive view of philosophy emerges ith the claim that philosophy is not a body of doctrine but an activity hich aims at 'the logical clarification of thought', and there is no ubt that Wittgenstein thought that deep confusions can be dispelled y exhibiting the logical forms of propositions, which are hidden, as it ere, by their surface grammar. However, some extremely cryptic marks suggest that he thought that philosophy did more than erely dispel confusions, for 'It must set limits to what can be ought; and, in doing so, to what cannot be thought' (4.114). But ow is it to do this if, as the picture theory claims, it cannot describe ose limits? Wittgenstein's answer introduces a distinction between

saying and showing to which he attached great importance. Certai
things cannot be *said* which nevertherless can be *shown*. For instanc
according to the picture theory one cannot say what a name, e.g
'John' stands for; nevertheless, that 'John' stands for John is som
thing that shows itself by the use we make of the name.

It seems that many of the most important things from a philosoph
cal point of view can be shown but not said. 'What the solipsist *mea*
is quite correct; only it cannot be *said*, but makes itself manifest. Th
world is *my* world...' (5.62). The self which is of interest to phil
sophy is not part of the world, but its limit. It is like the eye in relatio
to its visual field. When I perceive the contents of my visual field, I d
not perceive the eye which perceives, for all that visual field exists onl
in relation to that eye. Just as one cannot see one's own eye, on
cannot say anything about the metaphysical subject. The latter is n
part of the world any more than the former is part of its visual fiel
Nor can one say anything about what is of value. The only propos
tions are the ones of natural science, so there are no ethical propos
tions. What is of value must lie outside the world, and willing well o
badly cannot change the world. However, it can change its limits, i.e
it can change the metaphysical subject. So though I cannot change th
world, how I act is not a matter of indifference. The conclusion tha
there are no ethical propositions does not imply that matters of valu
are of no importance. Indeed, a positivist interpretation of the *Tract*
tus can be sustained only by ignoring the distinction between what ca
be said and what shown, and the influence of Schopenhauer in th
later propositions.[31]

It is, of course, a consequence of the picture theory that the 'prop
sitions' of the *Tractatus* are nonsensical, for they try to describe th
very relation between language, thought, and reality, which cannot b
described. But if the propositions of the *Tractatus* are nonsense,
perhaps does not follow, if the distinction between saying and showin
is accepted, that nothing has been conveyed, though nothing has bee
said. Certainly, Wittgenstein thought that something was to be learr
from the nonsense of the *Tractatus*:

> 6.54 My propositions serve as elucidations in the following
> way: anyone who understands me eventually recog-
> nises them as nonsensical, when he has used them –
> as steps – to climb up beyond them. (He must, so to

speak, throw away the ladder after he has climbed up it.)

He must transcend these propositions, and then he will see the world aright.

VIII

'Nature is a process.'   (A.N. Whitehead)[32]

The *Tractatus* has often been described as the death of metaphysics. Yet if dead it did not appear to know it. At least three imposing meta-physical systems were developed in works published in the 1920s, those of McTaggart, S. Alexander and A.N. Whitehead. Mention must be made again of Russell who wrestled with problems of mind in *The Analysis of Mind* (1921), and of matter in *The Analysis of Matter* (1927).

Undoubtedly, one thing these works have in common is the fact that they had little influence on British philosophy.[33] Alexander and Whitehead indeed admired each other's work, but their methods and conclusions were very different from those of McTaggart who complained that every chapter of Alexander's *Space Time and Deity* (1920) contained views which no one but Alexander had ever wished to hold. Certainly, it is difficult to think of a greater contrast than that between the personal idealism of McTaggart with its denial of the reality of space and time, and the realism of Alexander which sees space-time as the fundamental 'stuff' of reality. Alexander did not defend the reality of space and that of time, but that of space-time, for he thought that space and time are indissolubly related. The notion of pure time is a myth, as is that of pure space; what is real, and what we experience is the occupation of a place at successive times. Moreover, Alexander argues, the universe is fundamentally constituted by space-time, and a theory of emergent evolution enables us to explain the existence of matter, minds, etc. The essential idea is that activity of a certain degree of complexity at a certain level can result in the emer-gence of a quality not possessed *per se* by things at that level. For example, from very complex physiological processes there emerges consciousness, though consciousness itself is not a property of physical things. So when space-time reaches a certain degree of complex acti-vity such qualities as size and shape emerge (the so-called primary

qualities), and when things having primary qualities interact in certa
complicated ways there emerge such qualities as colour and taste (t
so-called secondary qualities), and so on. It is natural to ask wheth
mind is the culmination of this process, a question which Alexand
discusses in Part IV of *Space Time and Deity*. He concludes that it
not, and that deity is, as it were, the next stage in the process of evo
tion standing to minds as they stand to physiological processes. It
however, difficult to see that Alexander's deity has much to offer t
orthodox Christian, since it is not clear that we have 'got' to him y
or that if we have, that evolution must stop with him.

Whitehead agreed with Alexander about the fundamental impc
tance of space-time: 'It is hardly more than a pardonable exaggeratic
to say that the determination of the meaning of nature reduces its
principally to the discussion of the character of time and the charact
of space' (*The Concept of Nature*, p.33). Space and time ar
Whitehead argued, abstractions from space-time in the sense th
neither is self-subsistent. In line with his view about the fundament
importance of space-time he maintained that events are the ultima
stuff of nature, each event necessarily having both a spatial and
temporal location. This thesis is, he is aware, at odds with t
'ingrained tendency to postulate a substratum for whatever
disclosed in sense awareness, namely to look below what we are awa
of for the substance in the sense of concrete thing' (p.18). Th
tendency Whitehead resolutely opposes. To study nature is to stu
the *whole* of what we observe in perception. Clearly, we do not obser
substrata, which *ex hypothesi* cannot be observed, nor do we obser
ourselves observing. So the study of nature in no way involves that
our thought about it – nature is, as Whitehead put it, 'closed
thought', a conclusion which would seem to place him firmly in t
realist camp.

According to Whitehead what we see when we see, as we would p
it, a physical object, is an event. A physical object is merely a relative
stable factor in an event with which is associated a cluster of sen
objects, e.g., a colour, a smell, a sound, etc. An object is, of course, a
abstraction, since it is only a factor in an event, and cannot exist
isolation. Moreover, since an object can be an ingredient in mar
different events which belong to its neighbourhood, and since i
neighbourhood is indefinite, 'we are driven to admit that each obje
is in some sense ingredient throughout nature' (p.145). Th

torm is in mid-Atlantic, but news of it causes people on land to change their plans to travel tomorrow. At this point, Whitehead's position has a lot in common with that of those idealists who had argued that an object can be understood only in relation to the whole of which it is part.

A marked tendency in Whitehead's philosophy is hostility to atomism, to the view, for instance, that one can regard instants as fundamental and the continuous time which we experience as constructed from them. On the contrary, he argues, that what are fundamental are durations, i.e., periods of time, and that instants have to be constructed out of durations, not *vice versa*. He also opposed atomistic accounts of perception. What we perceive is a complex of related entities; moreover, a perception takes us 'beyond' our perceptual field, since when we perceive we are aware that the entities we perceive are related to ones which we do not perceive but which are significant for us in virtue of their relations to what we do perceive.

One of the fruits of the revolution in philosophy in the seventeenth century which accompanied the scientific revolution was the development of a thoroughgoing atomistic conception of nature. Complexes, whether complex things or complex ideas, were constructed out of simples. Taking into consideration the results of contemporary science, such as the theory of relativity, Whitehead tried to develop a radical alternative to this conception. His work is difficult, partly because of the unfamiliarity of his ideas, and partly because it often presupposes a familiarity with the results of science which many of us lack. It is to be hoped that his relative lack of influence does not stem from these difficulties.

IX

' . . . I am one of those philosophers who have held that the "Common Sense view of the world" is, in certain fundamental features, *wholly* true.'   (G.E. Moore)[34]

Though metaphysics did not die in 1921, the metaphysical systems of the 1920s had little lasting influence, and of the theses about the nature of philosophy propounded during our period the one which has had the most influence, in the short run anyway, is the view that philosophy is concerned with analysis. That one of the main tasks of philosophy is the analysis of propositions was argued by G.E. Moore in his influential, and much misunderstood paper, 'A Defence of Common Sense' (1925). Moore did not, of course, maintain that everything believed by common sense is true, but he did argue that a certain common-sense view of the world is wholly true. Roughly speaking, what Moore claims to know is that many human beings have *known* themselves to have a body, to have been born in the past, to have been spatially related to other things, etc., and that there exist other human beings. Attempts to deny that the common-sense view is true lead, he argues, to various kinds of inconsistency, though the claim that it is not true is not self-contradictory *per se*. By contrast, the view that we do not *know* the common-sense view to be true, though it may in fact be so, is actually self-contradictory. If Moore is right, philosophical theses which imply the falsity of the common-sense view of the world must be false. If, for example, 'time is unreal' implies 'it is false that Moore was born in the past', then since it is not false that he was, it must be false that time is unreal. In other words, Moore tried to break the back of sceptical *a priori* arguments by confronting their conclusions with the common-sense view of the world which he claimed to *know* to be true. Since, if Moore is right, one could not hope to establish *a priori* startling conclusions about the nature of space and time, etc., the question arises whether any task remains for philosophy. Moore's answer was that what was unclear about such propositions as 'Moore was born many years ago', 'there are human bodies', etc., is not their *truth*, but their *analysis.* One task for philosophy, therefore, though Moore never said that it was the only task, is the analysis of propositions.

One thing we might hope to gain by analysis is a full and explicit insight into conceptual distinctions, in the absence of which it is easy to fall into confusion and propound false theories about, for example, the meaning of 'good'. Another motive for practising a different, because linguistic, type of analysis, emerges from the influential work of J. Cook Wilson, Professor of Logic at Oxford from 1889 to 1915. Cook Wilson argued that logic investigates the forms of thought, and that grammar cannot be distinguished from logic on the grounds that it has a fundamentally different subject matter. It too treats of forms of thought, but only in so far as they have become recognized in linguistic forms. Thus though there are aspects of grammar which are of no logical interest, a grammatical inquiry can be of logical interest; the ogician 'deals with thought through its expression'.[35] Moreover, here is in Cook Wilson's view another reason for taking the study of anguage seriously, namely, that our fundamental data when we try to define a term or describe the meaning of a word are facts about usage. When we try to define *justice*, for example, we have to start by considering the sorts of things we call 'just' and those which we do not, and if our definition does not accord with usage, then we can be sure that whatever we have defined it is not *justice*. To the question what on earth we can expect to discover if we regard ourselves as tied down in this way by pre-existent usage, Cook Wilson's answer was 'explicit understanding'. One who can apply the term *justice* correctly in particular cases may still not be able to say what principle is involved in his application; but someone who can define *justice* can.

Linguistic analysis of Cook Wilson's kind is very different from that of Moore's. The former saw language as a source of insight, whereas for the latter it was rather something which gets in the way, often obscuring rather than revealing the form of a proposition. Indeed Moore once complained that language seems to 'have grown up just as if it were expressly designed to mislead philosophers; and I do not know why it should have. Yet, it seems to me there is no doubt that in ever so many cases it has.'[36]

X

'New movements in art are generally accompanied by muddle-headed but enthusiastic attempts to connect them with quite unconnected movements in philosophy.... There are people, for example, who try to connect cubism with Plato.'   (T.E. Hulme)[37]

Hulme's comment should remind us, if a reminder is necessary, of the difficulty of making connections between literary and artistic movements and philosophy. It is not my brief to try to do this, but something must be said about the general character of philosophy during our period. Evidently it is a rich one, which contains a strikingly large number of imaginative and independent thinkers. In a short survey sins of omission are inevitable. These are of two sorts, the omission of any reference to various individuals, e.g., Bosanquet, Ramsey, and Broad, and, arguably worse, the omission of any reference to whole branches of philosophy. The fact that there is no reference to the fast growing area of philosophy of science can, perhaps, be defended on the grounds that it is a specialism.[38] But the reader may well be puzzled by the absence of any reference, *Principia Ethica* apart, to ethical issues. However, Bradley's major ethical writings comfortably antedate 1900, and the work of the Ethical Intuitionists, Carrit, Prichard, and Ross, though undeniably interesting, seems to contribute a relatively minor tributary to the main streams of thought. Their writings lack the passion of Moore's, and had nothing like the same impact. Prichard's view, for instance, was that one cannot justify claims that one ought to perform a certain action. The judgement that one ought to do such and such is 'immediate' and 'self-evident' in the way in which judgements of mathematics are. If this is so, then moral philosophy must, as Prichard alleges, have rested on a mistake, that of trying to give reasons for what cannot be supported by reason. On the other hand, if he is right, there does not seem to be much work left for the moral philosopher. Ross's *The Right and The Good* (1930) was discussed a lot in the 1930s, but the issues which occasioned most philosophical interest at this time were undoubtedly ones in logic, metaphysics, and theory of knowledge. Other branches of philosophy were subsidiary.

In assessing an author's influence it must be remembered that thirty years is a short time in the history of philosophy, and that a philosopher's work may have to wait a very long time indeed to evoke a sympathetic response – Spinoza had to wait for a century. So those who had little influence at the time may yet have their day, and *vice versa*. Even so the enduring importance of Russell's work on logic is beyond doubt. It, together with the work of Frege, revolutionized the subject, and had a profound impact on the nature of philosophy. If one had to pick one outstanding achievement it would be this.

If there was a dominant philosophy at the beginning of the period, this was not so at the end. Clearly, idealism was no longer in possession of the field, and realism of various kinds replaced it. But the kinds were very different. Contrast, for instance, Moore's defence of common sense with Alexander's unabashed metaphysics, or Russell's atomism with Whitehead's thesis that an object is only a factor in an event. One very marked tendency which united Idealists and Realists, was anti-psychologism, and those who believe in subjectivist or relativistic theories of knowledge, truth, or value, will not find this a congenial period. The pragmatist theory of truth with its implication of the mutability of truth had a dusty reception. Bradley, who united with Moore and Russell in attacking it, was as keen as they were to insist on the independence of truth. And Moore's ethical theory, as were those of the Intuitionists, was strikingly objectivist. If there is an echo of this in literature it may be in Michael Bell's suggestion that modernism is distinguished from the idealism of the *symboliste* outlook by its insistence on impersonality, on the objectivity, for example, of Joyce's Dublin, even when viewing the world from an explicitly mental point of view.

Differences between the terms of philosophy and of literary form can be seen in their respective uses of the word 'realism'. T.E. Hulme saw a marked similarity between the realism of Moore and Russell and that of the Continental philosophers Brentano and Husserl. The rise of realism in his view signalled the end of a period of philosophy beginning at the Renaissance which was essentially humanistic, since it saw man as the measure of all things and, as such, the source of values. The orientation of Moore's ethics, and of Husserl's also, was, Hulme thought, profoundly different because of the emphasis placed on the objectivity of values. The growth of abstract art was, Hulme also thought, part of the same tendency; the move away from naturalism paralleling that from humanism. Certainly, since even the form of idealism dominant at the turn of the century had 'dethroned' the self, and was profoundly anti-psychologistic, there is much in what Hulme maintains. And there are parallels with literature too. For it becomes evident that what Hulme is describing as a movement *towards* realism are the same broad cultural shifts already described as a movement *from* realism in modern fiction, etc. As was pointed out in the essay on literature, though the modernist dissatisfaction with realism grew out of doubts about its truth, Woolf and Lawrence in attacking the old form were desiderating a kind of 'super'-realism. And although there are ways in which modern writers, like Yeats and Lawrence, pull against the dominant tendencies of contemporary thought, such as scientism, there are also ways in which they reflect it. Joyce's *Ulysses* is the striking and monumental example of the interplay of the real and the ideal, the objective and the subjective. That book at the same time challenges these categories and evades them, in a way which suggests both their continued importance for thought, and the difficulty in applying them to our experience of the world. Here, perhaps, a point

is reached at which one must acknowledge the separateness of th
artist's forms and of the philosopher's categories.

Notes

1 Sir Joshua Malleson in *Women in Love* and Eliot's 'Mr Apollinax'. Fc
   Russell's account of his friendship with Lawrence see *Portraits fron
   Memory*, London 1956. Cf. also Grover Smith, *T.S. Eliot's Poetry an,
   Plays*, Chicago, Il 1956, p.32.
2 Cf. Patrick Bridgewater, *Nietzsche in Anglosaxony: a study of Nietzsche
   impact on English and American Literature*, Leicester 1972.
3 *Appearance and Reality*, Oxford 1962, p.217.
4 Cf. John Valdimir Price, 'Religion and Ideas' in *The Eighteenth Century,
   ed. P. Rogers, London 1978, pp.131 ff.
5 *Collected Essays*, Oxford 1969, p.216.
6 The thesis, *Knowledge and Experience in the Philosophy of F.H. Bradley
   was published in London in 1964. A convincing account of th
   importance of Bradley for Eliot is to be found in Hugh Kenner's 'Bradley
   in *T.S. Eliot: A Collection of Critical Essays*, ed. Hugh Kenner
   Englewood Cliffs, NJ 1962.
7 Cf. J.W. Raleigh, 'Henry James: the Poetics of Empiricism', *PMLA
   LXVI, 1951, pp.107-23.
8 *Principia Ethica*, Cambridge 1959, p.222.
9 *My Philosophical Development*, London 1959, p.54.
10 *Philosophical Studies*, London 1948, p.27.
11 *Two Memoirs*, London 1949, p.94.
12 ibid., p.81.
13 For an account of Bloomsbury see Quentin Bell, *Bloomsbury*, Londor
   1968. The influence of Moore on Clive Bell is evident in the latter's *Art
   London 1923. An excellent account of this influence will be found ir
   Ruby Meager's 'Clive Bell and Aesthetic Emotion', *British Journal o,
   Aesthetics*, V, 1965, p.123.
14 One amusing story Keynes tells is about the visit of Lawrence tc
   Cambridge in 1914. Apparently Moore sat next to Lawrence at dinner,
   but 'found nothing to say to him'.
15 *The Principle of Mathematics*, London 1964, p.43.
16 ibid., p.8.
17 *My Philosophical Development*, op. cit., p.70.
18 *Contemporary British Philosophy*, vol. I. London, p.262.
19 Cf. Yeats' honorific reference to 'profound McTaggart' in his poem 'A
   Bronze Head'.
20 *Contemporary British Philosophy*, vol. I, op. cit., p.261.
21 *Autobiography, 1872-1914*, London 1967, p.152.

2 ibid.

3 'Mathematical Logic' in *Logic and Knowledge*, ed. R.C. Marsh, London 1956, p.63.

4 'Philosophy of Logical Atomism' in *Logic and Knowledge*, ed. Marsh, op. cit., p.270.

5 ibid., p.178.

6 *Our Knowledge of the Eternal World*, London 1926, p.42.

7 *Mysticism and Logic*, Harmondsworth, Middlx 1954.

8 A good account of Russell's construction is to be found in A.J. Ayer, *Russell*, London 1974, pp.78-82.

9 In *Logic and Knowledge*, ed. Marsh, op. cit.

0 *Tractatus Logico-Philosophicus*, translated by D.F. Pears and B.F. McGuinness, London 1961, 6.522.

1 For the influence of Schopenhauer on Wittgenstein see P.M.S. Hacker, *Insight and Illusion*, Oxford 1972, and A. Phillips Griffiths, 'Wittgenstein, Schopenhauer, and Ethics', in *Knowledge and Necessity*, ed. G. Vesey, London 1970.

2 *The Concept of Nature*, Cambridge 1964, p.53.

3 Though Wyndham Lewis took their ideas very seriously in *Time and Western Man*, London 1927. See p.59 of the essay on literature in this volume.

4 'A Defence of Common Sense' in *Philosophical Papers*, London 1959.

5 *Statement and Inference*, Oxford 1969, p.401.

6 *Philosophical Studies*, op. cit., p.217.

7 *Speculations*, London 1949, p.75.

8 A good account of the impact of science during the period is A.R. Ubblehode's 'Science' in *Edwardian England 1900-14*, ed. S. Nowell Smith, Oxford 1964.

Select bibliography

1 Ayer, A.J. *Russell*, London 1974.

2 Ayer, A.J. *et al. The Revolution in Philosophy*, London 1956.

3 Kenny, A. *Wittgenstein*, Harmondsworth, Middlx 1975.

4 Passmore, J.A. *Hundred Years of Philosophy*, Harmondsworth, Middlx 1970.

5 Pears, D.F. *Wittgenstein*, London 1970.

6 Quinton, A. 'Thought' in *Edwardian England 1900-14*, ed. S. Nowell Smith, Oxford 1964.

7 Russell, B. *My Philosophical Development*, London 1959.
——— *Portraits From Memory, and Other Essays*, London 1956.
——— *Autobiography*, Vols I and II, London 1967/8.

8 Warnock, G.J. *English Philosophy Since 1900*, Oxford 1969.

9 Wollheim, R. *F.H. Bradley*, Harmondsworth, Middlx 1959.

4 Myth and modern literature

CRISTOPHER NASH

Historical perspective

Myth has always had a privileged place in literature, whether it is
Beowulf, Milton, Pope and Tennyson we have in mind or Yeats, Eliot
Joyce and Lawrence.

Yet something quite different seems to be happening when, in the
nineteenth century, European artists with backgrounds and concerns
as divergent as those of Wagner and Gauguin begin to take up the
cause of what they think to be 'primitive thought', and men of letters
as far afield as H.G. Wells, Anatole France, Spengler, Freud, Bergson,
Jung and Wittgenstein pay special tribute – by means of extravagant
praise and/or by the lavish exercise of his ideas – to James Frazer's
The Golden Bough. And when, in the following decades, a T.S. Eliot
declares that 'the mythical method' can make 'the modern world
possible for art'. In order to understand how this shift in perspective
came about, it will pay to look back to earlier generations and their
developing attitudes towards the whole concept of myth.

'Civilized man' has tended to regard his myths according to one or
the other of two quite distinct overviews. These do coincide with
certain basic movements of ideas, yet they are not strictly tied to
specific historical periods; they have existed side by side as far back as
records go (Plato beside Aristotle, Pico beside Copernicus, Vico beside
Voltaire, Cassirer beside Bidney). And the first quarter of this century
in English literature is one of those moments in which circumstances
and hitherto divergent ideologies seem to combine under the cover of
one traditional but now revitalized mythologem – the evolutionary

ccount of existence – with intriguing and memorable consequences
or modern literature.

What are myths, taken on average, *about*? This is the question
osed by the first overview, which is fundamentally realistic (or at least
ational-materialistic) in outlook. Here, *myths* are regarded in terms of
heir contents, and are considered at bottom to be bodies of state-
nents, propositions; myths are either directly representational or alle-
orical narratives, whose meanings derive from their relationship to
natters of fact about the material universe.

What does myth *do*? how does myth *work*?, asks the second view.
Here, *myth* is a mode, a form, of thinking. It is a process – more often
han not non-rational – whose importance derives from its relation-
hip to the mind of God or to the mind of man himself, and whose
unction is basically symbolic and idealistic.

The realists' overview   In its struggle to work out some total concep-
ion of the universe, one of the first efforts of Western philosophy was
o come to grips with traditional mythology. Yet the Greek rational-
sts were not primarily motivated by any urge to attack mythology as a
rocess, so much as to provide a critique of mythology as a record of
he behaviour of the gods. How could the myths as portrayed by
Homer and Hesiod be accurate, if they described the gods as so vindic-
ive, jealous, ignorant, unjust and immoral? This will prove to be a
attern throughout history: myths come under fire first and foremost
t those points where they fail to reinforce some currently received set
f cultural values. Discussions of mythology all have buried within
hem this pragmatic concern, and it will shape all interpretations of
nyths' origins and functions. What varies among the realists'
pproaches to the matter is the area of human experience to which
nyth is taken to apply.[1]

In the *euhemerist* view (familiar to early modern writers through
he thought of Herbert Spencer and given literary expression by,
mong others, Robert Graves), myths are regarded as attempts at
history, in the course of which the confused memory and imagination
f early peoples have transfigured human leaders into 'gods' and the
ecord of their acts into theology.

Under the heading of *allegory*, on the other hand, realists have likewise described a variety of processes by which the originators of myths
perhaps an élite caste of priests or sages), having certain abstract

doctrinal concepts in mind, deliberately devised myths as metaphors t render these more immediately palpable to the laity. Myths migl thus be regarded as products of some 'cognitional' or 'aetiologica' approach to (an effort to discover and explain the causes underlying the natural universe. From the Sophists onwards, myth and languag itself were to be described as inextricably linked, the etymology (gods' names revealing their original identity with the physical object and forces which they had come figuratively to represent. Or eac cluster of myths might be meant to 'charter' some particular socia religious system and to promulgate its codes. For Philo Judaeus or fc St Augustine, for example, the characters and legends transmitted i the Bible might be seen as living laws or as metaphors representin states of the soul and exemplifying types of moral conduct. Philo's an Augustine's reverent exegetic approach to narrative, first directe backward toward mythology, came in fact to provide the classic mod both for the parabolic construction of literary works throughout th Middle Ages and the Renaissance (from *The Romance of the Rose* and *The Divine Comedy* to *The Faerie Queen, Paradise Lost* an *Pilgrim's Progress*) and for criticisms's own interpretive procedures i its response to literature.

It is peculiarly by their insistence on preserving the 'heathen myths of each preceding social order, and by treating them to thi pragmatic process of allegorical interpretation, that successive Nea Eastern and Western cultures have managed both to assimilate and t override the visions of their predecessors. By its reconstitutive, meta phorical approach to story, Christianity was able at will to dissolve o reconstrue in each Judaic or Hellenic myth whatever of its initia import may have proved doctrinally offensive.

Similarly, in later centuries, seeking to place what remained o 'natural religion' on a more solid philosophical footing, both Christia apologists and deists of the Enlightenment joined in the reassessmen of Judeo-Christian mythology. For a Voltaire, the Biblical narrativ turns out to be 'pure myth' in the sense of the word which is t become part of the popular idiom for many succeeding generations Opposed to reason, an insult to the majesty of Deity, rooted in delu sion and superstition, mythology's improbable propositions are to b seen as the source of war and of endless social injustice.

Yet at close range the Enlightenment reveals a striking and crucia ambivalence. This appears in the extraordinary passion with whicl

Iobbes, Spinoza and Bayle dramatize the fear and violence they see ehind the spawning of myths by the savage world; and in Hume's ondemnation not merely of the ignorant savage who is said to have reated mythology but of the rationalists and 'natural-religionists' vho rise up to destroy it. A similar ambivalence colours Voltaire's iscourse. He seems unable to decide whether to use the mythological asis of religion as an argument against it or for it; everywhere reliions divide men – yet everywhere men seem to prize the same eligious practices and the same myths. The eighteenth-century ationalist whose aim it is to determine the truth or falsity of myths' iteral *contents* seems committed to adopting an either/or stance vhich mythology itself appears ill-adapted to sustain. It is in this erplexed quality of their denunciation of it that the followers of both Voltaire and Hume leave open the door for myth's most extravagent levotees: those nineteenth-century post-Kantian and romantic dealists whose central response will be to propose that, instead, nyth's recalcitrance at the hands of reason only reveals that one must earn to think in 'a different way', the way that 'myth thinks'.

But rational materialism itself was to come up with yet another nswer. The either/or model became less and less appealing as the cientific method gained sway. By the second quarter of the nineteenth entury, writers like the German K.O. Müller, perhaps the preminent classicist of his time, had come to insist that myths were a ultural fact and must be studied as such and, in his *Introduction to a cientific System of Mythology* (1825)[2], he proposed to glean and efine what was most reasonable in the various extant rationalist heories. Philology and myth were to him the indispensable keys to .ny understanding of classical civilization, and myths were agglomeate products of euhemeristic, aetiological, and allegorical motifs; they rose out of religious worship as one of the two means available to the Greeks of explaining that part of human behaviour associated with vorship and the ideas associated with deity; 'the mythus relates an ction . . . the symbol renders it visible to the sense'. Here is one germ f the later British ritualist concept of myth's origins.

But it is F. Max Müller (1823-1900) who, in a specialized extension of this methodology, dominates English thought about myth in he second half of the nineteenth century. Initiating a school of comparative mythology' with Oxford as his base, he proclaims that nyth studies *are* in fact philological studies. He starts with the realists' traditional problem, 'how could the civilized Greeks tell such barba rous stories about their gods?' In a recombination and intensificatio of the more materialist postulates to be found in the Greek rationalists in Fontenelle, Vico and Heyne, Müller explains that in the mytho poeic age when the Aryan mothertongue was 'invented', men cam to ascribe to their deeper feelings the words they commonly used fo the profound concrete experiences with which nature surrounde them. At the centre of nature was the sun (the first wonder, the firs beginning of all reflection, all thought, all philosophy, all religion), an at the core of Western language lay an array of Aryan proper noun and epithets expressing the power of the sun in human affairs. As th family of Indo-European languages branched and spread, the form c the old words decayed and their original meanings were forgotten Stories emerged out of the proliferation of explanatory signification assigned to them.[3] Thus an initial impulse behind all mythology wa solar worship, and myths were the product of 'the disease o language'. The scene was set for controversy. The less Müller' theories accorded with contemporary poets' (and certain new scien tists') ideas of human nature, the more prestige they seemed at th time to gain with the academic establishment of myth-scholars; Quee Victoria sent Müller's widow a personal telegram when he died i 1900, the year with which our period begins.

The idealists' overview   In Plato's *The Laws*, one speaker says t another, 'God is the real ruler of men of enlightenment'. 'But who i this God?' says the other. 'Ah, there for a little', says the first, wh appears in many respects to speak for Plato himself, 'we must mak use of Myth.' And he proceeds, not to give a logical, conceptua description of this God, but to tell the *story* of a Golden Age, in whic men were governed not by earthly rulers but by a race of divinities Plato's work persistently embodies this tension between rationa philosophy and some form of 'thinking' through narrative images. A crucial moments in *The Dialogues* he introduces fables not simply t illustrate what he has already said in discursive terms but in fact t carry the reader's imaginative perception of the idea several steps further; the 'allegory of the cave' is a famous example.

Indeed, Plato personally distinguishes between myth and allegory in a way that roundly contradicts the interchangeable usage of the realists, and that will be central to the history of discussions o mythology. Allegory is for him a fictional narrative deliberately invented for its metaphorical message, and is *not* intended to be taken literally as 'truth'. Myth is a traditional, and not a necessarily fictitious, narrative which purports to embody the truth about the relations between the gods and men. While he excludes 'myth-makers' from his ideal state, unlike Aristotle and the rationalists he explicitly argues for the retention of as much of the mythology of Homer as he thinks is compatible with sound reason and morality. For myth calls upon a higher kind of consciousness that remains outside logic. In order to attain that plane, to penetrate into the realm of Idea behind sensory reality, one must cultivate a 'transcendental' sensibility. Myth works as an instrument to that end because it expresses in us the primeval condition, it restores in us our intuition of that divine Golden Age. The principle of correspondence implicit in this conception, as it is applied by Neo-Platonists ('Everything is in everything, but in each thing appropriately to its nature' – each aspect of reality contains within it its spiritual, ideal counterpart), will be vital to the idealist line of thinking about mythology and will prove quintessential to the *symboliste* and modernist literary modes.

In Francis Bacon, and in Bernard Fontenelle (1657-1757), a Frenchman writing a century after Bacon yet in many respects still well in advance of his time, we find the historical crystallization of two notions of prime importance. *First*, that myth may be the product of a special kind of mentality which has since been displaced and abandoned. To Bacon, the sin of traditional philosophy has been its desire to impose its own view upon reality, rather than to discover the imprint of God as it is manifested in the array of images by which ancient man reveals his wisdom to us; to Fontenelle, it is not the wisdom but the foolishness – the savage, childish wonder and terror – behind the ancients' way of thinking that is the source of myths. And *second*, that human minds are universally of the same nature. To Fontenelle, the only effective difference between the mythology of the ancients, the mythology of the natives living in America in his own time, and the physics of his late seventeenth-century European contemporaries was that those in the third group had the advantage of more accurate premises. From this time onward (with the dissolution of the absolute authority of Christian orthodoxy in the West), students of mythology were to seize upon the procedure of considering once purportedly spiritual or otherwise 'revealed' experiences as phenomena of social psychology, and of correlating the peculiar narrative format of 'the wisdom of the ancients' with the thought processes of contemporary 'primitive man'.

The influence on literary thought of Fontenelle's own complex and brilliant Neapolitan contemporary, Giambattista Vico (1668-1744) has recently become a favourite theme among the critics and biographers of writers as widely divergent as Goethe and James Joyce. Vico's 'new science' proposes a process by which man, seeking to discover himself, is to study not simply nature but history – not the objective world but the story of man making himself, man recreating his own spirit and subjective being. The key to this effort is poetry, and the key to poetry is myth. Man must, Vico says, 'descend' into the 'vast imaginations' of his own beginnings, and myth is a principal medium for the expression of the primeval and universal in human experience, and thereby for the direction of human consciousness. Myth is a story, not a statement. It seems false only when we try to extend it as an *idea* into other realms. Myth and idea are two distinct attitudes of human consciousness toward truth. Mythology *is* the seed-bed of idea – but as idea emerges, myth disintegrates. Philosophy, reflection and criticism, for example, are based on ideas; to the degree that they are applied to myth, adding to our conception of it 'physical, moral, metaphysical or other scientific interpretations', they falsify and dissolve it. The mythic image was thus, according to Vico, originally the material of a 'poetic logic' by which the spirit made itself present to itself. Metaphysics refers fundamentally not to nature but to the human mind itself. The world reflected in history is real because it is the human spirit itself which in-forms it.

Hence, myth as narrative is essential to human existence because it puts the diverse character-traits of mankind into a poetic time-frame. The narrative of myth is the history of the dynamics and evolution of the mind. In fact, Vico sees progressive liberation of the mind as both the process and the prize that come of man's critique of all myths. In this sense, the development of language from the vocabulary of the fables into the reflective terms of the philosophical sciences is a necessary process in the evolution of man's spirit.

English literature did not have to wait for Coleridge's now famous recitation of German romantic philosophy (with its special interest in Vico) before it could take up the idealist conception of 'the mythic vision'. Largely thanks to modernist criticism, we now perceive the

npact upon Anglo-American writing – through William Blake (and
3lake's deliberate attempt to create a total mythological cosmogonic
system'), Keats, Emerson and the Transcendentalists, Balzac,
3audelaire and the *Symbolistes* – of the illuminist ideology of
mmanuel Swedenborg (1688-1772). The natural and spiritual world
3gether 'form the Divine Being', says Swedenborg. 'All things
vhich exist in nature, from the least to the greatest, are correspon-
ences.' 'The Union of heaven with the world is effected by corres-
ondences.' Derived from Swedenborg by way of Baudelaire, this
oncept of the simultaneity and spontaneity of the intuition of both
naterial and transcendent truth through the symbol is the doctrinal
entre of Modernists' and Surrealists' technical preoccupation with
nyth. Unfortunately, Swedenborg's own practical explication of the
mport of specific 'correspondences', carrying with it the naiveté
ssential to certain stages of mystical experience, rings hollow to the
nodern ear, and it remains for nineteenth-century Continental
omantic theory to lend to the idealist position something of the air of
ritical sophistication so often sought by intellectual moderns.

A peculiarity, in fact, of the 'Enlightenment phase' in European
iterature was the conviction among philosophers and academicians that
1uman culture could and must be studied, and ultimately apprehended,
is a totality; and myth joined philosophy, religion, and art as one of the
rincipal thoroughfares to that understanding. For J.G. Herder
1744-1803), primitive and enlightened mankind are one; mythic
ruth is whole, and myth's meaning is not to be referred to concepts
utside itself. In an idea developed by Herder, Goethe (1749-1832) and
K.P. Moritz (1756-93) and that will be fundamental to Nietzsche as
vell as to D.H. Lawrence, myth (like religious music and dance) is the
:ommunal expression not of a morality but of the primal, ecstatic
:nergies of nature acting in the people, the Volk. The gods are not moral
:ssences but aspects of the inchoate organic force of life as it strives
:reatively towards universal fulfillment and wholeness in man. Myth
s – an elemental axiom in the idealist overview – a *symbolic* mode, in
he language of the imagination, and (as Schleiermacher will develop the
natter) is to be understood hermeneutically, not analytically. That is to
say, myth is not true only insofar as it is logically translatable into a
:ational statement as allegory may be, but rather it is true and active in
tself, as a whole, in its own terms; to apprehend its sense and wisdom,
)ne must enter into the spirit of those who gave birth to it.

Thus for A.W. Schlegel (1767-1845), 'art is thinking in images' 'poetry is speculation by imagination', and the poet is a myth-maker Myth is the system of symbols which 'possess a reality independent c concept', and by which the imagination 'plunges us into the univers ...in a magic realm of eternal metamorphoses, where nothing exist in isolation, but everything rises out of everything by a most marvel lous creation'. What is called the Enlightenment was rather a Darken ing, because it meant the extinction of the natural, primal myth iridescent inner light of man. August Schlegel and his brothe Friedrich (1772-1829) join with Herder and Klopstock in what is t become one of the shibboleths of modern thinking, the call for a return not only to Rousseau's Nature, but to feeling (which was the basis o thought, as Fichte would have it) and to the irrational unconscious a the mother-soil of the folk imagination, of human creativity, and o myth as their ultimate embodiment. The polemicists will violently quarrel as to whether a new myth can be found or created: has the indi vidual the power to invent myth or to capture its energies afresh through the unconscious? Or does man's only hope lie – as Jakob and Wilhelm Grimm believe – in the renovation of the anonymous collec tive lore of the ancients (which it becomes the self-appointed task o the Grimm brothers and other philologists to restore to their culture)?

In the philosophy of F.W.J. Schelling (1775-1854) the cult of myth attains an apotheosis which it has never since regained. For Schelling ideas are the subject-matter of philosophy; the matter of art and o myth is the gods and the Absolute, and these are accessible through imagination alone. Being a system of symbols, myth – unlike allegory (the particular signifying the general) and unlike abstract thought (where the general signifies the particular) – is completely 'indifferent', and provides in its self-contained world a union o general and particular, through a function which in psychological terms Lévy-Bruhl will introduce into common currency as a *partici- pation mystique*. Hence Venus *is* beauty. Arising not from strictly human invention but out of a supra-historical sphere which is the source of consciousness itself, myth's distinctive reality exercises prodigious power upon consciousness which historical or other rational analysis would altogether vitiate. Polytheistic mythology, then, was a manifestation of the indispensable process of cleavage, of gradual discrimination by which primitive consciousness was to come to perceive the objective actuality, the reality of God, by distinguishing

God from human consciousness itself and by observing the otherness, the distinctiveness, of God's many aspects. So this Janus thing, myth, like Nature, is at once an essential factor in, and a narrative revelation of, the self-development of the Absolute. An embodiment simultaneously of both divine and human consciousness, it refers at once to both spiritual and psychological truth. And its ultimate effect is to restore to man once again his wholeness and oneness with the primal, undivided, infinite cosmos. Schelling and the poets Hölderlin and Novalis will go on to argue that the poet-as-priest can create a new mythology for modern man.

*

We can now characterize more precisely the period in ·question. Between 1900 and 1930 there is an impulse toward synthesis, or at least some deeper mutual accommodation, of these two traditionally antagonistic modes of thought respecting myth, the realist and the idealist. Moreover, there is an agreement between myth-scholars and artists, for one final, climactic moment before they indefinitely part company, to consider the language of literature as a possible meeting ground.

Many of those who make up the background of this literary event were practitioners of two newly emergent 'scientific' disciplines, anthropology and psychology. The psychologist C.G. Jung subtitled his seminal work, *Psychology of the Unconscious* (1912)[4], 'a contribution to the history of the evolution of thought'. And in the following year, in his final edition of *The Golden Bough*, the anthropologist J.G. Frazer said of this his *magnum opus*: 'While nominally investigating a particular problem of ancient mythology, I have really been discussing questions of more general interest which concern the gradual evolution of human thought from savagery to civilisation.' The fact is that with the coming of the twentieth century, the tendency in the new 'human sciences' will be increasingly to consider myths as formal manifestations of the nature of man's thought itself — of mankind as a collective entity (as regarded by anthropologists) and of men as individuals (the subject of psychologists). For this brief phase a connection seems to have been found by which the *stories*, the *content*, of myths (that bugbear of the realists), may be seen to be organized according to a principle of *form* and *process* for which both eighteenth-century rationalism and romantic idealism contributed the philosophical groundwork. The restored eidolon of the evolution of man, itself a primal myth but at last apparently accredited by biological empiricism, now falls like a gift from the gods into the laps of the mythologists on both sides.

Modern syntheses

Frazer and ritual theory   Three years after Max Müller published in England his first startling essay on the linguistic sources of mythology (1856), Darwin's *Origin of Species* appeared. In 1900, largely owing to the continued efforts of Andrew Lang in support of a new, Darwinian approach to mythology studies, the solar theory died with Müller. The vital link and turning-point had been the work of E.B. Tylor (1832-1917).[5]

For Tylor, out of Darwin's conception of biological evolution there logically came the hypothesis of the evolution of human thought. All men evolved according to the same series of steps. The cultural history of man, Tylor suggested, must have followed a uniform pattern of development everywhere from savagery to civilization. Hence wherever the same behaviour and customs appeared, the same stage of evolution must be represented. The linchpin of Tylor's (and most future ethnological) explanations of the origins of mythology was the idea of a special kind of mentality, 'primitive mentality'. Primitives, says Tylor, attribute soul or spirit to all living things and to 'inanimate' objects. This 'animistic' proclivity is a rudimentary logical theory about things; religion has its genesis in the activity by which man attempted to establish a relationship with matter and events outside himself, an activity 'rising at its highest pitch to personification'. Myth was produced by men's failure to distinguish between subjective and objective data of experience, their consequent confusion of images and words with objective reality, and their urge to conceive their wonder and their evanescent abstract ideas in terms of concrete shapes and material incidents. Perhaps swayed by the classicist K.O. Müller, as well as by eighteenth-century theories (such as R.P. Knight's sex-orientated version) of the sources of mythology and religion in ritual, and soon endorsed by the biblical scholar W. Robertson Smith,[6] the proto-anthropologist Tylor argues that mythology is based on rites, 'a fiction devised to explain an old custom, of which the real meaning and origin had been forgotten'. Just as the evolutionary course of custom s 'to dwindle from solemn ritual into mere pageant and pastime', so myths linger as 'survivals' in the form of fairy-tales.

Here lay the initial impulse behind ethnology and the foundation, by Lang (1844-1912) and others, in 1878, of the Folk-Lore Society. Since 1872 in *The Birth of Tragedy*, Nietzsche (after Goethe and Moritz) had insisted that through an awareness of myth and the tension embodied in the Apollonian/Dionysian struggle, we might recover again the spirit of those forgotten rites – once found in music, dance and tragedy – which gave power and purpose to the lives of the ancients. But in fact, Lang insists, 'relics', 'survivals' of primitive belief and custom are there to be discovered in today's peasant, folk, and 'savage' ritual behaviour. Therefore, he says, if we leave behind our cumbersome philological speculations and look directly to the folk material in the living world around us, we shall – as Fontenelle long before suggested – understand classic myth.

With the Folklorists locked in public battle with the Comparative Philologists, J.G. Frazer (1954-1941) found himself free in the privacy of his study to devote three decades to the work which Lang's version of Tylor had thus called for. In the three editions of *The Golden Bough* with its sequel, *Aftermath*,[7] setting out modestly 'to explain the remarkable rule which regulated the succession to the priesthood of Diana at Aricia' in classical mythology, Frazer ended by producing a monumental encyclopedia of mythical motifs and 'primitive' and 'folk' customs, integrated into an overriding vision of the evolution of human culture through three socio-economic (hunting, pastoral, and agricultural) and psychological (magic-orientated, religion-orientated, and scientific) stages, from the dawn of pre-history to the Edwardian present. Tylor and Frazer argue that for primitive man the welfare of the tribe is supposed to depend on the performance of magical rites, and the magician rises to a position of influence and repute and may readily acquire the rank and authority of a chief or king. The tribe's existence depends on the vigour of its priest-king, whose individual ascendance and demise expresses both the yearly cycle of nature and the pattern-of-being of the deity who in society's religious phase is believed to rule both nature and man. Arising variably out of etiological speculation, euhemerist historiography, fetishism, mimicry of natural events, and allegorical thinking, myth is always a by-product of man's way of dramatizing and ceremonializing the pragmatics of Darwinian survival.

Given its new lease of life by the evolutionist reconstruction provided by men like Tylor, the ancient hypothesis of a special primitive mentality was eagerly adopted abroad. Following Durkheim (with his suggestion of the purely social origins and nature of religious feeling) Arnold van Gennep (1873-1957) and Lucien Lévy-Bruhl (1857-1939) were in turn to have a real share in the influence of the school of Frazer and Jung on future thought. In *Rites of Passage* (1909) van Gennep portrayed the individual in primitive society as a transient passing through certain successive life-stages, each of which was itself likened to a threshold of death and rebirth, and during which – with the vital assistance of certain communal ceremonies designed to secure the safe transition (passage) for him – man and nature joined in 'the great rhythms of the universe'. Rites hence celebrated birth, puberty, initiation, purification, betrothal, marriage, pregnancy, paternity, vocation, and death, and myths themselves might be seen by implication as reiterations of these and of the great overriding triadic pattern of the phases of 'separation', of 'margin' (in which the individual moves in darkness and anonymity between two worlds) and of 'attainment'. Meanwhile, Lévy-Bruhl[8] held that the thought patterns of primitives in groups (Durkheim's *représentations collectives*), having a special dynamic relationship with the whole of nature, followed an a-logical 'law of participation' which was indifferent to the notions of discrete entities, categories, identity and contradiction which are fundamental to our way of thinking. The realms of empirical knowledge and of magic were here indistinguishable, and myth was the product of a natural species of logic according to which all things flowed into and partook of the qualities of other things, so that, for example, the Brazilian tribe declaring themselves to be red parakeets were not simply borrowing a name or claiming a similarity but were asserting an actual felt identity with the red parakeets.

But it is to the famed Cambridge School of Anthropology's application of the ritualist interpretations of mythology derived from Tylor, Robertson Smith and Frazer that modern English literature most directly owes its repeated recourse to myth as poetic matter and rationale. In 1912,[9] Andrew Lang took with him to the grave the last traces of the Victorian Philologist/Folklorist quarrel over mythology, and the arguments that were to occupy English literary attention for the next twenty years where myth was concerned were simultaneously set in train with the publication of the first half of Freud's

Totem and Taboo, Jung's *Psychology of the Unconscious*, F.M. Cornford's *From Religion to Philosophy* and Jane Harrison's *Themis*. Harrison's book – which reports the first detailed evidence offered by Cornford, Gilbert Murray, A.B. Cook and Harrison for a ritual view of myth – is followed in 1914 by the first volume of Cook's massive encyclopedia of ritualist explications of classical figures, and Murray's lecture, 'Hamlet and Orestes, a Study in Traditional Types', opening the way from the classical context into the vast modern literary labyrinth of poetic constructions and critical reconstructions based on the ritual concept. Following Frazer and setting the model for her colleagues in the Cambridge School of Anthropology, all of whom were in fact not anthropologists but classical scholars, Jane Harrison proposed that myth always arises out of ritual. Traditional Greek verbal usage, she argues, clearly discloses that myth is 'the spoken correlative of the acted rite, the thing done'; myth is the 'things said over a ritual act'. 'The myth is not at first aetiological, it does not give a reason; it is representative, another form of utterance, of expression. When the emotion that started the ritual has died down and the ritual though hallowed by tradition seems unmeaning, a reason is sought in the myth and it is regarded as aetiological.' Working alongside Harrison, Cornford put forward a remarkably inventive reconstruction of the evolution of human thought according to which religion, law, philosophy, and scientific procedure all flowed from 'mythical cosmogony' and primitive man's ritualized collective functions. By 1920 Jessie L. Weston had published *From Ritual to Romance*. Unravelling in 'impenitently' Cambridge-Frazerian terms for literary minds the themes of the task of the hero, the freeing of the waters, the sword dance, the medicine man, the fisher king, the waste land, and so forth, Weston argues that the Grail romances – and, by extension, all Quest stories – were 'the fragmentary record of the secret ritual of a Fertility cult'. Her book is as much indebted now to Yeats, Hart Crane and Eliot for its renown as they were in their day to it for its imagery and narrative premises, and it is perhaps the only volume of poetic criticism in recent times to become the literal text of some of the most important poetry of a subsequent generation.[10]

Jung and archetype theory   In 1937 Lord Raglan would publish *The Hero*, an immensely popular attempt to show that the lives of the world's major mythological heroes fit a single ritualist narrative

pattern. More than one fictionalist would actually go so far as to char
his hero's exploits in terms of Raglan's tidy schema. But in 1909 i
Germany there had already appeared a book summarizing the appa
rently universally recurrent pattern of events in the lives of mytho
logical heroes. The summary is remarkably like Raglan's; the
interpretation is radically different. The book was Otto Rank's *The*
Myth of the Birth of the Hero. To Rank (1884-1939), a psychologist
failures to overcome the trauma of birth were the source of man'
neuroses, and myth was 'a dream of the masses of the people' in which
the effects of this trauma were revealed. The eternal myth of mankin
– and of the hero – was the story of man's deprivation of the 'pleasur
able primal situation in the womb' by the cataclysmic separation
which is birth, and of men's longing to restore the intrauterine condi
tion, to return to that Eden from which their birth had cast them out

For Rank, for Karl Abraham (who in the same year published his
Dreams and Myths), for Jane Harrison by 1921, and, to a great
extent, for C.G. Jung, the man to whom they all looked for much o
their initial inspiration, Sigmund Freud (1856-1939), was right when
he had said in 1908 that although 'the study of constructions of folk-
psychology . . . is far from complete . . . it seems extremely probable
that myths . . . are the distorted vestiges of the wish-phantasies of
whole nations – the age-long dreams of young humanity'. In his use of
the terms translated here as 'vestiges' and 'young humanity', we can
immediately recognize Freud's subscription to the evolutionary model
of human thought advanced by Tylor. Freud's one crucial work specifically devoted to myth, *Totem and Taboo*, was written to counter
Jung's developing ideology, and is built especially upon the evidence
and fundamental 'constructions of folk-psychology' of Frazer and
what Freud with open adulation calls 'Frazer's great book'.[11] The
1912 exchange represented in *Totem and Taboo* and Jung's *Psycho-*
logy of the Unconscious was the cause of the legendary and permanent
rupture between Freud and Jung, and their conflicting views regarding the forces underlying myth as well as dream are at the heart of the
matter.

Since to Freud the 'subconscious' is little more than a repository of
personal biographical material repressed from the consciousness of the
individual, symbols are merely signs or allegories meant to conceal
such otherwise disruptive psychic contents. For Jung, as we shall see,
the unconscious has its own autonomous dynamics, in which collective,

supra-personal matter plays an animated part, and which it is the function of symbols to reveal, to bring to consciousness. So while Jung believes in promoting the active formation of myth and symbols as a source of psychic growth for the group and for the individual, Freud (taking as his basis the evidence of contemporary neurotic behaviour) considers it the proper aim of both dream- and myth-interpretation to empty symbols of their content and power by a deliberately retrogressive process of reductive analysis. Mankind's efforts to suppress those anti-social, 'heedless sexual and primitive motives' inherent in the 'primal horde' – which was the original human condition – was the source not only of communal organization, moral restrictions, and religion, but also of myth, whose function was (via the 'substitutive gratification' of fantasy) to release repressed impulses through safe and socially productive channels. All myths are thus more or less disguised, regressive re-presentations of the primary 'Oedipal' story, made up principally of directly translatable 'symbols' standing as mechanical substitutes ('sharp weapons . . . stand for the male genital', etc.) for socially unacceptable sex-linked psychological relations and objects bearing on that 'family romance'.[12] The critical word here is 'regressive'. Myth, for Freud and his circle, is 'a fragment preserved from the infantile psychic life of the race, and dreams are the myths of the individual'. The symmetry of this German romantic notion has endeared it to modern students of myth ever since. In it lie the seeds of Jung's disillusionment with Freud and of one of Jung's own most fertile contributions to modern imaginative thought.

To C.G. Jung (1875-1961) 'one must certainly put a large question-mark after the assertion that myths spring from the "infantile" psychic life of the race'. Far from being neurotically regressive, men's myths provide them with a profoundly natural, potentially healthful, indeed a *necessary* connection with their past, a connection whose process is best expressed in terms of a further great Darwinian poetic concept which lurks within all that Jung comes to say about human mental life: ontogeny recapitulates phylogeny. The development of the individual is a re-enactment of the evolution of the species. The history of human thought – figured forth for us in the great monomyth which is the aggregate of human mythology – is the story of the emergence of consciousness out of the dark, undifferentiated sea or cave or womb of man's original unconscious state. Similarly, then, the biography of the individual is the drama of the progress of his psyche toward a state of wholeness ('individuation') in which the forces of the unconscious are to find harmony in and with the rational light of his consciousness. 'That seems to be man's metaphysical task – which he cannot accomplish without "mythologising". Myth is the natural and indispensable intermediate stage between unconscious and conscious cognition.'

Vital to this process is Jung's notion of the archetypes, a conception formed through the influence of Durkheim, Lévy-Bruhl, and Adolf Bastian[13], and remarkable for the interpenetration it reveals of Platonic and German idealism with Darwinian evolutionism. Unless we scientists are to claim that mind is implanted in each of us at the last moment by some purely supernatural force, Jung argues, the logic of genetics must entail that the individual inherits from preceding generations not only his physiological but his psychological structures. And in fact, the observation of art, custom, myths, dreams, fantasies, and patients' delusions reveals the existence of archetypes, inherited 'primordial images' 'living dispositions, ideas in the Platonic sense', which are 'more or less the same everywhere and in all individuals ... identical in all men'. Within the unconscious of each individual is a reservoir of 'archetypal personalities' disclosing 'manifold and unmistakable connections with mythological ideas'. Here are 'archaic strata' of situational predispositions deriving from 'the mind of our unknown ancestors, their way of thinking and feeling, their way of experiencing life and the world, gods and men', and which have become part of 'that phylogenetic substratum which I have called the collective unconscious'. The life of the psyche of the individual is rendered substantial by the progressive emergence, differentiation and interplay of these archetypal figures and situations performing dynamically as symbols in precisely the sense intended by Goethe, Moritz and Schleiermacher.[14] The whole works dialectically toward integration through a process of psychic transformation in a manner modelled neatly on Schelling's vision of the operation of myth in the development of a culture's spiritual awareness and its ultimate transcendent union with the Absolute.

Rite and dogma, then, 'were the dams and walls to keep back the dangers of the unconscious'. For 'the psyche contains all the images that have ever given rise to myths', which are

> first and foremost psychic phenomena that reveal the nature
> of the soul. ... Primitive man is not much interested in

objective explanations of the obvious, but he has an impera-
tive need...to assimilate all outer sense experiences to
inner, psychic events.... All the mythological processes of
nature...are in no sense allegories...they are symbolic
expressions of the inner, unconscious drama of the psyche
which becomes accessible to man's consciousness by way of
projection onto outer objects.[15]

Through 'several thousand years of civilization', Jung argues, we
have now nearly managed to detach those projections, those 'objective
explanations', from the unconscious which was their matrix. Primitive thinking, on the other hand, is 'not yet differentiated'. While 'the
archetype does not proceed from physical facts', neither does primitive
mentality '*invent* myths, it *experiences* them.... Not merely do they
represent, they *are* the psychic life of the primitive tribe, which immediately falls to pieces and decays when it loses its mythological
heritage, like a man who has lost his soul....'. This loss is always,
'even among the civilized, a moral catastrophe', and a primary cause
of mental illness. One of the principle tasks of modern psychology,
therefore, is that of 'finding a new *interpretation* appropriate to this
age, in order to connect the life of the past that still exists in us with
the life of the present'. In these apocalyptic tones we can of course
almost hear the voice of Lawrence, of Thomas Mann and of Eliot, who
will go so far as to say that the artist is and should be 'more *primitive*,
as well as more civilized, than his contemporaries'. The procedure of
analytical psychology will thus be the procedure appropriate to the
interpretation of symbols; it will not be strictly analytical but, rather,
hermeneutic. 'The ultimate core of meaning' of the archetypal
contents of myths may, by association and analogy, 'be circumscribed,
but not described', says Jung. 'The most we can do is to *dream the
myth onwards* and give it modern dress.'

So it happens that the two most influential myth-based texts in
English literary criticism written in the first third of the twentieth
century turn out to be Weston's *From Ritual to Romance*, an application of Frazer's view of the evolution of the mind and Maud Bodkin's
Archetypal Patterns in Poetry (1934), an application to poetic texts of
Jung's technique for the discernment of the forces inherent in the
evolution of the mind of the individual. As Weston examines literary
patterns in the context of Frazer's ideas on primitive social behavioural

configurations, Bodkin explores Jung's idea that certain literar
patterns persist and persistently carry special emotional significanc
because they activate primeval archetypal configurations in the indiv
dual reader's unconscious. While Erich Neumann (in his ofte
brilliant 'reconstruction', *The Origins and History of Consciousness*
Joseph Campbell (in *The Hero with a Thousand Faces*, a Jungia
response to the ritualist and psychoanalytic schematizations by Ragla
and Rank of the hero motif) and others go on to fill in the monomyt
outlined by Jung, Bodkin's work will have set in train for late
scholars of literature a whole mode of 'myth-' or 'archetype
criticism'.[16]

'Myth' and 'myths': background and foreground to modernism

While the 'comparative' analysis of the formal patterns of myths wi
always have its practitioners[17], more recent anthropology ha
disclosed the naiveté of general theories of myth based purely o
literary study. The view expressed in England at the close of ou
period by Bronislaw Malinowski (1884-1942) in *Myth in Primitiv
Psychology* (1926) – a work which he ardently dedicated to hi
avowed master Frazer – has taken hold in one form or anothe
throughout the world of extra-literary myth-scholarship. Mytholog
has come to be regarded as a matter to be investigated in the field an
in terms of the particular conditions and functions affecting its use i
each local context, whether one's final subject is the group or the indi
vidual. To many professionals, the entire conception of 'myth' witl
its implied applicability to a generic class of verbal artefacts has lon
been extinct and the word has been expunged from their workin
vocabulary.[18] Institutional anthropology and psychology thus mov
on to other pastures.

But the needs of literature are not always those of the sciences
From the theories reviewed here, one gains the impression of a cluste
of impulses and aspirations associated with myth which modern artist
found invitingly affined to their own preoccupations. In considerin
them we seem often almost to be recounting a catalogue of the theme
and yearnings of modern literature itself. Myth offers (the poet is told
to connect man with his past and to a tradition going back to 'th
cave'; and in so doing, it joins him as well with a lost Golden Age o
man, and with divinity. It binds him to Nature and 'the secret source

f life', and simultaneously links him to history's nobler civilizations nd hence to a higher beauty and moral resource. In this effect, by hich myth crosses both temporal and cultural bounds, it is taken in ddition to promise a more perfect future, for myths are also models of leal behaviour. 'Thinking through myth' secures the sense, in fact, f one's solidarity with what is 'universal' in human experience. Myth and ritual are thus portrayed for the poet as liberating men from ne present, and from the personal and the contingent and the material, from the 'spray of phenomena' itself, and as providing refuge n other, transcendent and timeless worlds. Among these is the world f dream, where the simple, eternal things are of the essence, and where personal heroism and progress remain possible.[19]

Yet, with myth's restoration of the grand, tragic or Dionysian pprehension of the efficacy of action, the renewed perception of the ontinuous, endless, cyclical quality of actuality also comes to deflate nd dissolve man's habitual catastrophism and self-aggrandisement, n a kind of sceptical Apollonian or Olympian calm, indifference, isinterest, or acquiescence. So it happens that the very duplicity of ne symbols by which myth addresses man is given to the poet as a eflection of the doubleness of man's acts, his experience, his place in ne universe, and the tension inherent in them. Thus, too (supple-nenting their rational intelligence), intuition into the ambiance of nyth promotes in men – in a spirit of simultaneous flagellation and elf-gratulation pleasing to the Puritan tastes of writers in Northern Europe and America – a mordant awareness of the 'savage', the cruel isceral reality beneath the skin. Just as myth and ritual may have ought, in looking back, to define causes, so in looking backwards men nay now see how myth and ritual have themselves become remorse-ess causes: received conventions and 'reasons' become more acces-ible targets, ready to waver and collapse in the perspective light of heir 'barbaric' origins.[20]

At the same time, myth is felt to release men from intellectualism nd the discriminations of logic and abstraction; it favours the dissolu-ion of false boundaries (individual/collective, natural/supernatural, I/ Thou, etc.), and opens the way for perception and communication via qually viable, non-rational modes of thinking and being that are ound to lure poets of an increasingly anti-positivist or at least relativ-st post-World-War milieu. As a means of activating and organizing hought, myth promises both a vision of a kind of order or pattern and

a liberated sense of dynamic impulsion – for example, through i
fusion of history with imagination, or through its hierarchical, cosm
logical disposition of natural or psychic forces in fluid dramatic, narr
tive form. And finally, myth justifies the role of the artist himself. T
act of poetic creation – by its association with the creative activity on
belonging to God, by its ancient ceremonial relation to both sacred a
profane imagery and to the ritual power which language is reported
have traditionally possessed – assimilates itself to mythopoesis (t
poet is told), and the poet may be conceived of as participating in
elevated and mysterious, ecstatic, potentially magical and prophe
process.

Undoubtedly the special place accorded in modern literature
thinkers like Frazer and Jung results to some extent from the
association with such ideas as these about 'myth' – about myth as
form and a process of thought. It is true that, as we have seen, a va
scattering of concepts were helpfully resolved and recast by theore
cians we've mentioned, into an attractive linear vision of myth
content (an old mythologem revitalized): of evolutionary man fightir
his way towards perfection, observed against the constant backdrop
nature's eternal round. Literature clearly appreciates Jung for adap
ing a theological model for salvation into a psychological model f
mental health, and Frazer for adapting a biological model for surviv
into a philosophical model for intellectual progress. Is there, howeve
a way of regarding the modern movement as a discrete and definab
attitude, and has 'myth' anything to do with it?

In *The Sirens of Titan*, Kurt Vonnegut, Jr, suggests that in fa
there is, after all, no such thing or place as a 'cromo-synclastic infur
dibula', 'where all the different kinds of truth fit together'. If any goo
reason exists for calling Vonnegut a post-modern or anti-moder
writer, as many do, here it is. The theoretical appeal of myth as
means to *synthesis* may explain a large part of its attraction early i
this century, and may be a key factor in our definition of modernisr

But if speculative concepts were all that such men as Frazer had ha
to offer, poets would scarcely have turned their heads to look. Th
evidence is pretty clear: historically, literature's real love affair wit
'anthropology' and 'psychology' was to last only for as long
'anthropologists' and 'psychologists' spoke in a language – and abo
texts – immediately assimilable into literature itself. It is just possib
that the ultimate basis for the rapport between theorists and artists w

ore textural and less conceptual than we are accustomed (or
epared, as conceptualizers) to think.

A final *caveat*, then, is in order. We are compelled to distinguish
nyth', someone's abstract notion of a way of thinking, from
nyths', a vast congeries of narrative images and events. There is
ways the chance that mythological materials – in yielding concretes
the service of abstraction (Eliot's objective correlatives), in clothing
e thought and providing for its sensuous articulation and amplifica-
on, in enriching and intensifying it with their own ambiguities –
ere is a chance that they contribute something which may effectively
ave the concept behind. Perhaps it is true, for example, that mythical
ferences do – to the chagrin of the critic who cries for precision –
ar about them (in addition to their expressive precision) some
mbus, some smell of import, or some numinosity, such as one might
pect for instance of objects immemorially associated with the nexus
tween community and power. Or perhaps they do render a prismatic
nction – fragmenting actual experience into its primary colours
ithout vitiating its overriding organic unity – which abstraction will
t allow. Or perhaps mythology does even perform as simple but
sential a task as to afford the poet, for both his visionary and his
nic aims, an iconography of dynamic motifs technically or psycho-
gically not viable in standard realism – direct motifs pertaining, let
say at random, to fate, creation, paradise, hell and purgatory, to
smemberment, rebirth and regeneration, to metamorphosis and
ansubstantiation, to crises (flood, famine, sterility, pestilence, holo-
ust) on a universal or apocalyptic scale, or to a fluent intercourse
tween human, chthonic and celestial forces. . . .

The fact is that it may well not be so much Frazer's and Jung's
nceptions of 'myth', but rather their 'myths', that captured the
inds of writers in the first half of this century. After all is said, the
aramount concept proposed by both ritual and archetypal theorists,
ncerning the attractive-power of myth-as-image, can find no better
pport than the evidence of modern literature's endless recourse to
ose imaginative constellations which the theorists themselves have
ought to the world's attention – the ritualist configurations, say, of
e king of the wood, the marriage of the gods, the waste land, the
stival of fire, the medicine man, the tree-spirit, the corn-maiden, the
ting of the god, the scapegoat, the rainmaker, the sword-dance, the
her king, the external soul, and the archetypes of the great mother,

the serpent Uroboros, the anima, the captive princess, the first fathe
the shadow, the divine child, the harlot, the *puer aeternus*, the terrib
mother, the spirit Mercurius, the wise old man, the trickster, the a
father, the eternal Sophia, the mandala, the self, the separation of t
world parents, the night-sea journey, the dragon fight, the treasu
beyond price. The real fascination of 'myth' for some Modernists ma
lie, in other words, in the foreground to which the foregoing discu
sion has been the background, and which only the immediate textu
and detail of the theorists' writings themselves (Frazer's texts, lik
Eliot's; Jung's texts, like Wallace Stevens') can properly commun
cate. There is a fair possibility that it is in the mass of integrate
images of which the mammoth canon of their interpretive work
composed, and not in their hypotheses, that they have given the visio
back to mythology.

Notes

1 The major 'realist' points of view touched on here form a customary pa
   of Western thought. They have been discussed at length in numerou
   standard works and form an important portion of K.K. Ruthven, *Myt*
   London 1976.
2 English titles are given in all cases, but dates cited are those of fir
   publication in any language. The reading background of an 'Englis'
   literary movement in which only one or two of the half-dozen leadir
   lights are English, and where others possess linguistic abilities of the ran
   of Pound's, Eliot's and Joyce's, is of a very cosmopolitan an
   sophisticated kind, in which the significance of translations (except t
   poets' own) is of a far more tangential sort than is normal in litera
   history. As to the writers from whom they got their ideas, they are I
   conviction linguists and/or comparatists to a man. Independent
   generation and nationality, thinkers as widespread as Max Mülle
   Bastiàn, Frazer, van Gennep, Harrison and Freud share reading matt
   and even correspondence, meet at conferences, and may, like Jung, I
   found writing or perusing papers in three languages in the course of
   working day. Published in 1909, *Rites de Passage* was imbedded in t
   daily and permanent parlance of British anthropologists by 1914, and w
   never translated into English – many may still be astonished
   realize – until 1960.
3 An erudite linguistician, Müller in an historic *coup de théatre* uncovere
   unexpected continuities in the mythology of Western and Easter
   cultures, e.g. the identity of the Vedic and Greek supreme deities (Zeus
   Dyaus, the Vedic sky-god). Hence, just as the tale of Dick Whittingto

and his cat might have arisen from a misreading of the French (and thus Middle English) word *achat*, trade, the source of Whittington's wealth, so one could see that Zeus' bizarre adventures were surely the result of corruptions of Aryan root-words for celestial phenomena. Müller's ideas find their twentieth-century elaboration (with its philological – and not without its naturistic – bias) in the 'new comparative mythology' of Georges Dumézil and its University of California variants.

4 Translated as such in English by B.M. Hinkle, 1916, from *Wandlungen und Symbols der Libido*; revised and published in 1952 by Jung as *Symbols der Wandlung (Symbols of Transformation)*.

5 *Researches into the Early History of Mankind and the Development of Civilisation*, 1865; *Primitive Culture*, 2 vols, 1871. Lang's initial publication on the subject, 'Mythology and Fairy Tales', appeared in 1872; his major, two-volume contribution to the Folklorist *vs* Philologist debate, *Myth, Ritual and Religion*, had its first edition in 1887.

6 Whose germane work, *Lectures in the Religion of the Semites*, was published in 1889, well after his influence on his disciple Frazer had made itself felt through personal contact at Cambridge.

7 1890, 2 vols; 1900, 3 vols; 1907-1915, 1936, 12 vols.

8 *Les Fonctions mentales dans les sociétés inférieures*, 1910 (*How Natives Think*, New York 1925); *La Mentalité primitive*, 1922 (*Primitive Mentality*, London 1923).

9 Which S.F. Hyman in 'The Ritual View of Myth and the Mythic' (*Bibliographical and Special Series*, Vol. 5, American Folklore Society, 1955) has signalled as 'the watershed year'. Hyman's article is so oft-reprinted as a basic survey of the ritualist position that it would be pointless to recite the School's history at greater length in the present essay than the following brief discussion entails.

10 A detailed exposé of the massive and explicit debt to Frazer and the ritualists is set well on its way by John B. Vickery in *The Literary Impact of The Golden Bough* (Princeton 1973), concerning Yeats, Eliot, Pound, Joyce, Lawrence, Aiken, Aldington, Rupert Brooke, Faulkner, Graves, Jeffers, MacLeish, Mitchison, T. Sturge Moore, J.C. Powys, Wain, and others. No comparable work on Jung's effect yet exists, nor is Vickery's definitive.

11 Freud refers continually not only to *The Golden Bough* but to Frazer's *Totemism and Exogamy*, from which his own book's title probably takes its shape. Ironically, among his constant Frazerian citations are ones received by Frazer from Bastian. Freud sent Frazer a copy of *Totem and Taboo* but the latter never acknowledged it and is said to have dubbed him simply 'that creature Freud'. Frazer was also frankly unable to digest that other great stepchild of his, 'The Waste Land'.

12 For classic explorations of the connections between literature and the psychoanalytic interpretation of myths see Ernest Jones, *Hamlet and Oedipus* (London 1949) – a nice parallel to Murray's ritualist study,

'Hamlet and Orestes'; P. Mullahy, *Oedipus: Myth and Complex* (Ne York 1948); G. Róheim, *Riddle of the Sphinx* (London 1934).

13 An early ethnologist, Bastian (1826-1905) has the unique distinction having been a crucial influence on the work of both Tylor and Frazer *a* of Freud (all of whom relied heavily on material evidence gleaned by h in the field) and Jung (who drew much from his ideology). Basti persistently maintained that a non-evolutionary principle of innate psych unity prevailed throughout mankind. That, independent of the state their civilization, among men everywhere certain permanent forms thought, certain elemental ideas (*Elementargedanken*) perdured; and th these psychic pre-formations were fundamental to any understanding folk thought and myth.

14 A number of archetypal patterns observed by Jungians and recurrent described in literature are noted on pp. 181-2.

15 'An allegory is a paraphrase of a conscious content, whereas a symbol the best possible expression for an unconscious content whose nature c only be guessed, because it is still unknown.'

16 E.g. that of Northrop Frye. It should be noted that the myth-orientat fiction of Eliot's friend Charles Williams expressly invites a variety archetypal interpretation quite independent of Jungian psycholog though of a tradition from which Jung readily claims descent: t procedure of hermeneutic explication of Scripture and of natural histo practiced by medieval scholastics.

17 E.g. in the formalist and structuralist approaches to mythology ma famous by Vladimir Propp and Claude Lévi-Strauss.

18 Cf., e.g., the work of such major folklorists as Stith Thompson.

19 This relation between myth and ritual on the one hand and the group drama or the individual's fantasy or dream on the other, so emphatica singled out by Murray and Harrison, Freud and Jung, will lead to A.F Krappe's notion (c.1930) that myths are the pure aesthetic inventions poets, Susanne K. Langer's notion that 'myth begins in fantasy' and h its primary origin in 'the entirely subjective and private phenomenon *dream*', and Richard Chase's conviction that myth *is 'narrative or poet literature'* and, as such, 'the aesthetic activity of man's mind'.

20 Contemporary criticism, so engrossed with the historical impact Freud's pronouncements on human sexuality, is inclined to forget ho Frazer's fundamentally pessimistic overview (concerning the 'round' nature) and his unstinting illustrations of the violent and erotic aspects *homo sapiens*' behaviour unsettled Victorian tastes and contributed to th language of disorientation and irony that was to emerge in the poetry Edwardian and Georgian England. It is undoubtedly in part due to th side of Frazer that Pound and Eliot speak of his 'art', of which Eliot ca him 'a very great master'. Vickery, op. cit., is able on this point.

lect bibliography

odkin, M. *Archetypal Patterns in Poetry*, London 1963.

assirer, E. *The Philosophy of Symbolic Forms*, vol. II: *Mythical Thought*, transl. R. Mannheim, London 1955.

eldman, B. and Richardson, R.D. *The Rise of Modern Mythology, 1680-1860*, London 1975.

azer, J.G. *The New Golden Bough*, rev. edn. T. Gaster, New York 1975.

eud, S. *Totem and Taboo*, transl. J. Strachey, London 1950.

ing, C.G. *Archetypes and the Collective Unconscious*, transl. R.F.C. Hull, London 1959.

alinowski, B. 'Myth in Primitive Psychology' in *Magic, Science and Religion*, London 1974.

eumann, E. *The Origins and History of Consciousness*, transl. R.F.C. Hull, London 1954.

eston, J.L. *From Ritual to Romance*, New York 1957.

5 Freud and English literature 1900-30

R. A. GEKOSKI

'The poets and philosophers before me discovered the unconscious. What I discovered was the scientific method by which the unconscious can be studied.'

Considerations of the work of Sigmund Freud, and of its implication for the arts, frequently begin with the above quotation,[1] from a sho speech given by Freud during the celebration of his seventieth birt day. The restraint and humility of the claim (however much implicitly places him with Sophocles, Shakespeare, and Goethe) a often felt to be a just indication of Freud's stature as a man at thinker. But it is, surely, a curious assertion; its modesty perhaps little disingenuous – as if made by an early American railway magna in deference to Christopher Columbus. For there is no rigorous sen of the term 'unconscious' which Sophocles or Shakespeare – in bot of whom Freud was well read – would have acknowledged himself tł discoverer of. That men are motivated by profound and frequent inexplicable surges of passion, and can be the unwilling agents of the own destruction, both knew and compellingly demonstrated. But neither would this have entailed the location of a distinct and isolatabl aspect of our humanity corresponding to what Freud was much late to label the 'unconscious'.

There is, however, ample evidence that a profound concern with, not the unconscious, then at least with unconsciousness, has been constant concern of artists and philosophers since the Greeks; Gale

AD 130-200) is believed to have felt that we make unconscious
ferences from our perceptions, while the Neo-Platonist Plotinus (c.
)4-70) suggested that: 'Feelings can be present without awareness of
em.' A lively sense of the unconscious components of human
tivity is widespread in Europe up to the time of Descartes, whose
dical distinction between mind and body has had commensurately
dical effects on the intellectual history of Europe since 1700. L.L.
hyte suggests that we only need a concept like 'the unconscious'
cause of the implications of Descartes' metaphor of 'the ghost in the
achine': if the mind is regarded as simply the ratiocinative faculty,
en irrationality needs explanation.[2] Freud stands, then, in a line of
velopment that culminates in what Whyte calls 'the discovery of the
nconscious not in the sense of a scientific discovery supported by
stematic tests, but of a *new inference*, the bringing to light of what
as previously unknown in a particular culture.'[3] Perhaps Freud's
eer originality has been somewhat exaggerated. Discussion of the
ature of the unconscious was a widespread concern in Germany and
ustria in the 1870s and 1880s. Certainly we can find in Nietzsche a
mber of formulations that might have been made by Freud:

> Every extension of knowledge arises from making conscious
> the unconscious.
>
> The great basic activity is unconscious.[4]

et Freud is commonly regarded as unique. If this is a misunderstand-
g, it is a significant and honorific one. Kant and Hegel are misunder-
ood only after a reading of their works, whereas Freud, like Marx,
as entered the common realm so thoroughly that it might be
garded as a sign of ignorance to *have* to read him. His terminology is
ow widely employed in everyday discourse, his concepts – neurotic,
nconscious, id, ego, superego, repression, projection, Oedipus
mplex, phallic symbol, and the rest – are used widely by a public
ho can talk confidently about the 'Freudian' implications of
ything from one banana to two peaches. And if many ignorantly
plore the 'results' of Freud's researches – promiscuity, permissive-
ess, the whole range of his supposed legacy – they still are somehow
mpelled to see the world in his terms: relating childhood to adult-
ood, motivation to behaviour, the intended or manifest to the
mbolic or latent. For Freud is not merely an abundantly brilliant
inker, he has radically changed the language and concepts with

which we do our thinking. And since this very pervasiveness of h
influence is itself a source of misconception, there will be a more th
summary value in briefly recapitulating his essential insights a
terms.

Freud's collected works are formidable both in length and co
plexity, and most demand some prior knowledge of the vocabulary
psychoanalysis. The most accessible of them are the two series
lectures delivered to lay audiences: the Clark Lectures of 1909 and t
Vienna Lectures of 1915-17. But both are limited in their range
clinical reference, and insufficient in the attention given to particul
topics. Furthermore, if one's acquaintance is limited to these work
the awesome inexorability of Freud's developing argument is lost; f
his work, fundamentally, is of a piece. Beginning with one set of que
tions in the early 1880s, his progress from work to work compelling
demonstrates (in the words of Ernest Jones) how 'the solutio
however brilliant, of one problem leads only to cogitation of othe
which the solution had exposed'.[5] I shall thus proceed chronologica
from *Studies on Hysteria* (1895) to the *Introductory Lectures c
Psychoanalysis* (1915-17) – that is, on the major works of the peri
1900-30 which would both have been available in English and ha
been likely to influence the important English writers of the period

It is as well, on first approaching Freud, to be clear about what que
tions one wishes answered. My focus (in the first part of this essay) w
be on Freud's developing views on the 'unconscious': what it is; ho
we can come to learn about it; how best we can intervene in its fun
tioning.

I

Though Freud's attention had been drawn to the subject of hysteria
early as 1882, when his friend Dr Josef Breuer related to him wh
was later to be known as the case of Anna O., his abiding interest i
the subject dated from his visit to Professor Charcot's Paris clinic i
October of 1885. Prior to Charcot's research, hysteria had been rega
ded as an inexplicable – and hence medically uninteresting – phen
menon. Because hysterical symptoms 'act as though anatomy did n
exist' (I, p.169)[6] (hysterical blindness is unrelated to damage to t
eyes; hysterical paralysis corresponds not to the anatomical nature of
limb, but to the ordinary *idea* of the limb), they had previously bee

egarded either as reprehensible forms of malingering, or as associated ince the disease was wrongly believed to be limited to women) with ome misfunction of the womb. Charcot's work suggested the nadequacy of both hypotheses: using post-hypnotic suggestion, he ould both create short-lived hysterical symptoms in non-hysterics, nd remove or transform previous symptoms in hysterical patients. he method was particularly effective with patients whose symptoms rst appeared following some traumatic experience. Though Charcot id not pursue the psychological implications of his findings, Freud's nterest was sharply engaged. If hysterical symptoms could be caused r removed by ideas – are 'ideogenic' – what did this suggest in terms f their treatment?

Freud's response to this question was to occupy the large part of the ext ten years, culminating in the work *Studies on Hysteria*, which he ublished jointly with Breuer in 1895, and of which he later said: 'I an give no better advice to anyone interested in the development of atharsis into psychoanalysis than to begin with *Studies on Hysteria* nd thus follow the path which I myself have trodden.'[7]

But before starting this investigation, and moving from the early rmulations of the *Studies* to the later sophistications of the theory nd technique of psychoanalysis (a word first used as late as 1896),[8] it s important to bear in mind four crucial assumptions that underlie reud's thinking – both at this period, and, to a large extent, through-ut his life:

1 The first is best stated in the *Introductory Lectures*, but was undoubtedly held firmly throughout his life; indeed, his work is impossible without some such premiss: he asks rhetorically if 'there are occurrences, however small, which drop out of the universal concatenation of events – occurrences which might just as well not happen? If anyone makes a breach of this kind in the determinism of natural events at a single point, it means that he has thrown overboard the whole *Weltanschauung* of science (xv, p.28).

2 The above principle applies as much to humans as to the rest of the natural world, and in exactly the same ways. According to Freud's teacher Ernst Brücke, himself a member of the school of Hermann Helmholtz: 'No other forces than the common physical-chemical ones are active within the organism.'[9] The

position is hostile not only to the vitalist theories of contem
porary biology, but also to those philosophers who posited forc
like the 'Will' which could not be reduced to a physical-chemic
explanation.

Freud was later to describe Brücke as the single maj
influence on his thinking.[10]

3 The third may derive from the philosopher Franz Brentano, a
is summarized by Richard Wollheim as follows: 'every men
state or condition can be analyzed into two components; an ide
which gives the mental state its object or what it is directed upo
and its charge of affect, which gives it its measure of strength
efficacy.'[11]

4 Associated with the principles above, we have what Freud muc
later termed the Principle of Constancy, which the editors of tl
Standard Edition call 'the most fundamental of Freud's theorie
(II, p.xix): 'The mental apparatus endeavours to keep the qua
tity of excitation present in it as low as possible or at least to ke
it constant' (XVIII, p.9). That is, feeling (or 'affect') is by
natural process of the mind in need of expression (or 'discharge'
without which it will continue, even unbeknown to the agent,
need expression in whatever way is available.

For present purposes I will not comment further on these assum
tions, other than to remark that it is not clear either that their status
as strictly 'scientific' as Freud would have supposed, or that they le
to new *explanations* of the processes of mental life, rather than ne
descriptions.

In 1893 Freud and Breuer published the paper known as the 'Pre
minary Communication', in which they laid out a revolutionar
approach to hysteria, which Freud (rather more than Breuer) believe
to entail a new theory of mind. The most trenchant of their formul
tions is the provocative 'Hysterics suffer mainly from reminiscence
(II, p.7). Hysterical symptoms, then, are understood as 'mnem
symbols' of a reminiscence which has, through a process calle
'conversion', become somaticized. But why does this process occur
The reason posited is simple, yet profound in implication: we a
dealing with a 'reminiscence' which is *not* remembered, having bee
(by a process termed 'repression') lost to conscious memory. Th
banishment from consciousness is the result of the traumatic quality

initial experience which has been 'insufficiently abreacted' – that been too painful to find discharge either in feeling or behaviour.

Some examples may bring home the human meaning of Freud and euer's theory. Anna O., a highly intelligent and lively woman of enty-one, was referred to Dr Breuer suffering from a remarkable talogue of complaints contracted while nursing her terminally-ill her: intermittent paralysis of three limbs, inability to take food, a rvous cough, and a remarkable symptom whereby she was unable to eak German (her native tongue), but instead spoke only English hich she did not know well previously). In addition, she manifested o distinct personalities, the one her normal self, the other that of a oublesome little girl. Breuer observed that when Anna told him of e first appearance of one of her symptoms, she found that the mptom immediately vanished. He tried to make her repeat the ocess: taking each symptom in turn, he tried to elicit from her when had first appeared. When this could be done, the symptom disap- ared. The technique, which Anna called 'chimney sweeping', was e basis of what Breuer was to refer to as the 'cathartic method'.

Two crucial problems now emerged. First, it appeared that the moval of the symptom was not permanent. But second, and more nportantly, the previously girlish Anna began to manifest a distinct xual attraction to Dr Breuer, which he found himself reciprocating. considerable alarm, he dropped the case. Only many years later did is patient make a full recovery.

Freud's treatment of his (exclusively female) hysterical patients was itially heavily reliant on the use of hypnosis, but he gradually began use Breuer's cathartic method, which he modified by encouraging is patient to give voice to whatever came into her mind, with no ttempt to censor the apparently irrelevant or irreverent: a technique ter called 'free association'. He found that when such a flow of asso- ation was blocked, and the patient remained silent or obviously vaded voicing what was on her mind (which he called 'resistance'), it as always because of the presence of some idea or feeling incompat- le with the patient's consciously held notions of propriety. In the case Elizabeth von R., this idea involved a strong sexual attraction to her other-in-law, which had caused her to feel (and immediately to press) pleasure at the incipient death of her sister. The cause of her ysterical symptom (intense pains in the right thigh) lay in the repres- on, and subsequent conversion, of this feeling. Encouraged by Freud, she was reluctantly led back to the 'traumatic' moment at her sister' death bed when she had thought, 'Now he is free again, and I can b his wife' (II, p.156). Having discharged the affect attached to th: reprehensible wish, by recalling it to consciousness, she no longer ha need of her symptom, and could return to the unhappy, but adul ambivalence of her grief. In Freud's phrase, 'much will be gained if w succeed in transforming . . . hysterical misery into common unhapp ness' (II, p.305).

He was able, too, to reassure Breuer, who continued to feel that h had mishandled the treatment of Anna O., for Freud had also observe that, as the treatment of his hysterical patients progressed, the frequently manifested strong, and entirely unsolicited, sexual feeling towards him. Unlike Breuer, he was not shocked, but interested. Sinc nothing occurs without a cause, this evidence of inappropriate sexua attraction, like the supposedly trivial meanderings of a free associatior needed to be interpreted. He labelled the phenomenon 'transference the analysis of which was to become an essential feature of psychc analytic procedure. Somewhat later, he was to postulate that in th case of hysterical patients, the root of this sexual feeling lay in earl childhood (between the ages of five and seven) when the patient ha been molested by her father: a conclusion based on the evidence tha patient after patient, reluctantly and unsolicited, reported memory c such a scene.

The 'seduction theory' of hysteria, which Freud framed in 1896 was designed to answer the difficult question: why is it that som people develop hysterical symptoms in response to adult trauma, whil others do not? He argued that such symptoms are in fact over-deter mined, the critical factor lying not in the trauma, but in the represse childhood memory, the dormant feeling of which is reactivated b some particular quality in the adult experience.

But *Studies on Hysteria*, largely due to the reluctance of Breuer hardly reveals the importance of sexuality in the aetiology of hysteria Though the work begins the crucial task of framing a conceptua apparatus to discuss unconscious processes, it leaves unanswered tw overwhelmingly important questions: how are we to gain reliabl access to the unconscious? and, what is the importance of sexuality i unconscious functioning? These questions, then, become the bases c Freud's next three books: *The Interpretation of Dreams* (1899), *Th Psychopathology of Everyday Life* (1901), and *Three Essays on*

Theory of Sexuality (1905), the first and last of which being the only works that Freud troubled to keep up to date during his lifetime.

The Interpretation of Dreams, published in 1899, is Freud's most ambitious and important work. It was designed to restore to dreams the status attached to them in the pre-Cartesian world: as meaningful mental acts, in need of detailed and prolonged attention. Though dreams were hardly neglected phenomena in the nineteenth century (as the first chapter of Freud's work amply demonstrates), they were generally considered as the trivial results of daily routine or somatic disturbance – the residue of a day at the office or a bout of indigestion. Indeed, Freud denied neither of these causes, the first of which he stressed as an important contributing factor in every dream. Further, he was happy to admit that a stomach-ache, for instance may well trigger a dream in which the digestion figures. But one question, simple, yet previously unanswered, remained to be considered: why does the dreamer dream the particular variant of the stomach-ache dream that is uniquely his own? Freud, responding to the works of previous writers, put the problem quite clearly:

> They have underestimated the extent to which psychical events are determined. There is nothing arbitrary about them. It can be shown quite generally that if an element is left undetermined by one train of thought, its determination is immediately effected by a second one. For instance, I may try to think of a number arbitrarily. But this is impossible: the number that occurs to me will be unambiguously and necessarily determined by thoughts of mine, though they may be remote from my immediate intention. (V, pp.514-15)

The complex implications of this are best understood if we recall an additional factor in Freud's interest in dreams. He had previously noticed, in his work with hysterical patients, the regularity with which they reported their dreams to him – and had observed the important connection between dreaming and free associating, in both of which the contents of the mind are revealed without conscious censorship. But the most significant spur to his interest in dreams came through his self-analysis, which began in 1896, and (though it continued throughout his life) had its most intense period over the next three years. It is impossible to overestimate the difficulty of such an

endeavour; self-analysis is even now regarded as exceptionally haza
dous, for the desire to maintain a pleasant (and hence a distorte
picture of the self is hardly an unusual human trait. Insofar as it is th
purpose of analytic procedure (in Freud's words) 'to make the unco
scious conscious', one can easily see how strong the resistance to suc
a process is likely to be, and how necessary the help of a therapis
Indeed, the results of Freud's introspections were far from delightful t
him, and it is a testimonial to his genius that he was able to assimila
them, not only to his growing theoretical awareness, but also to h
view of himself.

Self-analysis convinced Freud of the importance of dreams as the *v*
regia to the unconscious; it was through interpretation of his ow
dream material that he was reluctantly led to the abandonment of th
seduction theory. He had recovered within himself that complex an
distressing matrix of infantile hostility and desire, towards his fathe
and mother respectively, that was later to be termed the Oedipu
complex. Audaciously, he decided that this apparently idiosyncrati
disposition must represent a universal human tendency – an intellec
tual procedure equally characteristic of exceedingly intelligent peopl
and of remarkably stupid ones. But it was, in any case, a constant i
his method that the 'neurotic' or pathological are to be distinguishe
from the 'normal' not by kind, but degree.[12]

The consequence of this self-observation was the unregretted deat
of the seduction theory, which had become an embarrassment becaus
of the number of sexually perverse fathers that it led Freud to postu
late. His recasting of the theory, however, had its own unfortunat
consequences, at least in terms of Freud's standing amongst hi
medical colleagues (for, at the time, he had no psychoanalytic ones).
his patients' memory of an early seduction did not recall a truth, it wa
presented as if it did. It was, Freud postulated, a fantasy, a recapitula
tion of an infantile wish. But how could children, universally (in th
medical profession at least) regarded as innocent of sexual feeling
produce such wishes? He concluded – and any nanny could hav
confirmed that he was right, had she been asked – that children hav
not that sexual 'purity' conventionally ascribed to them. Upon bein
told this truth, in a lecture of Freud's, most of his colleagues walke
out in disgust. It had been sufficiently revolting to be told (on th
model of the seduction theory) that certain pathological states wer
rooted in early perverse experience, but to hear it affirmed that al

urotic states are related to the universal occurrence of infantile xuality was the final outrage. Freud was never again widely teemed in Viennese medical circles.

His self-analysis had revealed the murky world of the unconscious its unacceptable desires, its perverse strivings – largely through his veloping understanding of the nature of dreams. *The Interpretation Dreams* draws widely and courageously on this material, in an tempt to make intelligible the following assertion: '[Dreams] are sychical phenomena of complete validity – fulfilments of wishes; ey can be inserted into the chain of intelligible mental acts: they are nstructed by a highly complicated activity of the mind' (IV, p.122). wo discrete activities are thus distinguished: wishing (in this se, unconsciously), and dreaming (which supplies the disguised lfilment of that wish). What is at issue is the *nature* of this disguise, r its necessity (to conceal an unacceptable wish) may be taken for ranted.

A dream, like a neurotic symptom (IV, p.101), is the result of a ompromise between the ego and the unconscious. By analogy with eurotic symptoms, then, we establish the existence of a repressed ish in conflict with the conscious ideals of the self: '*a normal train of bought is only submitted to abnormal psychical treatment of the sort e have been describing if an unconscious wish, derived from infancy nd in a state of repression, has been transferred on to it*' (V, p.598). It the purpose of the 'dream work', as Freud called it, to produce the hallucinatory' quality of dreams, whereby the affect attached to the nconscious wish is discharged, while at the same time sufficiently istorted to make the real purpose of the dream unintelligible. Freud hus deviates from contemporary commentators insofar as his interest not in the 'manifest content' of the dream (the dream itself, or, at east, the dream as it is remembered), but in the 'latent dream houghts' that, in disguised form, underlie the manifest content. Properly understood, his interest is not in dreaming, but in wishing.

The apparent unintelligibility of dreams is the result of two, closely llied, factors. The first of these is the process that Freud called 'secon- ary revision', which is the ego's share in the censorship of the dream houghts. This process ensures both a degree of disguise, and also that revity which is the characteristic of most dreams – it takes much less ime to have a dream than to interpret it. The three most important nethods of secondary revision are condensation, displacement, and

symbolization. Condensation, the chief cause of the relative shortne
of most dreams, is the process whereby a dream image or figure ma
be the result of the amalgamation of a number of further images c
figures. Through free association, the composite nature of a condense
dream image may be traced back to its constituent elements. Displac
ment is a process whereby a '*transference . . . of psychical intensitie*
occurs in the process of dream formation' (IV, pp.307-8); throug
displacement strong feeling towards one person, (for instance), may b
displaced onto another, and presumably less significant, figure
Symbolization, of these three processes, is the most difficult t
evaluate, since the correct interpretation of a symbol is (as mos
literary critics will know) hardly a scientific procedure. Indeed, in
dream (as in a poem) it is not always easy to know when to interpre
symbolically – a procedural difficulty that Freud himself acknow
ledged. Nevertheless, clinical experience had demonstrated to hir
that certain dream symbols have recurring referents. Thus images of
King and Queen usually refer to the parents, 'all elongated objects
tend to refer to the penis, while 'hollow objects' of various sorts ma
represent the uterus (V, p.354). But every such interpretation, Freu
warned, ought not to be a simple matter of 'decoding' (IV, pp.97-8
but must proceed directly from the dreamer's particular associatio
with the image.

But there is a further, and much more profound, difficulty
Through the processes of secondary revision, the ego attempts t
preserve sleep from the sharp and unwelcome intrusions of the uncon
scious. Dream material itself, unimpaired by conscious interventior
is presented in a peculiar, one might say foreign, manner. If the uncon
scious may be said to speak to us, it speaks in a tongue with which w
are largely unacquainted. Its images, thoughts, and wishes, expresse
in what Freud calls the 'primary process' (V, pp.588-609), appear 'i
a manner which is in the highest degree bewildering and irrational
(V, p.597). Because it functions so differently from conscious think
ing, which Freud called 'secondary process', the unconscious ca
seem as if it were talking gibberish. It takes no note of contradiction, o
identity, of the normal workings of time and space. And yet Freud wa
adamant – the very assertion of its 'primacy' suggests this – that th
unconscious 'is the true psychical reality': ' . . . *in its innermos*
nature it is as much unknown to us as the reality of the external worla
and it is as incompletely presented by the data of consciousness as i

ие *external world by the communications of our sense organs'* (V,
613). The metaphor is striking, but perhaps ill-considered. If the
nconscious really does bear strong analogy with Kant's noumenon,
иen it is not difficult to know, but impossible. Whereas it is the
urpose the *The Interpretation of Dreams*, and most of Freud's later
ork, to give us clear, reliable, and profound access to the world of the
nconscious.

That he was able to do so cannot be convincingly demonstrated here
or, some would argue, at all). To the extent that *The Interpretation of
Dreams* offers evidence for the validity of Freud's view of the uncon-
cious, it does so through his interpretations of particular dreams in
иe context of the lives of the people who dreamt them. The theore-
ical structure that I have sketched above is, in itself, compelling, but
s real vitality is derived from its human source. Which is true of all of
reud's theoretical writing. And only someone who has himself
иndergone the kind of rigorous self-inspection that *The Interpretation
f Dreams* records and recommends is likely to be a fit judge of its
nerits.

Freud's next book, *The Psychopathology of Everyday Life*, has
lways been one of his most popular. It is among his least demanding
vorks theoretically, yet gives a reasonably clear idea of his conceptual
оosition; and though it is filled with a vast number of detailed
xamples, these are amusing, and easy to relate to everyday experi-
иnce. It is a cosy book, free from pathological concerns, and unforth-
coming on the troublesome topic of human sexuality. Its subject – the
иsychic determinants of parapraxes, or everyday errors like forgetting,
lips of the tongue or pen, misreading – was first mentioned by Freud
и a letter to Fleiss in 1898. The book followed in 1901. Perhaps its
najor interest to us now, aside from its accessibility, lies in its rhetori-
al strategy, in the subtlety with which the reader may find himself
nexorably compelled to assent to premises in which he had no idea
hat he believed. Readers are offered an attempt to work with examples
lrawn from their own experience, a chance to confirm Freud's
оosition by resorting to their own interpretive work. For while the
leepest motivations of some errors may be profoundly submerged, in
nany cases an interpretation need meet with no very strong resis-
:ance.

But nothing in Freud's work is as simple as it may sound, or without substantial implications. Consider a sceptical reader, who was able

to analyse some of his own errors according to Freud's procedures: a interesting parlour trick, he might conclude, though of no signi cance. But the final chapter of *The Psychopathology of Everyday Li* is cunningly placed to challenge such complacency. It contai Freud's longest statement on the nature of psychic determinism:

> Many people, as is well known, contest the assumption of complete psychical determinism by appealing to a special feeling of conviction that there is a free will. This feeling of conviction exists; and it does not give way before a belief in determinism. Like every normal feeling it must have some-thing to warrant it. But so far as I can observe, it does not manifest itself on great and important decisions of the will: on these occasions the feeling that we have is rather one of psychical compulsion ('Here I stand: I can do no other.'). On the other hand, it is precisely with regard to the unimportant, indifferent decisions that we would like to claim that we could just as well have acted otherwise: that we have acted of our free – and unmotivated – will. . . . But what is thus left free by the one side receives its motivation from the other side, from the unconscious; and in this way determination in the psychical sphere is still carried out without any gap. (VI, pp.253-4)

Having assented to the particulars, our reader may find himse well on the way to becoming a Freudian without having wished to d so.

But he would be wrong to do so uncritically. The structure of *Th Psychopathology of Everyday Life*, like that of the later *Introductor Lectures on Psychoanalysis*, depends on a slow build-up from commonplace problems, to their analyses, and only then to a set o strictures which seem to gain validity from the evidence previousl presented. In the above passage, for instance, two particular problems which are not at first obvious, may come to mind: (1) though it i possible to discuss the question of free will with regard to *why* w should feel that it exists, does any analysis of the cause of our feelin throw light on its validity? The fact that a feeling may have hidde psychic determinants does not mean that it may not make a vali claim. (A similar problem underlies the later book, *The Future of a Illusion*, in which Freud traces the infantile roots of the belief in God

nd suggests that this establishes that God does not exist except in our
egressive need for him. But if God exists, he does so whether or not
eople believe in him, and whatever their reasons.) (2) Is the concept
f 'determined' as it is used here a clear one? It seems that it is used
ynonymously with 'motivated', but there is a distinction to be drawn
etween the two concepts: an error, for instance, may not occur for no
eason, but to say that there are reasons why it occurred (that it was
notivated) is not to entail that it, and only it, could have occurred (that
: was determined).

After the book on dreams, Freud's work on errors represents a
lling in of the argument, and not any substantial extension of it. The
ame might be said of *Jokes and their Relation to the Unconscious*
1905), though this richer and more ambitious achievement is
articularly interesting in that it contains Freud's first analyses of
tructures framed according to considerations that are as much aesthe-
ic as psychological. It is not Freud's purpose to discuss the factors that
ormally and linguistically constitute a joke, but instead to analyse our
notivations in telling them, and the effects that they produce. The
uestions – why do we create jokes? and what is the nature of the
leasure that we get from them? – have striking analogies with the
orts of questions that are asked about works of art; Freud's concept of
he 'work' that goes into the making of jokes thus repays study for
hose looking for a latent aesthetic theory in his works.

A book published in the same year, *Three Essays on the Theory of
Sexuality* makes substantial new theoretical contributions, moving
nto material that had been of critical importance to Freud since the
niddle 1890s, but which he had not, as yet, considered in detail. *The
nterpretation of Dreams*, in spite of its later additions, had in fact
underplayed the importance of sexuality as the key to latent dream
houghts – perhaps because Freud had used his own dreams as
naterial for discussion, but also because he had, at that time, no
dequately developed understanding of sexuality.

Though the book on sex followed that on dreams by six years, there
s no question that the one led directly to the other in Freud's mind; as
arly as 1899 he wrote to Wilhelm Fleiss, whose theory of innate
numan bisexuality had an important part to play in Freud's thinking
it the time: 'A theory of sexuality might well be the dream book's
mmediate successor' (VII, p.129). It is Freud's densest and most
courageous book, and he was at pains, in his successive prefaces to it,

to defend himself from the charge of morbid and exaggerated interest in sexual matters. Thus he reminds his reader that 'it is some time since Arthur Schopenhauer, the philosopher, showed mankind the extent to which their activities are determined by sexual impulses' (VII, p.134). Freud's attempt, within this context, was not to insist on the importance of sexuality *per se*, but to widen and deepen our understanding of its workings and ramifications.

He begins the *Three Essays* by distinguishing sexual aims (that is the various kinds of sexual activity) from sexual objects (the being with whom the activities take place). From observation of human sexual life from infancy to adulthood, it seemed clear to Freud that there is no adequate biological evidence to assert either that human beings are innately heterosexual or that they naturally incline towards genital intercourse: that is, that neither sexual object nor sexual aim are determined, at least in the first instance. In fact, 'the sexual instinct and the sexual object are merely soldered together . . . . It seems probable that the sexual instinct is in the first instance independent of its object; nor is its origin likely to be due to the object's attractions' (VII, p.148).

Freud did not regard all sexual object choices, and all sexual aims, as equally mature, yet his definition of 'perversity' is, properly understood, intended as value-free – as a deviation from a 'maturity' which is developmentally rather than morally understood. Were a sapling, by some quirk of nature, to fail to grow to its full height, no moral blame could be attached to it; equally, an adult neurotic who fails to develop along the natural path of sexual maturity (to genital heterosexuality) may be 'abnormal', but is certainly not to be regarded as immoral.

We need, then, a full characterization of the sexual nature of the child, from which we begin, and a description of the stages through which we pass on our way to sexual maturity. By 'sexual' nature of the child, Freud clearly does not refer to the capacity for that 'genital' pleasure that adults experience: he refers, instead, to the child's experience of sensual enjoyment through the erogenous zones. An infant, he argues, passes through a series of stages in which sensual pleasure is initially associated with the fulfilment of a somatic need, and later (in the absence of that fulfilment) with the area with which the need was associated. Thus, the mouth, anus, and genitals, originally in feeding, toilet-training, and bathing or urinating, are the respective foci of sexual pleasure. Any of these areas may, either in masturbation or with a sexual partner become the focus of perverse

activity – that is, activity not designed to lead directly to genital intercourse. Hence he concludes: 'the disposition to perversions is itself of
no great rarity but must form a part of what passes as the normal
constitution' (VII, p.171).

All of these stages occur in infancy, after which a 'latency period'
intervenes until the arrival of puberty, in which 'changes set in which
are destined to give infantile sexual life its final, normal shape'. The
genitals become the primary area of sexual pleasure, the aim of which
now lies in finding a (hetero)sexual object for the purposes of reproduc-
tion. In this transformation from the autoeroticism of childhood, two
'streams' of feeling – the 'affectionate' and the 'sensual' – which split
apart as a result of the Oedipal injunction against sensual intimacy of
parent and child, once again (ideally) come together in the choice of a
sexual partner.

This does not, of course always happen; nor does it always result,
when such maturation fails to occur, in sexual perversion. A variety of
inner and outer forces may combine to oppose the enactment of
perverse sexual longing: forces that Freud calls 'shame, disgust, and
morality'. But energy seeking discharge in perverse sexual activity,
however censored and redirected, must find its outlet. That outlet is
neurosis. Neurotic symptoms 'constitute the sexual activity of the
patient' (VII, p.163); psychoanalytic treatment of neurosis, therefore,
inevitably leads away from the particular symptom to its underlying
cause: the sexual 'fixation' from which the individual has been unable
to free himself. It is the purpose of psychoanalytic treatment to allow
the release of this energy, and thus to allow normal maturation to
recommence.

To understand the therapeutic intervention necessary to cause this
undamming of 'libido' (or sexual energy), it is necessary to look to
Freud's next major work, the *Introductory Lectures on Psychoanalysis* (1915-17), which concludes with a comprehensive discussion of
the nature of psychoanalytic treatment. The difficulty, as Freud
himself remarked, is that a proper understanding of psychoanalytic
therapy is almost impossible where one often has not undergone it
oneself, for psychoanalysis as therapy is based on talk between two
people – one of whom does the bulk of the talking. It is the role of the
analysand that is the most interesting, and most commonly miscon-
ceived. He does not seek understanding – either of the nature of his
illness or of the treatment he is undergoing – if understanding is

conceived as that rational activity designed to generate answers. Indeed, such attempts to intellectualize the process (except towards the conclusion of an analysis) are generally interpreted as signs of resistance. Instead, his role is an intellectually passive one: he attempts to become a sort of conscious filter through which unconscious material can find an undistorted expression. He reports dreams, memories, fantasies, and freely associates to the material he produces. To describe such an activity as 'passive' ought not to lead us to think, however, that it is easy. It is difficult enough to do merely by oneself; in the presence of a stranger (as the therapist initially will be), the constraints of propriety alone can be almost overwhelming. Yet without the eventual casting-off of such restraint, significant progress is impossible.

Psychoanalysis originated, and is still practised, as a form of therapy, though Freud often wondered whether this constituted its major contribution to human welfare. As he acknowledged, 'there are many ways of practising psychotherapy. All that lead to recovery are good.' But though analysis as therapy is but one means amongst many, it has stronger claims as a theory of mind:

> Psychoanalysis began as a method of treatment; but I did not want to commend it to your interest as a method of treatment but on account of the truths it contains, on account of the information it gives us about what concerns human beings most of all – their own nature – and on account of the connections it discloses between the most different of their activities. (XXII, pp.156-7)

This is not to minimize the claims of psychoanalysis as a curative procedure, nor to regard it as merely a by-product of a speculative meta-psychology. It is to point out that the importance of psychoanalysis lies also in its practical confirmation and exploration of the Freudian model of the human mind. Although his hypothesis grew out of a commitment to scientific assumptions concerning the determination, and hence potential explicability, of psychic life, these hypotheses are hardly susceptible to scientific verification. It is a peculiar aspect of Freud's genius to use in a powerful way a scientific world view without quite being contained within it. The corroboration of his general hypotheses lies in their efficacy as experienced many times over, yet individually, in the inner lives of patients. To see the status of his hypotheses in this way is to suggest its effective power, and also a reason for the unease with which Freud has been viewed by both scientists and artists; the latter relationship particularly providing the focus for the latter part of this essay.

A reader who has followed the discussion this far, working his way through the major texts from the *Studies on Hysteria* to the *Introductory Lectures*, should have no difficulty in understanding Freud's later work, which consists largely of further developments of the themes we have been following – *Beyond the Pleasure Principle* (1920) and the *New Introductory Lectures on Psychoanalysis* (1933)) and meta-psychological speculations based on already established argument (*The Future of an Illusion* (1927) and *Civilization and its Discontents* (1930). Valuable, indeed essential, as such work is to a comprehensive understanding of Freud's development, I will nevertheless stop at this point, having discussed those works which were likely to have an impact on English writers of the period 1900-30. I will close this section, then, with some short remarks on Freud's views on literature, and go on in the next section to discuss reactions to his work from influential writers in the period.

Freud's own views on literature are spread throughout his works, which contain little sustained reference to aesthetic problems, at least insofar as these can be considered in themselves. Psychoanalysis he considered a universal science both insofar as it applied to everyone, and also because it could be applied to all varieties of human experience. As psychic phenomena, the arts needed no special vocabulary, though Freud certainly acknowledged that psychoanalysis had no particular contribution to make to the questions surrounding artistic technique. The following passage accurately represents his view of the artist:

> For there is a path that leads back from phantasy to reality – the path, that is, of art. An artist is once more in rudiments an introvert, not far removed from neurosis. He is oppressed by excessively powerful instinctual needs. He desires to win honour, power, wealth, fame and the love of women; but he lacks the means for achieving these satisfactions. Consequently, like any other unsatisfied man, he turns away from reality and transfers all his interest, and his libido too, to the

wishful constructions of his life of phantasy, whence the path might lead to neurosis. There must be, no doubt, a convergence of all kinds of things if this is not to be the complete outcome of his development; it is well known, indeed, how often artists in particular suffer from a partial inhibition of their efficiency owing to neurosis. Their constitution probably includes a strong capacity for sublimation and a certain degree of laxity in the repressions which are decisive for a conflict. (XVI, pp.375-6)

Freud's interest, then, is not really in the manifest content of the work, but in those latent repressions that constitute the fantasy life that the work deviously enacts. Even acknowledging this limitation, the passage is still disappointing. The description of the 'artist' – do we really believe in the psychological typology that generates the term? – is on a level too general to offer us much; it doesn't allow, for instance, a clear distinction between artists and that host of other men who share their (I would have thought universal) clamorous needs. Indeed, the passage carries the implication that what psychoanalytic approaches to works of art *do* is make them go away – transform them back into the psychic contents that generate them, and which they come to represent in disguised forms.

Freud's comments on literature are largely by way of illustration of some particular pathological phenomenon. The passages that comment briefly on *Hamlet*, in *The Interpretation of Dreams* (IV, pp.264-6), could be cut from that text without loss of content; but they serve as the basis for the most famous of all Freudian readings of literature, Ernest Jones' *Hamlet and Oedipus*.[13] But Freud's many followers, both professional and amateur, have since produced a great range of psychoanalytic interpretations of works of art that seek to preserve the work's autonomy from the reductive qualities of Freud's own procedures. Psychoanalysis can be used not merely to explain the relation of an author to his work, but also facets of that work itself: the inner lives of its characters, the nature of its imagery, its fundamental themes. Hence the impact of Freud on the reading of literature is often most visible where it is at its weakest: in the monolithic and reductive application of Freudian ideas and material. It has had its most vital import where it enters the general quality of the reader's consciousness (his willingness to pick up the signals of latent and oblique meanings) and is thus not immediately and exclusively attributable to Freud. A case in point would be the essay 'Regulated Hatred: An Aspect of the Work of Jane Austen' [14] by the psychologist and literary critic D.W. Harding. This study of Jane Austen's ironic humour as a controlled manifestation of negative feeling is inconceivable in a pre-Freudian context, and yet the essay works from the non-specialist standpoint of an educated reader rather than implying the privileged insight of the Freudian disciple. It is in this more pervasive, although less visible, way that Freud had his strongest, if oblique, impact on the reading of literature.

II

The period from 1900 to 1930 is the richest and densest in English literature since the Renaissance, astonishing for the wealth of its major figures and works, and for the extraordinary range and vitality of its creative achievements. The novel maintains the narrative traditions of the Victorians not so much in the continued presence of Hardy (who writes largely poetry during this time) as in the figures of Galsworthy and Bennett, who are the (not always easy) contemporaries of modernist figures like Lawrence and Joyce. In poetry, a similar distinction emerges between the traditional voices of the Georgian poets, so like in vocal range to those of Arnold and Tennyson, and the experimental forms and rhythms of Eliot and Pound. Literature in the period both maintains and enlarges its traditions, and also breaks with them. Though the great diversity of the work produced during these three decades makes generalizations risky, it might nevertheless be observed that the 'influence' of Freud on the writers of the period is greatest with those whom we regard as most 'modern'. That I should need to use inverted commas here indicates the nature of the difficulty: the 'modernity' of Joyce, or Lawrence, rests partly in the ways in which each inhabits the same intellectual ground as Freud does – but what is most interesting in pursuing the topic is not to trace a putative 'influence', but to discover the different ways in which each explores the new terrain.

Freud's work had posed, in a most compelling and detailed manner, the problem of the unconscious, and of the kinds of introspection needed to have reliable knowledge of it. It was not necessary to accept Freud's version of the nature of the unconscious, even in some modified form, to share his concern for the deepest privacies of our being. It is one of the characteristics of what we may call modernism that it combines an acute interest in the nature of introspection with the apprehension that such an interest requires new forms to accommodate it. For the modern novelist, to continue in the narrative modes of Dickens or Trollope would be to accept a version of the inner life that fundamentally falsified its verbal and emotional rhythms – if the two can be clearly distinguished at all. And though connections can be made between Freudian theory and, say, *Sons and Lovers* or *Ulysses*, in neither case would it be accurate to regard the work as 'Freudian'; it is enough to say that both – and the same is true of 'The Waste Land', Pound's *Cantos*, Virginia Woolf's *Mrs Dalloway*, and a host of others – are moving, as Freud was moving, towards greater creative understanding of the nature of the unconscious.[15]

Let us accept, then, that 'influence' – especially when we are dealing with complex ideas and complex minds – is by no means an unambiguous process, but even granting the kinds of indirection that it characteristically displays, there remain two difficulties in assessing Freud's effect on the literature of this period: (1) we must make a sharp distinction between what Freud actually said, and what he was taken to say, or reported to have said. Most early commentators, if they had read Freud at all, did so in translation, and many had not even done that. Contemporary accounts of his thinking were often limited to a consideration of selected Freudian concepts (particularly the unconscious, repression, and the libido), with all too little attention to their theoretical superstructure. By the 1920s – *The Interpretation of Dreams* was published in England in 1915 – a widespread familiarity with Freudian jargon served as a kind of intellectual slang, but entailed no necessary accompanying comprehension of Freudian theory. (2) Even when Freud was taken carefully, no comprehensive picture of his work could emerge because that work was incomplete; Freud was constantly refining formulations of old concepts, and introducing new material to an understanding that was, during this period, increasing in breadth as well as depth. The important text, *Civilization and its Discontents*, was published in 1930, and thus postdates all of the important literary works of the period in question.

The London Psychoanalytic Society was founded in October of 1913 – the year of publication of *Sons and Lovers* – with Ernest Jones as its President; of the original nine members, only four actually practised psychoanalysis. At the time only one book on the subject of psychoanalysis existed in English, and none of Freud's works had yet been translated. Yet from this quiet beginning, and within only about a decade, psychoanalysis captured the imagination of a number and range of people that must have been astonishing to even its most enthusiastic adherents. The primary reason for this, of course, was the war. To a generation dazed by the contemplation of that nightmare – the senseless brutality which seemed to shatter the cultural assumptions of an entire era – Freud seemed to offer a variety of conceptual pegs on which to hang the hats of freedom, individualism, liberation and modernity. And if the nature of the hat invariably obscured the contour of the peg, that was fair enough. Freud was championed and pilloried with equal verve and misunderstanding; he was topical, provocative, and apparently easy to use in defence of virtually whatever new position one wished to maintain. In retrospect (perhaps this is always true in such cases), it is the satire that the 'Freudians' were subjected to that is most memorable; thus we have G.K. Chesterton's remarks on the effects of psychoanalysis on the literature of the period:

> Some ridiculous mythology about every man having inside him a sort of aged and microcephalous monkey. Wistful and melancholy poems were written about how trying it is to have a monkey inside him, and ethical essays earnestly debate whether the man should own the monkey or the monkey the man.[16]

However misguided a summary, its cunning assimilation of the Freudian to the Darwinian – designed to invoke anxieties not merely of a sexual but also a metaphysical kind – makes a connection not unusual in critiques of psychoanalysis: that it represented yet another step in the intellectual rejection of the Divine that has characterized modern Western thought. And in this, of course, Chesterton was quite right.

For the novelists and poets of the time inhabited, largely, a godless world, and the energy freed from the search for grace found its uneasy new goal in the search for self-knowledge. The generalization is, of course, too broad. But if it would be extreme to argue that the novel of the twentieth century is more mature than its predecessors – is Leopold Bloom more convincingly adult than Elizabeth Bennett? – it is unquestionably more comprehensive in its consideration of their

adultness. This is not a matter simply of explicitness, of the opening o
the doors of the lavatory and bedroom, though it may entail that, bu
of a seeking for that wholeness that demands integration, rather than
renunciation, of the unclean, undignified, and unacceptable.

Lawrence is an interesting case here. There is no need to disbelieve
his claim that the first drafts of *Sons and Lovers* (first entitled *Pau.
Morel* – the change is itself significant) were written before he had
read Freud. Yet on his first exposure to the Freudian theory, Lawrence
could only have found the results of his introspection substantiated
enlarged, and generalized. Equally, the early English Freudians were
quick to spot in Lawrence a potential ally in the exploration of the
psychic terrain opened by Freud's research. *Sons and Lovers* so
explicitly enacts the Oedipal situation, and its result in the schism that
Freud called the complex of the Madonna and the Prostitute, that it
might almost serve as a case study for aspiring psychoanalysts. Consider the following:

> He looked round. A good many of the nicest men he knew
> were like himself, bound in by their own virginity, which
> they could not break out of. They were so sensitive to their
> women that they would go without them forever rather than
> do them a hurt, an injustice. Being the sons of mothers
> whose husbands had blundered rather brutally through their
> feminine sanctities, they were themselves too diffident and
> shy. They could easier deny themselves than incur any
> reproach from a woman; for a woman was like their mother,
> and they were full of the sense of their mother. They
> preferred themselves to suffer the misery of celibacy, rather
> than risk the other person.[17]

This (like so many of the attempts to extrapolate generalizations from
the narrative in Lawrence) is weak in context, because those nice other
young men have no existence in the novel, but its attempt to univer-
salize a particular psychic situation recalls Freud's similar effort in the
1890s.

There is plenty in Lawrence to suggest a debt to Freud; indeed, his
mature effort seems designed explicitly to promote that making of the
unconscious conscious that Freud had recommended. But when
Lawrence said 'we must grow from our deepest underground roots,
out of the *unconsciousness*, not from the conscious concepts which we

alsely call ourselves',[18] his alliances were rather with Blake and Nietzsche than with Freud: with the romantic tradition in which the ruition of the unknown brings with it freshness and energy, not stale, f pungent, reincarnation of the past.[19] Freudianism, then, sees only half truths', correctly gauging the importance of the unconscious, but misrepresenting its nature. Lawrence's *Psychoanalysis and the Unconscious* (1921), a confused, rambling, and intermittently brilliant book, makes this point attractively:

> Once we can admit the *known*, but incomprehensible, presence of the integral unconscious; once we can trace it home in ourselves and follow its first revealed movements; once we can know how it habitually unfolds itself; once we can scientifically determine its laws and processes in ourselves: then at last we can begin to live from the spontaneous initial prompting, instead of from the dead machine-principles of ideas and ideals. There is a whole science of the creative unconscious, the unconscious in its law-abiding activities. And of this science we do not even know the first term. Yes, when we know that the unconscious appears by creation, as a new individual reality in every fertilized germ-cell, then we know the very first term of the new science. But it needs a superscientific grace before we can admit this first new item of knowledge. It means that science abandons its intellectualist position and embraces the old religious faculty. But it does not thereby become less scientific, it only becomes at last complete in knowledge.[20]

The search for the integral unconscious, for that 'spontaneous initial prompting', becomes the basis of all of Lawrence's work in the 1920s. The wholeness that it affirms is certainly not that described by Freud, though it has striking affinities with the thinking of C.G. Jung. In the later Lawrence, the stress on myth, ritual, and religion, the tendency to see the world in polarities rather than causal networks, the insistence on the collective nature of the unconscious (and its difference in men and women), and the concern with the drama of the mature individual struggling to become himself, are remarkably similar to themes in Jung which treat the archetypal nature of the collective unconscious, and its role in what Jung called 'the individuation process'. But Lawrence, who may have anticipated such a connection

being suggested, nowhere writes of Jung at any length, and always
slightingly: 'Freud is with the scientists. Jung dodges from his univer
sity gown into a priest's surplice till we don't know where we are.'[21]
Lawrence was frequently accused, sometimes by himself, of similar
sleights of role.

A remark of James Joyce's is similar in tone: Jung is 'the Swiss
Tweedledum who is not to be confused with the Viennese Tweedle-
dee, Dr Freud.'[22] Unlike Lawrence, who was struggling for some way
to place and profit from Freud without having to become a disciple,
Joyce's comments on psychoanalysis are only occasional, and
unremittingly hostile. This may suggest, if we have learned our
psychoanalytic lessons, an even deeper connection between Joyce and
Freud than between Lawrence and Freud – an interpretive procedure
that psychoanalysis not only sanctions, but frequently requires.

A Portrait of the Artist as a Young Man shares with *Sons and
Lovers* a concern with the importance and strength of the instincts,
the terrible explosiveness engendered by frustration of sexual need, the
formative influence of childhood on the adult psyche, and the inhibi-
tions and anxieties caused by the neurotic possibilities of the nuclear
family. But in the case of Joyce we can see a second area in which
psychoanalysis may have influenced the fiction of the period: for Freud
not only suggests new areas of inquiry, but also a new language – or, at
least, a new view of language. There are striking analogies between
Freud's use of free association and the literary 'stream of consciousness', a term which needs more clarification than I can give it here,
but which generically describes that style which attempts to present
the mind in unmediated flux, capturing the rhythms of the process of
thought itself. This at once suggests a certain disorder in thought, in
its apparently random meandering, and yet at the same time (here the
analogy with free association is most interesting) is capable of demonstrating new sources of orderliness whereby the transition from the
important to the general, may be explained with reference to the
underlying affective states that language expresses. Take the following
passage from *Ulysses*:

> STEPHEN: (Abruptly) What went forth to the ends of the
> world to traverse not itself. God, the sun, a commercial
> traveller, having itself traversed in reality itself, becomes
> that self. Wait a moment. Wait a second. Damn that

fellow's noise in the street. Self which it itself was ineluct-
ably preconditioned to become. *Ecco!*[23]

The freedom from normal conventions of syntax, the easy movement
as thought follows thought – reacting both to internal processes and to
apparently gratuitous external stimuli – suggest that associative
principles other than those governing normal discourse are at work.
And, certainly, there is considerable psychological interest in the
meditation, particularly in the suggested continuity between the
procreative principle and the movement of the seasons. As in a free
association, nothing is gratuitous – but for a different reason. Here,
the principle of continuity, linking thought to thought, is found not
with reference to the particularities of Stephen's psychic condition,
but only in Joyce's overriding aims as a novelist. Thus for instance,
the reference to the sun is designed to remind us of Stephen's earlier
implied pun of 'sun' with 'son',[24] and to prepare us for Molly's later
meditation on the meaning of a day;[25] the apparently accidental 'noise
in the street'[26] reminds us that Stephen has previously defined God as
just that; indeed, the passage is densely connected at all points with the
overriding symbolic dispositions of the novel. In this it is no less free
than a 'free' association, but the constraints are crucially different.

I have chosen to quote this passage, from among any number of
possibilities offered by *Ulysses*, because its placement in the 'Circe'
chapter suggests a second way in which Freud may have affected
Joyce's use of language. We may observe a significant parallel between
Freud and Joyce with respect to what Freud called 'the primary
process'. In the 'Nighttown' episode, Joyce clearly intends a dramatic
presentation that captures the feeling of the world of dreams: hallucinatory images appear and disappear, genders shift, identities fade into
and out of each other, time moves backwards or forwards – all with a
terrifying but not irrational arbitrariness. This is the 'true psychic
reality' that Bloom and Stephen inhabit, and which inhabits them –
and the phrase is Freud's, not Joyce's. Indeed, by the time of publication of *Finnegans Wake*, the concern with a day in the life has shifted
to one for a night in the life: its protagonist is asleep throughout his
own narrative, which is dominated by those processes that make up
Freud's 'dream work' – condensation, displacement, symbolization.
But H.C. Earwicker, like Bloom, is both convincingly human and a
fictive construct: ultimately all is art, not life – filtered by the secondary

process, mediated by authorial considerations throughout. From Joyce's work we can best learn how Freud can help us in reading literature, and also the extent to which that aid is limited.

It is not a difficult step to see the ways in which these adjustments of linguistic possibility may have affected a generation of modernist poets in whose work imagery is increasingly freed from even the minimal commitments to narrative of the traditional lyric. In the imagist poets, in Eliot, in Pound, the image, while still cemented into the aesthetic foundation of the whole (except when the image is that whole), can attain to that numinous particularity that we associate with the products of the unconscious. The Surrealists used Freud (wrongly, I think) to support a theoretical allegiance to the autonomy of the unconscious image; more fruitfully, Freud may be seen to have sanctioned the possibility whereby the poem is released from its obligation to some compressed attenuation of the syntactic conventions governing prose. The transitions in 'The Waste Land' are stark, unpredictable, confusing, but never without purpose, never arbitrary. Freud allows us (in Kenneth Burke's phrase)[27] to see the 'poem as dream' – not as *a* dream, but as the product of a communicative process, governed by its own modes of coherence. Lionel Trilling makes a related point:

> For, of all mental systems, the Freudian psychology is the one which makes poetry indigenous to the very constitution of the mind. Indeed, the mind, as Freud sees it, is in the greater part of its tendency exactly a poetry-making organ. . . . Freud has not merely naturalized poetry; he has discovered its status as a pioneer settler, and he sees it as a method of thought.[28]

The comment is intended to apply to all poetry, but it has, I feel, particular relevance to the modernist poems of our century.

Freud's concern with dreaming, then, suggests certain new possibilities for the freeing of language from the normal demands of logical progression as they are embodied in our syntactic conventions. His interpretive procedures in dealing with dreams involve taking particular images, and then paying careful and prolonged attention to the hidden ambiguities, the depths of feeling, the whole range of suggestion and nuance, that they may be made to reveal. At this point my reader may observe that the procedure sounds a good deal like literary

riticism as it is now practised. For modern critical methodology, like
Freud's interpretations of dreams, is concerned to attend in detail to
hat about which previous commentators remained silent. Of course,
t would be absurd to argue that Johnson, Coleridge, or Matthew
Arnold did not read acutely and with due attention to the intricacies of
he text; my point is that the fruits of such attention find their way into
heir criticism only indirectly. We trust their generalizations, to be
sure, because they confirm that prolonged attention to the text has
gone on – but the criticism is not concerned to point out to us the
ntricacies of particular passages in the text. It is only since the publica-
ion of I.A. Richards' *Practical Criticism* (1929), and the impetus
given it by the later work of William Empson in England, and the
'New Critics' in America, that it has been felt to be the critics' major
ask to give us 'a reading' of a work – to take us through it, like a
sophisticated guide, discovering its byways, mapping connections,
exploring the detail of different passages.

Though Richards was interested in psychology, and in the poem as
a communication from a particular man to a reader, that interest is not
a psychoanalytic one, except in one important sense: literary criticism
and psychological interpretation are based on modes of attention that,
Richards suggests, have more in common than had previously been
recognized:

> Compare now the attitude to speech of the alienist attempt-
> ing to 'follow' the ravings of mania or the dream maunder-
> ings of a neurotic. I do not suggest that we should treat one
> another as 'mental cases' but merely that for some subject
> matters and some types of discussion the alienist's attitude,
> his direction of attention, his order or plan of interpretation,
> is far more fruitful, and would lead to better understanding
> on both sides of the discussion, than the usual method that
> our language-habits force upon us.[29]

The connection between the reading of a poem and the 'reading' of a
dream is apt insofar as both are dense means of communication, but
we may see similar connections between the methodologies of a great
variety of modern disciplines which are committed to analytical procedures and structural analysis, whether those structures be poetic,
psychic, anthropological, philosophical, or whatever. Freud is hardly
the founder of this analytic tradition, but no consideration of the

development of nineteenth-century positivism into contemporary analytic methodology can ignore his seminal role.

But why, then, should such significant modern writers as Lawrence and Joyce (and one could easily instance others) have been hostile to Freud, who seems so clearly to have anticipated and shared so many of their concerns? Having asked the question in its particular form is to suggest its general version: have artists rejected psychoanalysis? We are frequently assured that the answer to this is 'yes', particularly by individual artists who wish to do so. And this is manifestly false. I have suggested that the category 'artists' is itself not a very clear one, and observed that what a particular writer may reject, in rejecting 'psycho-analysis', may bear only a very distorted relationship to what psycho-analysis actually is. In any case, the question as to the relationship of literature to psychoanalysis – implying the greater question of the relations of the arts and the sciences – seems to me wrongly framed. To speak of the possible 'influence' of Freud is to suggest his difference from the artists of his time; but I would like to close by once again remarking his similarity. Freud is not, finally, so much an influence on a generation of creative writers as a colleague of theirs, whose picture of the nature and plight of man is in its own way as compelling and deeply felt as that of any modern writer. Lionel Trilling makes just this point in beginning his well-known essay on 'Freud and Literature':

> The Freudian psychology is the only systematic account of the human mind which, in point of subtlety and complexity, of interest and tragic power, deserves to stand beside the chaotic mass of psychological insights which literature has accumulated through the centuries.[30]

As I began with a quotation from Freud's seventieth birthday party, I shall end with one from his eightieth: this time, with the text of a letter of congratulations sent to Freud as a birthday tribute, signed by 197 prominent European artists. Signatories included H.G. Wells, Virginia Woolf, Jules Romains; the text was delivered to Freud by Thomas Mann, in whose style it would appear to be written:

> The eightieth birthday of Sigmund Freud gives us a welcome opportunity to convey to the pioneer of a new and deeper knowledge of man our congratulations and our veneration. In every important sphere of his activity, as physician and

psychologist, as philosopher and artist, this courageous seer and healer has for two generations been a guide to hitherto undreamt-of regions of the human soul. An independent spirit, 'a man and knight, grim and stern of visage' as Nietzsche said of Schopenhauer, a thinker and investigator who knew how to stand alone and then draw many to him and with him, he went his way and penetrated to truths which seemed dangerous because they revealed what had anxiously been hidden, and illumined dark places. Far and wide he disclosed new problems and changed the old standards; in his seeking and perceiving he extended many times the field of mental research, and made even his opponents indebted to him through the creative stimulus they derived from him. Even should the future remould and modify one result or another of his researches, never again will the questions be stilled which Sigmund Freud put to mankind; his gains for knowledge cannot permanently be denied or obscured. The conceptions he built, the words he chose for them, have already entered the living language and are taken for granted. In all spheres of human science, in the study of literature and art, in the evolution of religion and prehistory, in poetry itself his achievement has left a deep mark; and, we feel sure, if any deed of our race remains unforgotten it will be his deed of penetrating into the depths of the human mind.

We, the undersigned, who cannot imagine our mental world without Freud's bold life-work, are happy to know that this great man with his unflagging energy is still among us and still working with undiminished strength. May our grateful feelings long accompany the man we venerate.[31]

It is a powerful testimony. Two generations later, acknowledging the cultural and intellectual perspectives into which we must now place Freud, I would still not change a single word.

Notes

1   See, for instance, Lionel Trilling, 'Freud and Literature', in *The Liberal Imagination*, New York 1950, p.32.

2 L.L. Whyte, *The Unconscious before Freud*, London 1962.

3 ibid., p.60.

4 Cited in Whyte, *The Unconscious before Freud*, op. cit., p.176.

5 Ernest Jones, *Sigmund Freud: Life and Work*, vol. I, London 1957 p.392.

6 This and other volume and page references are taken from *The Standard Edition of the Complete Psychological Works of Sigmund Freud*, ed James Strachey, London 1953-74.

7 Preface to the Second Edition of *Studies on Hysteria*, 1908, in *The Standard Edition*, op. cit., II, p.xxxi.

8 For an account of the first uses of the term, see Jones, *Sigmund Freud: Life and Work*, vol. I, op. cit., p.217.

9 Cited in Jones, *Sigmund Freud: Life and Work*, vol. I, op. cit., p.45.

10 ibid., vol. I, p.31.

11 Richard Wollheim, *Freud*, London 1971, p.35.

12 For a discussion of this point, see Paul Roazen, *Freud and his Followers* New York 1975, pp. 124-5.

13 *Hamlet and Oedipus*, New York 1949.

14 *Scrutiny*, VIII, 1940, pp.346-62.

15 The most comprehensive, and still the best, discussion of this subject is F.J. Hoffman, *Freudianism and the Literary Mind*, Baton Rouge, LA 1945.

16 G.K. Chesterton, 'The Game of Psychoanalysis', *Century*, CVI, 1923 pp.41-2.

17 *Sons and Lovers*, London 1960, p.341.

18 *The Collected Letters of D.H. Lawrence*, ed. H.T. Moore, London 1970 p.396.

19 For a discussion of the relation between Freud and the romantic tradition see Trilling, 'Freud and Literature', op. cit., pp.32-54.

20 *Psychoanalysis and the Unconscious*, New York 1921, pp.43-4.

21 *Fantasia of the Unconscious*, London 1923, p.15.

22 *Letters of James Joyce*, ed. S. Gilbert, London 1957, p.166.

23 *Ulysses*, New York 1961, p.505.

24 ibid., p.207.

25 ibid., p.782.

26 ibid., p.34. (The reference is to a 'shout in the street', but the parallel is clear enough.)

27 Kenneth Burke, 'Freud – and the Analysis of Poetry', reprinted in *Psychoanalysis and Literature*, ed. Ruitenbeck, New York 1964, p.121.

28 'Freud and Literature', op. cit., pp.49-50.

29 *Practical Criticism*, London 1973, p.7.

30 'Freud and Literature', op. cit., p.32.

31 Cited in Jones, *Sigmund Freud: Life and Work*, vol. III, op. cit. pp.219-20.

Select bibliography

Hall, Calvin S. *A Primer of Freudian Psychology*, New York 1954.
Hoffman, F.J. *Freudianism and the Literary Mind*, Baton Rouge, LA 1945.
Jones, E. *Hamlet and Oedipus*, New York 1949.
——— *Sigmund Freud: Life and Work*, London 1957.
Kris, E. *Psychoanalytic Explorations in Art*, London 1953.
Nelson, B. (ed.) *Freud and the 20th Century*, London 1958.
Rieff, P. *The Triumph of the Therapeutic: Uses of Faith after Freud*, New York 1966.
Roazen, P. *Freud and His Followers*, New York 1975.
Ruitenbeck, H.M. (ed.) *Psychoanalysis and Literature*, New York 1964.
Storr, A. *The Dynamics of Creation*, London 1972.
Trilling, L. 'Freud and Literature', in *The Liberal Imagination*, New York, 1950
Wollheim, R. *Freud*, London 1971.

6 Revolutions in the visual arts

CYRIL BARRETT

I

The period 1900-30 witnessed revolutions in the visual arts such as had not been seen since the Renaissance. Indeed, they were more radical than the Renaissance revolution. The Renaissance harked back to precedents of what in classical antiquity had been considered fine art. The revolutions of the early twentieth century may have had precedents, but on the whole they were in areas which had not hitherto been regarded as art. Moreover, the scope of these revolutions was wider, since they included film and photography, as well as painting, sculpture, print-making and the so-called applied arts.

It is hard to say when these revolutions began. One could date them from impressionism or even further back. But to keep within our period we must begin with the cubist revolution, which in any case is more radical and more far-reaching in its consequences than any of the others within the period. Indeed, some would say that it was *the* revolution and that all the others followed from it. I shall discuss this view in due course.

One important feature of the cubist revolution, which revolutions immediately preceding it shared to some degree, was that it took the artificiality of art seriously. All artists (as opposed to critics and public) have recognized this, at least implicitly. But, since the time of the Renaissance, some have behaved as if they believed that the function of art was to 'hold the mirror up to nature' in some literal sense. This, of course, was what Plato accused painting of doing; and persistent misinterpretation of Aristotle's notion of *mimesis* (usually translated 'imitation') encouraged the view that this is what representational art does (each art imitating in its own manner, but all imitating). In fact, though visual art draws on nature, it does not duplicate it. Indeed, as Ernst Gombrich in *Art and Illusion* and elsewhere, and as others too, have shown, it is not possible to duplicate nature in any artistic medium (though it may be possible to deceive the spectator, in certain special conditions, into thinking you had done so). At most, art can give an analogue or equivalent of nature, with the ratios of light and shade, colour values and shapes similar to those in nature, much as a plan of a building relates to the actual building. A picture or a piece of sculpture constitutes at most a reconstruction of nature; but essentially it is a construction. As a construction it is governed by laws and requirements of its own, which may conform to those in nature, but do not have to. It was the full realization of this, and the ability and courage to act on this realization, which was the essential feature of the cubist revolution as a revolution. Once the revolution had succeeded, naturalism in visual art could never again be the sole acceptable theory or practice.

The revolution, like most revolutions, came about slowly (contrary to popular belief); though when it came it seemed abrupt and shocking. One can plot its advance through a series of minor revolutions. The Impressionists, for all their preoccupation with the scientific observation of the effects of light on coloured objects, succeeded in liberating colour from its traditional function of defining solid objects and distinguishing near from distant objects – the bright green fields which ultimately appear blue as they recede into the distance. The liberation of colour was carried further by the Post-Impressionists, each in his different way. Van Gogh built up his compositions with vibrant, strongly reacting colours such as few of us see in nature. Gauguin placed colour flat on the surface of the picture as it is in heraldry or tapestry. Cézanne returned to the solidity of objects and their relationship in depth, but without losing the vibrancy of colour of the Impressionists or returning to the old techniques of naturalism. Thus he could make objects – a mountain, a rock, a table, fruit, a human being – look solid without using contrasts of light and shade (chiaroscuro). And he could make them appear distant without losing their colour – a field on a far-away mountain would be as freshly green as one in the foreground.

Although Van Gogh, Gauguin and Cézanne gave cause for alarm

among those who were aware of their existence, they at least approxi
mated to 'local' colour in their paintings. A tree was green and brown
a cow was black, white or brown; the sky was blue, etc. In the firs
decade of the twentieth century, however, artists began to take greate
liberties with colour. In France a group known as *Les Fauves* (Th
Wild Beasts), which included Matisse, Braque and Vlaminck, and ir
Germany a group known as *Die Brücke* (The Bridge) were abandon
ing local colour. The trunk of a tree could be bright red, a face brillian
yellow or a cow blue. Moreover, these artists became very conscious o
the surface of the picture or the so-called 'picture plane'. As Mauric
Denis had said in 1890: 'Remember that a picture . . . is essentially :
flat surface covered with colours arranged in a certain order.'
Although these artists probably did not do so, we must distinguish
between the surface of the canvas (wall, panel, paper or whatever) tha
the picture is painted on and the picture plane: the two do not coin
cide. A picture restorer examining it for flaking or some other form o
deterioration will look only at the surface of the paint, and, for him, :
shepherd in the foreground is neither nearer nor further away than :
distant mountain. To someone looking at it as a picture the pain
surface is of no interest as such, nevertheless he must be consciou
that the picture has no real depth – you cannot walk towards th
pictorial distant mountain. He has, therefore, to *take* some part of the
picture as the plane or foreground from which the rest appears tc
recede. To give a simple example. These letters seem to lie on top o
the white paper and it acts as their background. They form the *plane* o
the page, but the white 'background' lies on the same *surface* as the
print; plane and surface differ.

The Cubists, as well shall see, were to make much of this. Indeed
they exploited it for reasons of their own. This emphasized the artifi
ciality of art. But their revolution, as I have said, was more radical still.

All the movements or minor revolutions which I have mentioned –
impressionism, post-impressionism, fauvism – sedulously preserved
traditional orientation. Traditionally both painting and sculpture
assumed either a fixed or a principle viewpoint. In other words, if you
looked at a landscape, it would appear to be the view you would have i
you stood in a certain spot on a hill or in a room. You might be able to
walk around a statue, but there was usually a point from which it
looked best, an optimum viewing-point. Moreover, a good picture was
one in which spatial relationships were coherent that is, you could

place things in relationship to one another – floors were flat, table-legs were at right-angles to them, table-tops parallel to them, and so on. If there was any divergence from the norm – an uneven floor, a wobbly or falling table – this could be detected. The Cubists changed all that. If a cubist picture is coherent, it is on its own terms, and not because it represents the coherent spatial relationships of the world in which we live. In place of the single viewpoint, they introduced the multiple viewpoint, so that an object or even a face could be shown from many angles at the same time.

But the Cubists did not stop there. What I have so far described, while breaking with traditional methods of painting or making sculpture, could easily be related to them in the way people relate non-Euclidean geometry to Euclidean geometry by saying that the former can be seen as the latter applied to a curved surface. In other words, one can say that the multiple viewpoint of cubism is a more dynamic way of representing an object, that is, it represents the object as it appears when either you walk around it or it turns (or is turned). This will work well enough (though it is far from adequate) if one is talking about the period of what is called 'analytical' cubism, from 1907 to 1912; but it cannot be applied to the subsequent period of 'synthetic' cubism.

Synthetic cubism operated from an entirely different basis from that of analytical cubism, even though the end products may not have been greatly dissimilar. During the period of analytical cubism the Cubists systematically broke down the appearance of objects into their simplest recognizable geometrical shapes as seen from various angles (not only left and right, in the traditional sense, but also above and below). But, however odd the result, and however difficult it was to recognize the original object, the point of departure in the analysis was always an existing object, whether a girl playing a mandolin, a table covered with bottles and glasses or the landscape at Estaque, in the south of France. For reasons which will be discussed presently, the Cubists from 1912 reversed this process. In other words, they ceased to take the object as their point of departure. Instead they began with the materials of their art. And here we have another deviation from tradition, since these materials were as likely to be old newspapers, wallpaper, sand, hair or pieces of wood as to be paint. Starting from these materials they constructed a composition which gradually came to resemble some recognizable object – a man with a pipe, a gorilla with young or a bull (made out of the saddle and handle-bars of a bicycle).

The cubist revolution was now complete. The painter and sculptor was finally liberated from his role as imitator and free to follow his art in whatever direction it might take him. Not that artists of the past had not followed their artistic inclinations nor that this newly won independence was any guarantee of superior quality, but, for what it was worth, it was a new stage in the history of painting and sculpture. Others were to carry the implications of the revolution further than the Cubists themselves. But, before considering these other revolutions, I should like to say something more about cubism.

II

Cézanne had a profound influence on the Cubists. Between 1904 and his death in 1906 there had been frequent exhibitions of his work, and in the following year there was a major retrospective. Another influence was African and Oceanic masks. Many of the Cubists collected them. What prompted them to do so is not certain. It seems to have been a fashion among artists at the time. Les Fauves also collected them. Indeed, judging from some paintings of Matisse of the time and some by Derain, in which the influence of Cézanne as well as primitive art is evident, it is somewhat surprising that it was not they, but Picasso and Braque, who were the originators of cubism. The appeal of these objects is clear. They represented human features without any attempt at fidelity of detail. Indeed they were not the result of observation but of art: their makers had built from the inside out, so to speak; that is, they had made a construction which resembled but did not copy the features of a human face. Picasso was also interested in Catalan art. He came from Catalonia and had visited it in 1906. From the amalgam of all three (Cézanne, and Negro and Catalan sculpture), plus Egyptian art, emerged what may be regarded as the most important painting of the twentieth century, Les Demoiselles d'Avignon (1907).

Les Demoiselles d'Avignon, which is now in the Museum of Modern Art, New York, is not a completely coherent picture, and shows signs of its revisions. But this is its strength rather than its weakness. When Picasso showed it to his friends, they were taken aback. Derain said: 'One day we shall find Pablo has hanged himself behind his great canvas.' Although nothing more than the seeds of cubism were in it, it still remains a shattering picture. Its ostensible subject is a brothel scene in the Calle Avignon, a street in the red-light district of Barcelona. But the inmates have become, reading from left to right, Egyptian, Catalan and African. The Africans are not only the latest additions, but the most interesting. We are accustomed to the ambiguous poses of Egyptians; the Catalan girls in this context look almost normal; it is left to the Africans (I cannot call them girls, since the one in the right foreground is nothing more than a mask) to draw our attention to the ambiguity of the picture. In the case of the Negro-masked figure in the bottom right-hand corner we are looking at back-view and full-face at the same time, and this is something no contor-tionist can achieve. Therefore we are confronted with a picture which claims to present simultaneously several different perspectives or viewpoints.

One of the first to grasp (at least partially) the implications of what Picasso was doing was Braque. Some people consider his *Maison à l'Estaque* of 1908 the first truly cubist painting; others accord this distinction to Picasso's *Nude with Drapery* of the previous year. There is also controversy over the origin of the term 'cubism'. Some attribute it to Matisse, others to the critic Vauxcelles. None of this matters, though it may be significant that the term was first used to describe Braque's picture. What matters is that a radical change had taken place in art. After 1908 things would never be quite the same again.

Picasso and Braque worked in very close collaboration during the early, heroic days of cubism; first the period of analytical cubism, and then, after 1912, synthetic cubism. It is worthwhile tracing the transi-tion from one to the other since it marks an important stage in the evolution of twentieth-century art.

During the last phase of analytical cubism (referred to as 'hermetic cubism') the analysis of objects had been carried to such a length, they had become so facetted, so geometrical, that it was exceedingly diffi-cult to recognize them any more. To aid recognition Braque and Picasso added certain clues. It might be a pipe or a bottle or even a row of buttons. In 1911 they began to add lettering – *BAR, PERNOD, JOURNAL*, etc. This had a double effect. It not only aided recognition of such objects as tables and chairs, bottles and newspapers, but it was also a means of establishing a picture plane, a nearest point of reference from which all perspectives and deviations of perspective could be judged. It is assumed that lettering lies flat, whether on the page or on a bar window; if it is on a curved surface, such as a bottle it becomes distorted.

The use of lettering led, in the following year, 1912, to the introduction of collage and *papier collé*. The distinction between them is subtle. Both refer to sticking on, pasting or gluing (*coller* in French), but, whereas in a collage all kinds of things, sand, wood, hair, linoleum, can be stuck on a canvas or panel, a *papier collé* consists invariably of paper of various kinds (newspaper, wallpaper, coloured paper, etc.). *Papier collé* might be regarded as a subdivision of collage, but the matter is not quite so simple. A collage may incorporate paper, but a *papier collé* has no other material *but* paper. This is not just a linguistic point. *Papier collé* was used almost exclusively for aesthetic purposes. It was first introduced by Braque. Its advantages were numerous. You could build up a basic abstract composition with the paper, and then superimpose the painting of a guitar or bunch of grapes or the inevitable bottle. Coloured paper brought back the element of colour without restricting it to local colour. In other words, you could make a colour composition and then draw in the representational bits as you thought fit. Collage was a different matter. It was often used to shock (whiskers on a print of the *Mona Lisa*), to give the feeling of a particular time or period (the use of tram-tickets and other bric-a-brac by Schwitters), to show one's virtuosity (Picasso turning a model motor-car into a gorilla with young), and so on; all of which I shall discuss in due course. But the most important thing about both *papier collé* and collage is that they enabled an artist to construct a picture *out of materials*. It was no longer a question of finding the appropriate means to represent a subject. It was something vastly more exciting, namely, what image will emerge when we have put this piece of paper here and that piece of wood there?

It was Juan Gris (who joined them in 1911) who really understood what Picasso and Braque were doing. In *L'Esprit nouveau*, no. 5, 1921, he wrote: 'Cézanne turns a bottle into a cylinder.... I make a bottle, a particular bottle, out of a cylinder.'

III

This divorce of form from content was carried much further by such abstract painters as Mondrian in Holland and Malevich in Russia. Both had been influenced by cubism, but by 1913 Piet Mondrian, who had come to Paris to study cubist painting at first hand, and Kasimir Malevich, who knew it through exhibitions organized by Larionov, had both become disenchanted with it. In their eyes it had not carried its own principles to their logical conclusion which was to free pictorial art and sculpture from all forms of naturalistic representation.

The evolution of Mondrian's art is instructive. He moved steadily towards abstraction from fairly naturalistic drawings and paintings of trees and churches and seascapes, to more abstract versions of an apple tree which, between 1910 and 1913, became less and less recognizable. The trunk and some of the branches became more and more vertical and other branches were resolved into curved (mostly oval) shapes. The seascapes had, by 1914, become a network of disparate horizontal lines crossed with verticals. There was a further period around 1917 when the composition consisted of rectilinear blocks of colour, sometimes incorporating the broken vertical and horizontal lines. Finally, by 1918 Mondrian had evolved the grid of vertical and horizontal lines, filled in with the primary colours, red, blue and yellow, or left blank with which everyone is familiar. Many of his works between 1911 and 1913 resemble cubist paintings of the analytical period, the facetting and the handling of paint which unified the facets often soft and sensuous. Indeed, they might be taken for cubist paintings of the hermetic stage, so difficult is it to detect any resemblance to a tree, church or whatever object the abstraction had been made from. But in fact Mondrian was going in a quite different direction from the Cubists. He was bent on carrying analysis to its ultimate conclusions. Therefore he was not concerned with planting clues towards recognition, such as pipes, bottles, buttons or lettering. Nor was he at all interested in the synthetic aspect of cubism. That, in his opinion, would be retrograde. It means a return to the object, to nature, however freely, imaginatively and creatively reconstructed. Mondrian did not reject representation as such, but for him it was directed to something more universal than a pipe and a bottle of Pernod: it was concerned with the basic forces which govern the universe and the equilibrium between them.

The evolution of Malevich's art was rather similar to that of Mondrian's, except that it was far more abrupt and dramatic. Between 1911 and 1913 he evolved a kind of mechanistic cubism, not unlike that of Léger, in which the facets, instead of being just hard, or soft and sensuous, were like curved metal plates. In 1913 he went through a brief phase akin to synthetic cubism. Then suddenly in that year he went entirely abstract, drawing, and later painting, his famous black square on a white ground. This was soon followed by a black circle and a black cross on a white ground. Malevich did not, however, exhibit them until 1915 and at that exhibition he issued his Suprematist manifesto, which began:

> Only when the perceptual habit of seeing bits of nature, madonnas and shameless nudes, in paintings has vanished shall we witness the composition of pure paintings . . . Only an artist's cowardice and lack of creative power leads him to deceive and make him stop short at natural forms: he is afraid to undermine the basis of primitive and academic art.

Malevich was not prepared to stop short at natural forms, and he certainly did not lack creative powers. Between 1917 and 1918 he did a series – the 'White on white' series – in which white squares were painted on a white ground. This must surely be about the ultimate in abstraction. But it was neither perverse nor ironical. Malevich believed that he had at last cut through the veil of representation of objects to the true nature of art which has to do with sensibility. Of suprematicism he says: 'Suprematism is the rediscovery of pure art which, in course of time, had become an accumulation of objects. . . . Sensibility is the decisive factor.' As the contemporary Venezuelan artist, Soto, remarked: 'By painting white on white Malevich was saying: *Let us paint light as light*.' But, for Malevich, as for Mondrian, abstraction was not merely a matter of aesthetics or sensibility. It had a profound symbolic and mystical significance. Of his first black square on a white ground Malevich says: 'It was the absolute night I felt in me: in that I perceived the creation.'

One abstract movement, however, may be said to have developed out of cubism. It was given the name 'Orphic Cubism' by the writer Apollinaire, and has come to be known as orphism. Robert Delaunay, who, together with his wife, Sonia, Picabia and Kupka, was one of its chief practitioners, defined it as a 'pure art', 'an art of painting new structures which have not been borrowed from the visual sphere, but have been created by the artist himself'. In fact he borrowed heavily from the visual sphere – motifs such as the propellor-blade and the

Eiffel Tower – and from cubism. Sonia Delaunay, however, achieved a truly abstract form of art in which the facets and interrelated planes of cubism were used as purely abstract shapes. She also reintroduced the vibrant colour of the Impressionists by using their technique of simultaneous contrasts of colours (a term borrowed from the great pioneer of colour theory, Chevreul). This has given rise to a confusion. The word simultaneity came to mean either the simultaneous viewpoints of the Cubists or the simultaneous contrasts of colour of the Orphists. The confusion was confounded when the Futurists used both senses almost simultaneously. But before coming to the Futurists, I must disentangle some further confusions and make a few general points.

First, it must be remarked that this tendency towards purity of content in art – or more accurately, the elimination of the distinction between form and content, in which the form becomes the content – was not confined to painting. It is found also in the music and literature of the period, in the theory that art is nothing more than pure sensation – a notion which can be traced back to Walter Pater incorrectly interpreted. This theory flourished most strongly in Russia. It was known as 'formalism' and came under heavy attack from Marxist theoreticians during the 1920s until it was forced to go underground when the doctrine of socialist realism was proclaimed in 1934. Unfortunately the practitioners of this formalist art, whether in painting or literature called themselves 'Futurists' – and why not? theirs was to be an art of the future – and thus gave rise to endless confusion, since 'futurism' as used by the Italians meant something different, but not entirely different. The Italians, like the Russians, were Formalists in literature and, in theory, in music (they issued a manifesto about sound but had not the technological ability to put their ideas into practice). Here, side by side, is a Russian and an Italian futurist poem:

driving	Lulla, lolla, lalla-goo
ruffian	Leeza, lolla, lulla-lee
fluff	Pines, shoo-yat, shoo-
so	yat
baby	Gee-ee, Gee-ee-oo-oo[3]
reason	
rat	
unshoed the armchair[2]	

In the visual arts they had very little in common beyond the name, a
became apparent when Marinetti visited Russia in 1914, though the
both had their origins in impressionism, wished to shake off the dead
weight of tradition and academicism, and brought literature and art (a
least in the form of design and typography) closer together in such
way as to anticipate concrete poetry. They both drew on cubist tech
niques, but, whereas the Russian Cubo-Futurists were interested in
cubism for predominantly formal or aesthetic reasons, the Italian
Futurists had other ideas.

The preoccupation of the Italian Futurists was with all thing
modern, particularly speed. In their first manifesto in 1909 (and the
wrote over a dozen formal manifestos and many more informal
Marinetti wrote: 'We affirm that the world's magnificence has been
enriched by a new beauty: the beauty of speed. A racing car whose
bonnet is adorned with great pipes...is more beautiful than the
Victory of Samothrace.' By 1911 they had achieved some success in
conveying the dynamism they sought by using the impressionist technique of 'pointillism', that is the juxtaposition of small dabs of colour
which interact with one another and give a lively effect of movement
and vibrance. They also found that facetting gave an even greater
effect of movement, as anyone who has seen multiple-exposure photographs of humans or animals in motion will appreciate. It is certain
that they were influenced in this by cubism, but when they visited Paris
in that year they were bitterly disappointed, as Mondrian had been,
but for a different reason. Mondrian could not understand why the
Cubists would not pursue the logical conclusion of their revolution (as
though there are any 'logical' conclusions in art or, for that matter,
why should a revolutionary be expected to realize all the implications
of what he has done on his own?). The Futurists could not understand
why they would not exploit the dynamic possibilities of their technique. Boccioni wrote in 1913: 'though the Cubists showed objects in
all their complexity...the spectacle itself did not change.' Having
created the conditions for representing an object in motion by showing
it in various facets, they locked it back into a solid composition.

There is no doubt about the dynamism of futurist painting and
sculpture subsequent to their contact with the Cubists. The most
famous example of this is Balla's *Leash in motion* of 1912 which
shows not only the leash in its various phases, but also the different
phases of the legs and tail of the little dog on the leash. By way of

compensation this adaptation of cubist technique was either introduced into cubism or arrived at by an independent development in the famous, not to say notorious, painting by Marcel Duchamp, *Nude descending a staircase*, of 1912, in which a somewhat mechanical nude is shown in many phases of her descent. But it was quite different in spirit from futurist painting. It was rejected by the Cubists when sent to the *Salon des Independents* and attacked by most *avant-garde* critics when it was shown at the *Section d'Or*. Unlike the Cubists, Duchamp was not primarily interested in picture-making; and unlike the Futurists he was not interested in the celebration of movement. Indeed, Duchamp is the link between cubism and the other movement which was to dominate the inter-war years, dada-surrealism. Unlike the other cubist painters he commented on life; and, unlike the Futurists, he commented unfavourably on life in a machine age. Before abandoning painting altogether in 1914, Duchamp painted a number of pictures in which he depicted love-making as a mechanical process.

Duchamp was by far the most intellectual of the Cubists. In 1913 for his own amusement he placed the wheel of a bicycle on a stool in his studio and this gave rise to what he was to call a 'readymade'. A readymade was an object in common use – it might be a bicycle-wheel, a bottle-rack, an iron or an urinal – which was made into a work of art by being signed. As he said of the *Fountain* (1917), an up-turned urinal signed 'R. Mutt' (the name of the manufacturer of such objects): 'Whether Mr Mutt with his own hand made the fountain or not has no importance. He CHOSE it. He took an ordinary article of life, placed it so that its useful significance disappeared under the new title and point of view – created a new thought for that object.' In presenting such objects Duchamp was raising fundamental questions about the nature of art. But he was also questioning the position which art had assumed in society and somewhat mischievously poking fun at collectors and connoisseurs of art. Duchamp was comparatively relaxed about the sociological implications of what he was doing. Not so the Dadaists, with whom his name is inextricably bound up.

Dadaism originated in the *Cabaret Voltaire* in Zurich in 1916. The name, which means 'gee-gee' in French, was hit upon by leafing through a Franco-German dictionary and considered sufficiently primitive, irrational and infantile to express what Hans Arp, Tristan Tzara and the other founder members had in mind. They were protesting against the so-called rationality which had led Europe into increasing materialism and finally a disastrous and senseless war. If that is rationality, then onward the progress of irrationality. As Richard Huelsenbeck wrote in *En avant Dada* (1920):

> None of us had much appreciation for the kind of courage it takes to get shot for the idea of a nation which is at best a cartel of pelt merchants and profiteers in leather, at worst a cultural association of psychopaths who, like the Germans, march off with a volume of Goethe in their knapsacks, to skewer Frenchmen and Russians with their bayonets.

In itself dadaism was not likely to make any contribution to art, since, if it was to be true to its principles, it should be anarchic, nihilistic and destructive. However, the techniques which the dadaists adopted – Arp's 'chance' compositions, photomontage as used by John Heathfield and dada collages – were assumed into a truly artistic movement, surrealism.

Surrealism, together with cubism and various forms of abstract art, dominated the 1920s. By now cubism was a spent force as a revolutionary movement. Braque went on quietly developing along the lines he had established in the heroic days of the 1910s and Picasso adapted his cubism to whatever wind was blowing, including surrealism. Surrealism grew out of dadaism, which in any case could not perpetuate itself indefinitely, since a protest endlessly reiterated eventually falls on deaf ears and a purely destructive movement runs out of objects to destroy. By 1922 dadaism was to all intents and purposes finished. But the poet, André Breton, rescued something of its spirit and techniques, particularly the part played by chance, free association and automatism. Breton had worked in the Charcot Clinic where Freud's techniques of automaticism and free association had been used. He had also studied Freud on the interpretation of dreams. He saw both these techniques as a means of bypassing reason and conscious control in order to arrive at a more natural and primitive state of consciousness, beyond everyday reality. He borrowed the term 'surrealism' from Apollinaire and in 1924 defined it in the first *Surrealist Manifesto* as follows:

> Surrealism is based on the belief in the superior reality of certain forms of association heretofore neglected, in the omnipotence of the dream, and in the disinterested play of

thought. It leads to the permanent destruction of all other psychic mechanisms and to its substitution for them in the solution of the principal problems of life.

This use of automaticism and dreams ran counter to that of Freud who wished to use them to restore, not destroy, rationality; but it was in accord with the spirit of dadaism. The difference between the two was mainly that of emphasis. Whereas dadaism was destructive, anarchic and negative, surrealism was positive, with a definite goal and purpose.

Surrealism was initially a literary rather than visual movement. In the first place, free association lends itself more easily to bizarre literary imagery, such as the repeatedly quoted line from Isidore Ducasse (Comte de Lautréamont), 'As beautiful as the chance encounter of a sewing-maching with an umbrella on an operating-table', which appears in the sixth canto of *Les Chants des Maldoror*, written in 1868. (He has come to be regarded, along with Rimbaud, Mallarmé and Apollinaire, as an ancestor of surrealism.) Secondly, the visual imagery has the look of something borrowed from literary sources. Thirdly, even when the object is the result of a chance encounter, such as an *objet trouvé*, or 'found object' – a pebble picked up on the beach or a piece of weathered stick found in a field – or the imagery results from taking a rubbing from wood or some other substance (Max Ernst's technique known as *frottage*), it is usually 'worked up' to make it aesthetically satisfying. Surrealism was very satisfactorily applied to the cinema by Buñuel in *L'Age d'Or* and *Le Chien Andalou*. But few surrealist works in the visual arts have an imagery quite comparable to these lines from Breton: 'The street lamps, moist, make sound, framed in the nebulae of blue eyes', or 'The air in the room is blue like drumsticks' (both from *Le revolver à cheveux blancs*). For one thing, the lines evoke sounds as well as visual images; for another, some of the elements are mutually exclusive. One might get away with depicting air in a room as blue (a blue haze), but not as a drumstick as well.

Surrealist poetry helps us to find a link between all these movements of the pre-war and first half of the inter-war period. If we compare those lines by Breton with poems by poets who were associated with the cubist, dadaist and surrealist movements, we will find certain important similarities. Where the Cubists established once and for all for everyone to see the independence of visual art from the demands of verisimilitude, Apollinaire, Pierre Reverdy, Gertrude Stein, Paul Eluard, Max Jacob, Cocteau and Blaise Cendrars established the independence of poetry from sense in the narrow meaning of the term, that is, consequential or rational thought (one idea *following from* another). In place of rational sequences of ideas they substituted the juxtaposition of ideas or of images. Take this, to my mind not very good, poem by Cendrars:

> A tie
> Six dozen handkerchiefs
> Three underpants
> Six pyjamas
> Kilos of white paper
>
> Kilos of white paper
> And a fetish
> My trunk weighs 57 kilos without my grey hat

Here we have a juxtaposition of items (it is hard to call them ideas, and such as they are, they are not exactly consequential). They might have been written by a 'cubist' or surrealist poet. In principle the method is the same, though the aim may be different. And so it was in visual art. The Cubists used juxtaposition (facetting) in their analysis and synthesis of objects: they were principally interested in producing works of art, but, after that, in objects. For the Surrealists, on the other hand, juxtaposition was a means to slip through the guard of rationality. One might say that, while surrealism did not arise out of cubism, cubism itself and its technique, if it did not make the path of surrealism possible, at least made it easy.

IV

The impact of cubism and surrealism on Britain was delayed, and when it came, it was oblique. Until the 1950s both movements were considered crazy by the general public, who talked jokingly of futurism (a global term) and modern art, and even by many eminent critics. They were as disturbing as the Copernican system was to sixteenth-century churchmen, and Einstein's theory of relativity or the philosophy of Russell, Moore and Wittgenstein was to their contemporaries. They disturbed the accepted order of things. A cubist picture of a woman did not look like a woman; and a surrealist picture

f a watch painted like a fried egg was neither funny nor serious: it was
illy; yet, somehow it could not be written off. It was not as though the
British public was unaware of what was going on elsewhere. There
were small exhibitions of cubist art in London, and even in Dublin,
ong before war broke out, and by 1912 its influence was apparent in
Wyndham Lewis's picture, *Kermesse*, exhibited at the Allied Artist's
salon and later described as the English *Les Demoiselles d'Avignon*.
But the impact was muted.

At the time there were two main groups in England. There was the
Camden Town Group, inspired by Sickert and interested in post-
impressionism. And there was the 'Bloomsbury' group much
influenced by fauvism. The Bloomsbury group were closely related, in
every sense, to the Bloomsbury literary set. This is illustrated in the
persons of Vanessa and Virginia Stephen, daughters of Sir Leslie
Stephen. Vanessa became a painter and married Clive Bell, the art
critic and theorist; Virginia became a writer and married Leonard
Woolf, a theorist of politics. The other members of the group
concerned with the visual arts were Duncan Grant, the painter, and
Roger Fry, the critic and painter. Others associated with the group
were the writers, E.M. Forster, David Garnett and Desmond
MacCarthy, and the economist, John Maynard Keynes. The genius
presiding over the group was the philosopher, G.E. Moore, whose
Principia Ethica had a powerful influence on the men (Cambridge
men), particularly Bell and Woolf. Moore's method is reflected to
some extent in Bell's influential book, *Art* (1914), and his
values – love, knowledge and aesthetic experience as the constituents
of the prime object of life – were shared by the group as a whole.

At first the Bloomsbury group and Lewis, soon joined by Fredrick
Etchells and Edward Wadsworth, exhibited side by side. They even
joined Fry's Omega workshop when it was set up in 1913, because
they thought what he and Bell meant by 'pure form' (or, as Bell called
it, 'significant form') was abstract form. But they soon parted
company, Lewis describing the Bloomsbury group as a family party of
strayed and dissenting aesthetes, whose efforts would not rise above
the level of a pleasant tea-party or attract more attention. It was a
parting by mutual consent, since the Bloomsbury group had little time
for the Futurists with whom Lewis and his colleagues had become
associated. Fry claimed that they had developed an aesthetic out of a
misapprehension of Picasso's 'difficult and recondite works', and Bell

that their works were intended to convey information rather tha
provoke aesthetic emotion, neither of which accusations was accurat

In 1913 Lewis and his colleagues, joined by David Bomberg and th
sculptor, Jacob Epstein, came to be called the London Group. A
Lewis pointed out in the catalogue to an exhibition in Brighton tha
year, where they occupied a 'cubist room', they were not accidentall
associated, but formed a 'vertiginous but not exotic, island in th
placid and respectable archipelago of English art'. Ezra Pound (whos
wife was to join them) was soon to translate the term 'vertiginous
into 'vorticist', the title by which they have come to be known.

The Vorticists may have had their origins in cubism and futurism
and have been regarded as a sub-class of one or the other; but in fac
they cannot be identified with either movement. Vorticism was a
original, *sui-generis* movement; one of the few to be indigenous t
Britain. Unlike cubism and futurism it was abstract. Unlike othe
abstract movements, such as the De Stijl movement in Holland, exem
plified by Mondrian, or Malevich's suprematism in Russia, it wa
neither flat nor relatively static, but dynamic and in depth (lik
futurism, and, to a lesser extent, cubism). Lewis considered that the
had changed the artist's mission. Henceforth he would penetrate '
transposed universe, as abstract as, though different from, th
musician's'. The philosopher, T.E. Hulme, in a famous lecture
'Modern Art and Its Philosophy' (1914), defended vorticism. H
distinguished it from the Futurists' 'deification of flux', on the on
hand, and the Cubists' 'theories of interpenetration', on the othe
Vorticism was something else. He, then, singled out as its essentia
characteristic an abstract precision of line and colour, like a
engineer's drawing, 'absolutely distinct from the messiness, th
confusion and the accidental details of life'. But Hulme was not reall
at home with absolute abstraction, and soon disassociated himself wit
the movement. Pound deserted them during the war, and they were
subjected to rather senseless jibes by Clive Bell, accusations of provin
cialism, etc.

Vorticism did not survive the war. For one thing the Vorticists wer
employed as war artists, which meant that they had to return to figura
tion. Their greatest contribution to the war effort, however, wa
abstract: the camouflaging of ships, in which the use of dynami
abstraction broke the line and form of a ship so that it became less eas
to recognize. After the war, Wadsworth, the creator of thi

amouflage, was to use it in a series of semi-abstract pictures of ships in
ockland; so vorticism recouped a little.

After this short-lived excursion into the mainstream of European
t, British art in the 1920s settled back into its quiet ways. It was not
ntil the influx of Continental artists into Britain following the Nazi
up in Germany in the 1930s that British artists began to pick up
here the Vorticists had left off. Before then they were hardly touched
y surrealism, for instance.

There are two aspects of vorticism which remain to be mentioend.
ne is its literary connection. Its leader, Wyndham Lewis, as every
ader of this book is aware, was no less important a literary figure as a
ainter. It is not surprising, therefore, that he and his colleagues and
ssociates should express themselves in print as well as paint. In 1914
ewis and Ezra Pound founded the periodical *Blast*, which ran to only
vo numbers; the second was a war number (1915). It might have
een called *Counter-blast* since it was in large part a manifesto in the
tyle and format of futurist manifestos, but counter-futurism. But that
not its importance, however. What was most important and of most
asting value was that it introduced into Britain a typography which
as comparable to that of the Italian Futurists and the Russians, and
nat, irrespective of the quality of the literary content, was an achieve-
ent.

Secondly, it made a contribution to photography. This was largely
ue to an American, Alvin Langdon Coburn, of Boston. Coburn's
vortographs', which must have been among the first series of abstract
hotographs, 'facetted' objects out of recognition. Ezra Pound wrote
he catalogue to his first exhibition, and George Bernard Shaw at the
pening contributed in his usual brilliant manner to make the evening
nemorable. But Coburn did not continue the experiment for long.

V

This brings me to the final revolution of the period, namely, in photography and in particular in moving pictures or cinematography.

Ever since the invention of the daguerreotype in 1838 there has
een an interplay between painting and photography of such
omplexity that it is rarely possible to say which has influenced the
ther at a given time. There can be little doubt that photography
ncouraged the move away from the so-called photographic realism of

such painters as Bastien Leplage. But when we examine photographi realism we find that it, strangely, reflects the style of painting currer at the time. There can be no doubt, however, that cubism marked decisive step away from photographic realism in any narrow sense however interpreted. But, though there is no hard evidence for this, is possible that the extraordinary series of humans and animals i motion, and birds in flight by Muybridge and Marey in the 1870s an 1880s may have, if only subconsciously, suggested the cubist use c facetting to show various viewpoints of a figure simultaneously. Bu even if this were so, the aim of the Cubists was to present static figures not the phases of motion. We know however, that Marey's 'chronc photographs' influenced both Duchamp and the Futurists. Wherea Muybridge showed the successive phases of a moving object as sepa rate pictures, Marey superimposed the phases in a single, multipl image, which gives not only the phases of a movement, but th impression of movement. A typical example today would be a photo graph of a golfer starting and completing a drive. In the 1920s Picasso, in a surrealist mood, seems to have been influenced by th kind of disorientated photograph which amateurs take on the beach particularly of people playing with a ball or otherwise disporting them selves.

The new art movements, on the other hand, influenced photo graphy in a number of ways. I have already mentioned the influence c vorticism on Coburn's vortographs, and the influence of collage or the evolution of photomontage. Photomontage is particularl interesting. It was used in the cinema by two of its pioneers, Méliè and Zecca, in their film fantasies. Dadaists, such as Man Ray, Hanna Höch and Grosz, and Surrealists, such as Max Ernst, used it to create fantasies of a different sort. John Heartfield, a Marxist, used it for the purpose of anti-Nazi propaganda. It is a particularly effective propa ganda weapon, and has been used as such ever since.

The art movements also had an influence on the cinema, ever though this was not felt by the ordinary cinema-going public. In hi book, *The Film Sense* Sergei Eisenstein, speaks of the influence o cubism – multiple viewpoint, interpenetrating forms, ambiguou: perspective – on the cinema. The technique of montage, which Eisen stein pioneered, depends on juxtaposition, which, as we have seen, is fundamental to all art, but more blatantly so in cubism and surrealism. Of this more in a moment. Duchamp in 1924 interested himself in the inema, making an abstract film which he called, almost palindromic- lly *Anemic-Cinema*. In the same year Léger made a semi-abstract lm, *Ballet méchanique*. Throughout the 1920s Man Ray, Hans ichter and Viking Eggling experimented seriously with abstract lms.

Meanwhile the mainline development of film had undergone impor- ant changes. Indeed, it can be said that, between 1900 and 1930, it ras transformed from entertainment with occasional flashes of artistry nd more than occasional charm, into an art form in its own right. The ioneers of film – Lumière (a strangely appropriate name) and Méliès – produced charming and beautiful film fantasies in the 1890s. But rhen the cinema became a popular form of entertainment addressed to mass audience of millions throughout the world, the artistic quality lummeted. The stories were taken from the romantic or melodrama- ic novelettes which appealed to the masses at the time. The only real laim to artistry was in slapstick comedy, Charlie Chaplin (who made is first film in 1913), the Keystone Cops, Buster Keaton, and so on. ven the great D.W. Griffiths, whose *Birth of a Nation* in 1915 and *ntolerance* in 1916 were to transform the cinema by their technical rilliance, still worked within the limitations of the novelette and the lemands of popular entertainment, even if its demands and those of art net in spectacle. It was the Germans, French and Russians who raised or restored) film to the status of an art form in the 1920s. *The abinet of Dr Caligari* (1921), an expressionist film produced by ladaist artists, alerted the art world to the artistic possibilities of film, ut the chief credit goes to the Russians.

The Russian attitude towards the cinema after the revolution of 917 was serious. Film was to be used as a means of propaganda, to nform the masses about socialism and whip up their support for it. As enin said: 'Film is for us the best means of instruction of all forms of rt.' This seriousness of purpose involved a degree of research and xperimentation, an exploration of the possibilities of the cinema which few, if any, French, German or American film-makers had ndertaken. But, though seriousness of purpose might lift the cinema ut of the category of mere popular entertainment, it would not have een sufficient to raise it to an art form but for the genius of Eisenstein, Pudovkin and Dovzhenko. They studied the psychology of perception, n particular our tendency to make connections, often erroneous and llogical, on the basis of juxtaposition of images or ideas. Eisenstein

was much taken by the extreme example of this, in Lewis Carroll'
portmanteau words ('two meanings packed into one word like a por
manteau'), in which the fusion of two ideas was most complete ar
economical. Juxtaposition enabled the film editor to convey ide
visually. The image of a woman in black, weeping beside a grave w
convey the idea 'widow', even if, as in Ambroce Bierce's story, she
weeping for a dead lover, not a dead husband. Pudovkin discovere
that by juxtaposing an expressionless face with, say, a shot of a child
a bowl of soup, it 'took on' a tender or hungry expression. But none
these discoveries and devices alone would have produced *Battlesh*
Potemkin (1925) or *October* (1928). It was the artistic genius
Eisenstein, who was able to both create a formal structure and conve
ideas by means of juxtaposition of images (or, as he called i
'montage'), that brought this about.

VI

The revolutions in the visual arts during the period 1900-30 we
part of a much wider revolution which began at the turn of th
century. They represent collectively a new way of viewing the worl
in the broadest, metaphysical sense, and of perceiving it closer to one
nose, so to speak. As at the time of the scientific revolution of the la
sixteenth and early seventeenth centuries it involved thinking th
unthinkable and imagining the seemingly impossible. It was the perio
in which, for instance, Einstein expounded his theory of relativity,
theory which gives us a multiple perspective on the universe. There
no absolute view – no God's eye view – of events in the universe: th
relationships of before and after, and simultaneous with, depend on th
observer's position in relation to the events.

This awareness of the part played by the observer is to be found i
the experimental sciences generally. Bohr and de Broglie discusse
this in relation to quantum theory. It was realized that not only was a
object of investigation altered by being investigated, but the outcom
of the investigation depended on the standpoint which was initiall
taken. This line of discussion might be said to have culminated i
Heisenberg's indeterminacy or uncertainty principle. According t
this principle it is impossible to determine *both* the position an
velocity of an object *at a given moment*. If you know exactly where
is, you cannot tell how fast it is moving (for all intents and purposes

ight as well not be moving); in order to tell how fast it is moving, you
ave to consider its movement over a given distance, that is, an indefi-
ite number of possible positions. So, once again, one is thrown back
n the viewpoint of the observer or spectator.

That psychology, whether experimental or depth psychology, con-
erns itself with the observer or the subject (the 'observer' unobserved
nd unobserving) is hardly in doubt. The relationship between the
isual arts of the period and the works of Freud have already been noted.
arallels between art and the psychology of perception as expounded by
ne Gestalt psychologists, Koffka and Köhler, could be explored. Their
neory assumes that our perception of the world is from the inside out,
nat we have innate (geometrical) forms of perception into which we try
o fit the data of experience in order to make it intelligible. It is not a
uestion of looking out on the world and trying to comprehend what is
nere. The 'world' is to a large extent of our own making. It is seen
nrough our eyes, and these are not windows, but active agents of
eception. There was an old scholastic tag, *quidquid recipitur, per
nodum recipientis recipitur* (which may be loosely translated: 'what
ach one takes in, he takes in after his own fashion'), and this seems to
um up the more recent findings in the psychology of perception.

Finally there were the contemporary philosophical tendencies and
novements. These included the preoccupations with perception by
ergson and the phenomenologists, Heidegger and Merleau Ponty,
vhose interests in art included the art of Cézanne and the Cubists. But
nuch more important, to my mind, was the preoccupation with
anguage of Frege, Brentano, Russell, Moore and Wittgenstein.
anguage is that artificial medium by which we hope to come to terms
vith our environment. Though Aristotle, Aquinas, Leibniz and Kant
vere aware of the importance of language, it was not until the twentieth
entury that philosophers grasped the full implications of language.
Vhen Wittgenstein stated in the *Tractatus Logico-Philosophicus*
1919) – which he wrote while he was a soldier in the Italian campaign
nd carried in his knapsack – that 'the world is the totality of facts, not
f things', that is, of what we take to be true and believe that others
lso take to be true ('my world'), he was merely asserting what
ainters and sculptors had come to take for granted, namely, that we
onstruct the world, build from the inside out, and do not merely adapt
urselves to a putative, 'given' world outside, even though the 'out-
ide' exercises certain constraints on our constructing.

This does not mean that science, philosophy and art had become subjective during the first half of the twentieth century. Indeed, as has been argued in the introductory essay with respect to literature, the had become more objective insofar as they had come to terms with the realities of thought and perception, and the creative and personal nature of both. It is not for me to judge the extent to which literature was in line with these developments but unquestionably some writers were. For, without doubt, the period between the beginning of the century and the Second World War, particularly the 1920s, was one of the most exciting and exploratory in the history of human thought and cultural experience, and, as ever, the visual arts reflected these developments.

Notes

1 'La définition de neo-traditionalisme', *Art et critique*, August 1980. It came to be regarded as the manifesto of the *symboliste* movement.
2 D. Kruchenykh; 'Battle of India and Europe' (1915).
3 Quoted by N. Bukharin in 'Poetry, Poetics and the Problems in the USSR'.

Select bibliography

Arnason, H.H. *History of Modern Art*, New York 1968.
Barr, A.H. (ed.) *Masters of Modern Art*, New York 1954.
—— *Cubism and Abstract Art*, New York 1936.
—— *Fantastic Art, Dada, Surrealism*, New York 1937.
Eisenstein, S.M. *The Film Sense*, London 1943.
Golding, J. *Cubism: A History and an Analysis, 1907-1914*, London 1968.
Hamilton, G.H. *Painting and Sculpture in Europe 1880-1940* Harmondsworth, Middx 1967.
Jacobs, L. *The Rise of the American Film*, New York 1939.
Martin, M.W. *Futurist Art and Theory, 1909-1915*, Oxford 1968.
Rhode, E. *A History of the Cinema*, Harmondsworth, Middx 1976.
Richter, H. *Dada, Surrealism and Anti-Art*, New York 1965.
Wright, B. *The Long View: An International History of Cinema*, London 1974.

ndex

b) *Subjects*